MW01058771

Oct. 25, 2014 (7)
Nov. 14, 2014 (6)
NOV. 19, 2014 (4)

Winning My Wings

Marion Stegeman Hodgson

Naval Institute Press / Annapolis, Maryland

Winning My Wings

A Woman Airforce Service Pilot
in World War II

Library of Congress Cataloging-in-Publication Data
Hodgson, Marion Stegeman.
    Winning my wings: a woman Airforce Service pilot in World War II.
/ Marion Stegeman Hodgson.
        p.   cm.
    ISBN 1-55750-364-8 (cloth: alk. paper)
    1. Hodgson, Marion Stegeman. 2. World War, 1939–1945—Aerial operations, American. 3. World War, 1939–1945—Personal narratives, American. 4. Air pilots, Military—United States. 5. United States. Army Air Forces—Biography. I. Title.
    D790.H63 1996
    940.54'4973—dc20   96-12643

Printed in the United States of America on acid-free paper ∞

03 02 01 00 99   9 8 7 6 5 4 3 2

In Memoriam _____

The following WASPs (Women Airforce Service Pilots) were killed in crashes in the line of duty while flying Army Air Forces airplanes:

Champlin, Jane*
Clarke, Susan P.
Davis, Margie L.*
Dussaq, Katherine
Edwards, Marjorie D.*
Erickson, Elizabeth*
Fort, Cornelia
Grimes, Frances
Hartson, Mary
Howson, Mary H.*
Keene, Edith
Lawrence, Kathryn B.*
Lee, Hazel Ah Ying
Loop, Paula
Lovejoy, Alice
McDonald, Lea Ola
Martin, Peggy
Moffatt, Virginia
Moses, Beverly

Nichols, Dorothy
Norbeck, Jeanne L.
Oldenburg, Margaret*
Rawlinson, Mabel
Roberts, Gleanna*
Robinson, Marie N. (Mitchell)
Scott, Betty
Scott, Dorothy
Seip, Margaret J.*
Severson, Helen Jo*
Sharon, Ethel Marie
Sharp, Evelyn
Silver, Gertrude (Tompkins)
Stine, Betty P.*
Toevs, Marion
Trebing, Mary E.
Webster, Mary L.
Welz, Bonnie Jean
Wood, Betty L. (Taylor)

*Killed while in training

Contents

Preface

We didn't know we were making history. We were liberated but not feminists. Equal pay and benefits were not a consideration then. We only knew that our country was deep in war, and there was a serious shortage of pilots. We were licensed female pilots, and the Army Air Forces needed us. They were going to train us and let us fly their planes, and that was enough.

This is one girl's story—my story. Every WASP's story is different; I've told mine mostly through letters to my mother and to Ned, a Marine pilot fighting for his life after a fiery crash, and through his letters to me.

Why would I share something so blushingly personal as some of these letters? Because this is history, an eyewitness account of events and emotions of a bygone era. It was a time of patriotism, idealism, romanticism, and something almost approaching inno-cence—by today's standards, anyhow—in spite of the cussing and hard-drinking partying that masked the anxiety that accompanied war and death and airplane crashes.

I can hardly remember the giddy, boy-crazy girl pilot revealed in these letters, but I do remember that she was an agnostic, and a lot of the time, just plain scared.

That long-ago wartime military pilot—was it really me?—would have cleaned up her act and watched her language if she'd realized that these letters would someday be read by her grand-children.

Nevertheless, to them their "Oma" dedicates this book.

Winning My Wings

1

3812 N. Pine Grove, Apt. 102
Chicago, Illinois
February 18, 1943

To: Maj. Edward M. Hodgson
U.S. Marine Corps Air Station Hospital
Cherry Point, North Carolina

Dearest Ned:

Well, it has happened. I'm so thrilled I don't know how to put it into words. If I pass the physical on the 23d of this month, I'm in the AAFFTC's [Army Air Forces Flying Training Command's] Women's Flying Training program! Then I report for duty on the 24th of March.

Ned, you just don't know what this means to me. I didn't honestly believe it would ever happen. All I know is that one night when I came home from work, there was a telegram for me from the chief recruiting officer, and it said, "If interested in WFT for Ferry Command, contact me Palmer House, etc." I was so excited that I couldn't sleep that night. Then the next day when I went down for my interview, all that she asked me was if I had my private license. I showed her my license and my log book, and she said, "You're in." So here I am, walking on clouds, waiting for the physical . . . .

I'll either be assigned to Houston or Sweetwater, Texas. We train right at the Army field. In Houston they are building barracks for us. In the meantime we live in motels. In Sweetwater the girls will live in Army barracks. We're in the Army and yet we aint. Technically, we're Civil Service employees.

Theoretically we don't have any say-so about where we prefer to be sent for training, but the recruiting officer hinted that if I stated my preference, I might get it. . . . Meanwhile, I don't really know why I did this, but I requested Houston. I spose it was because I had never heard of Sweetwater and didn't want to be stuck way off in the middle of nowhere.

I'm not expecting any picnic, but I know this is the chance I've been waiting for, and I wouldn't miss this wonderful opportunity for nuttin. Don't you agree it's the chance of a lifetime? Or do you think I'll break my neck? Which?

Lotsa love,
Marion

Ned, to whom I was writing the letter, was a Marine pilot from home. Our families were closest friends in our small university town, but I really didn't know Ned very well since he was eight years older. I was writing him now because he was lying in a hospital bed, horribly burned. I hoped the letter would make him smile—the poor grammar and deliberately misspelled words were a shared joke with the younger generation of Athens, Georgia, considered country bumpkins by visiting Easterners.

As I licked the stamp for his envelope, I reflected on the irony of life. Ned, the person who had convinced my mother (and me!) that it was safe to fly, was now fighting for his life because of an airplane crash. My mind went back, and for a moment I felt the old sickening fear of flying engulf me, the fear I thought I had overcome.

My very first experience with airplanes, when I was five years old, was a disaster. A tri-motored Ford *aeroplane* had flown into

Athens on a barnstorming tour. My family and I were at the airport that Sunday afternoon, watching airplanes take off and land. When it was announced that we could take a ride over town for a dollar a head, our family voted to go for it, a wild extravagance for us in those days.

My father, mother, brother, sister, and I climbed aboard. But when the pilot started up the engines, there was such a terrifying roar that I clapped my hands over my ears and bellowed. My father—my hero, my comforter—took me on his lap and held me close to make me feel safe, but for the only time in my life, it didn't work. As we taxied out to takeoff position, my screams grew louder, until the pilot was forced to turn the plane back and let me off.

But first, Mother gave me one more chance to save face. "If all your family are killed, don't you want to go with us, Marion?" she asked, as they opened the door for me to get out.

"No!" I shrieked, leaving no doubt.

People were laughing at me as I was told to wait with a cluster of strangers, and I couldn't stop sobbing. I stood alone at the edge of the group and watched, terrified, as the plane took off without me, wondering who would take care of me when it crashed. My thumb sneaked into my mouth.

When my family returned to earth safely, my great relief was matched only by my shame.

I attempted to overcome my dread of flying early in 1941, during my senior year at the University of Georgia. An old friend, John Ashford, home from med school for a weekend, showed up at our door. He was a CPTP (Civilian Pilot Training Program) alum who had his private pilot's license and enough money saved up for half an hour of flying time in a Cub: three dollars. Would I go along for the ride?

Determined to conquer the near-pathological fear and shame I still carried, I failed to notice the devilish gleam in John's eye. After all, he was practically an older brother to me, one of my brother's best friends.

As I crouched through the little door of the J-3 Cub, my heart was jumping. John climbed into the front seat, and as he closed the door I felt trapped, claustrophobic, but determined to see this thing through. As we jounced along toward a takeoff, I tried to breathe normally. But once we became airborne I grabbed the inside supports with a death grip, thinking I might be somehow holding the plane up with my bare hands.

After we had climbed several thousand feet, the engine sputtered and stopped, and John cried, "Uh, oh! The engine's quit. Find us a field to land in."

There weren't any good fields. I was in total panic, much to his satisfaction. He advanced the throttle and the plane throbbed back to life. He repeated the prank several times, laughing fiendishly as I reacted every time, even though I finally figured out that his perverted sense of humor was causing the "engine failure." Once safely back on solid ground at the airport, I pummeled my "friend" and vowed to myself that I would overcome the paralyzing fear that had overwhelmed me in the air.

As the spring of 1941 approached, the University of Georgia gave me that chance. Because of the war in Europe, the government was stepping up its training, through colleges, of civilian pilots, just in case we were drawn into the war. But it wanted its CPTP to appear innocent of military implications. So Georgia obediently opened its cockpits to girls that spring: one female to every ten males, five girls in all, for a free course in flying, with five hours' college credit for ground school thrown in.

Here was my chance! There was just one roadblock: my mother. I had to have her signature on the papers because I was only nineteen, and she didn't want to sign. "I might be signing your death warrant!" she cried.

Mother was still hopelessly grieving for my father, who had died two years before, and she said she just couldn't sign away the life of her "baby girl." My heart was still broken, too, more than anyone guessed.

I had adored my father. Bad enough was the memory of his

suffering, something that still woke me up in the middle of the night in tears. I felt totally inadequate to meet my mother's emotional needs, when I myself was drowning. My siblings had flown the coop—my brother to medical school, my sister to a teaching job in South Carolina—and I was beginning to feel smothered as I struggled for independence and tried to overcome my own grief and loss. Spiritual education had not been part of my otherwise idyllic childhood. With my father's death I felt my security, financial as well as emotional, had slipped away. Now that I needed something solid and permanent to support me, it was not there.

One beautiful morning that spring of 1941, I awakened with fierce determination to get on with my life, to try my wings—literally—in the big, wide world. I had things to prove and actions to take and the world to conquer, as well as myself. I wanted that free pilot's license the University of Georgia was dangling in front of me.

In another few months I'd have my diploma and would have lost my chance for the CPTP course; it would be too late. (And, it turned out, they never again offered the course to girls.) After graduation I would have to support myself. There were no good-paying jobs in Athens, a small town dependent upon the university, that died in the summertime. Most everyone went to Atlanta to find work. And surely in Atlanta, potential employers would be impressed with a pilot's license! I had to grab this opportunity now.

Grannie, Mother's mother, was visiting us at the time, and she was on my side. She had tried unsuccessfully to get Mother to sign the permission form, and if it hadn't been for her and for our old family friends the Hodgsons, it never would have happened.

Ned Hodgson was flying for Eastern Air Lines out of Atlanta but was home for the weekend, visiting his parents, at that crucial paper-signing time. He had dropped by our house after church on Sunday to say hello and good-bye—he was reporting back to Eastern that night—and Grannie collared him. "Marion wants to fly and Dorothea won't sign," she told him. "Tell her that flying is safe, Ned. She trusts you."

Ned was too honest to tell an outright lie, but he also was on my side and, like Grannie, had a spirit of adventure. He said to Mother, "Mrs. Stegeman, would it make you feel better about signing if Mother and Dad came over to talk to you?" He seemed to understand that Mother was missing my father's counsel.

"Oh, yes!" Mother cried. Since Ned's parents were two of her best friends, she could share her qualms and fears with them. The Hodgsons themselves must have been through much of the same anguish when they had mentally released two of their sons to the sky. Both had service training and now flew for different airlines. The Hodgsons knew how to let their children go; maybe they could teach her.

Mr. and Mrs. Hodgson came right over and talked to Mother. Ned talked to Mother. She finally signed, weeping.

The decision made, it was time to celebrate, so we all went out to Sunday dinner at the Holman Hotel. I rode there in Ned's little coupe with him.

"A lot has changed around here since I left Athens," he said.

"You think so? Like what?" Athens seemed exactly the same to me, only deader and duller than ever, now that the war in Europe was causing more activity in the cities in the rest of the country. All the action seemed to be elsewhere.

"Like you, for instance." Ned looked at me sideways, smiling. "You were just a beady-eyed stick of a child the last time I saw you."

"Has it been that long?"

"Long enough. You were a late bloomer, weren't you?" It was a delicate way of saying that I'd reached the age of puberty much later than most girls. "And now," he added, "you're a long-stemmed American beauty."

"Too long-stemmed," I said. "I can't get any extra-length stockings anymore." Shortages were beginning to show up in prewar America.

Ned regarded my legs and nearly ran through a stop sign. "Well, it may create a problem—your height, I mean—but I like the way you stand tall, as if you're proud of it. Don't ever stoop just because people like me are shorter than you."

"Okay." I wished he were taller or I, shorter. I had always admired Ned through the hero-worshipping eyes of a child, first when I'd cheered him on from the bleachers of the old polo field at Georgia as I watched him ride with a trick horseback team, and later as I watched him box in Woodruff Hall, or perform on the tumbling team, or walk on his hands at picnics, or dive for the university swimming team. There was something extra about Ned, something beyond his clean-cut, athletic bearing. It probably came under the heading of manners, the bred-in-the-bone kind that come naturally. He was just plain nice.

For one thing, Ned had always been gracious to me, unlike many older sons of family friends, especially the ones who were attracted to my older sister and swarmed around her like fruit flies around a ripe Georgia peach. Ned always seemed to enjoy talking to me, or maybe he was just trying to draw out the beady-eyed child who hung back in the shadow of her beautiful big sister and who played alone much of the time with her dog, cat, rabbits, turtle, white mice, duck, and baby alligator. Whatever the reason, he had earned my undying gratitude and affection.

And now he had smoothed the way for me to make a giant step forward, a step that would take me far beyond my wildest dreams.

2

It wasn't easy, learning to fly. The little yellow Cub J3F drifted through the air like an autumn leaf, and when I tried to land it, it would float off again all by itself. Nevertheless, after the required eight hours I soloed, a numbing experience as I looked ahead at the empty seat where my instructor had sat and saw the dual controls moving as if by a ghost's hand. Then I realized that *I* was moving those controls from the back of the stuffy little cockpit, and I didn't know what I was doing. Help!

I made a terrible landing complete with bounces, but nevertheless my instructor waved me on to make more. At the conclusion of the landings, several boys and another girl student, along with two other instructors, rushed out to my plane with the traditional pair of scissors, to cut off my shirttail (or rather my brother's outgrown shirttail), an old ritual for first-time solo students. I was hysterical with relief and rejoicing. I had done it.

But there was still the required solo cross-country to contend with, down the line. In heavily wooded Georgia, it was hard enough for an experienced pilot to tell where he was by reference to the ground, and for a novice like me, born without a sense of direction, it was close to impossible. I knew I was going to get lost before I took off, strapped into my backpack parachute—which I had on backward, making it useless, I found out later. It didn't help that my compass was thirty degrees off, or that I had a strong crosswind, which nobody bothered to tell me about and I didn't have enough sense to ask about.

On the first (and as it turned out, last) leg of my journey, I missed the first checkpoint, panicked, and flew around trying to read the names of towns on water towers until my gas ran low. There was no airport anywhere around that I could see, and the last water tower I checked out said "Sparta" on the side nearest me, and I assumed with horror that I had flown into Spartanburg, South Carolina. I tried to remember everything I'd been taught about picking a good field for a forced landing, and I put the Cub down in a cotton field. It was the only good landing I ever made in that little airplane. My slack suit was drenched with nervous sweat and the heat of a hot May day.

I caught a ride to town with a farmer and found out that I was in Sparta, Georgia, which I had never heard of. I called the Athens airport, and my instructor answered. He let out a whoop and yelled to all present, "Stegeman's down! Stegeman's down!," and I could hear raucous laughter in the background. From that moment on, I was Cross-Country Stegeman.

Perhaps that was the day a ferry pilot was born—once again, not out of a love for flying, especially cross-country, but out of determination to overcome obvious deficiencies.

Miraculously, by June I had my private pilot's license and also a bachelor of arts degree in journalism. Trouble was, neither accomplishment impressed anybody in Atlanta who was hiring. The only available jobs for girls, it seemed, were secretarial, and I could only hunt-and-peck on a typewriter with two overworked fingers, and knew no shorthand at all.

I had to get a job. I rented an old typewriter for two dollars a month, stuck a tiny patch of adhesive tape over each key so I couldn't cheat, and began to teach myself the touch system out of a secondhand typing book. With an equally used Gregg shorthand book that cost fifty cents, I taught myself enough shorthand to apply for work later in that summer of 1941 as a stenographer. But I knew the competition for jobs was fierce, and I had no experience.

One day in Atlanta while waiting for a job interview, I came across an article by Jacqueline Cochran in the June 1941 issue of *Flying* magazine. In it, she proposed that the government create a corps of women to be used as instructors and pilots, to ferry fighters and bombers and perform other flying duties. It was an impossible dream I didn't identify with.

Meanwhile that June, the war was beginning to seem more real to me, especially since Britain warned that German submarines were getting nearer to our shores. I joined the Ninety-Nines, an international organization of women pilots that Amelia Earhart had helped start before she'd disappeared over the Pacific. The Ninety-Nines, so named because there had been ninety-nine original members, received a plea from the Civil Air Patrol for volunteers to patrol the eastern coastline in light planes—without pay. I yearned to answer the exciting call, but without an airplane and without pay, how could I?

Toward the end of the summer, while the war raged on in Europe, I landed a temporary job as receptionist in Atlanta for the Athletic Department at Georgia Tech, with the proviso that I never, ever divulge the fact that I had attended the University of Georgia, their hated rival. Jubilantly I moved into a rented room in a private home with one of my best friends, Margaret "Mac" McEver, who later married Ned's brother.

As I worked daytimes at Tech and practiced typing and shorthand at night, Hitler was boasting that he had destroyed most of the Russian army. Germany continued to make advances everywhere. But the Soviets fought on heroically, and the USSR and Great Britain alternated in nightly air raids on Berlin.

The Russians were not yet using women pilots, but many of their teenage girls had joined paramilitary flying clubs where they were given free flying lessons, first in gliders, then in prop-driven planes. Later they would be used as combat pilots, when the Nazis were at the gates of Moscow. The British, however, had been using women ferry pilots since 1940 in their ATA (Air Transport Auxiliary).

On Sunday, 7 December 1941, I was working overtime at the Federal Reserve Bank of Atlanta, where I had finally landed a good job, at seventy-two dollars a month, working as a stenographer. My world seemed ordered and secure for the first time since my father's death, and the war was still an ocean away. That afternoon a bank employee ran breathlessly into our office and said that we were all to gather in the cafeteria, immediately.

The announcement that we were at war left us stunned and silent. Most of us didn't even know where Pearl Harbor was. All I could think was, Miss Bocock was right, after all. Miss Natalie Bocock had been my civics teacher in high school, and she had made the startling prediction that we would go to war with Japan before we went to war with Germany.

Nothing in my lifetime before or since has united our country like the attack on Pearl Harbor. Since we were forced into war, we were all in it together, and there were virtually no dissenters. But for the first six months of 1942, the United States took a terrible beating. We had been forced to surrender at Bataan, and I had a good friend over there, so suddenly the war became very real to me.

While World War II was escalating, I was going through a personal crisis. An attractive man, two years older than even Ned, was pressuring me to marry him. Although I was fascinated by his convertible, his Chris-Craft, his airplane, and even him, I knew it was all wrong. I recognized that I had to distance myself from that situation, lest I drift into something I did not want.

I explained to Mother, who didn't want me to marry him, that I had to leave town to get far, far away from him and find work elsewhere. Since we had relatives in and around Chicago who would put me up while I hunted for a job and an apartment, we decided that should be my destination.

The Federal Reserve Bank of Chicago hired me at a much better salary than I had been making in Atlanta. But everything cost more, so it came out about the same at the end of the month: zero. I seldom saw the sun in the Windy City. I stood shivering in a raccoon coat a generous cousin had given me, waiting for the bus. Then, after the sun went down, I sloshed through melted snow to get back to my pitiful little apartment to fix something to eat, wash my hair, sleep, and go back to work—overtime—the next day.

The Fed had hired me to work as a secretary in the War Department liaison office there in the bank, which delighted me because I wanted to be involved in the war effort. But I worked killing overtime hours, often seven days a week, and had no social life. However, my bosses, a major and a captain, were fun, even though they teased me mercilessly about my southern accent.

One day the phone rang at work, and I heard another most welcome southern accent on the line. Ned Hodgson! He was now a proud Marine, in town while carrying out the coveted assignment of ferrying around the war's first Marine aces, Marion Carl and John Smith. They were on a tour of war-bond rallies, using a Navy transport plane. Ned and one of his cousins took me out to dinner after work that night. I was sorry I had worn my high heels because it made the difference in Ned's and my height more obvious.

He was gone the next day, and neither of us wrote. I started a letter to Ned when I read in the paper that his old boss with Eastern Air Lines, Eddie Rickenbacker, had been picked up in the South Pacific, where he had been drifting on a raft for three weeks. But I never finished the letter.

I tried to keep up with the war and Ned's part in it, though it was difficult. Overseas news was heavily censored and I didn't often get to see a newspaper. But when I did, I always looked for news of the Marines. Ned was headed for the South Pacific any day now, with a night fighter squadron, and I wanted to know what was going on. I rejoiced when the campaign in Guadalcanal seemed to be coming to a successful conclusion, at last.

I was reading about it on the train one weekend toward the end of January, as I headed for nearby Winnetka to see Mother. She was there visiting my Uncle Carleton and their mother, my beloved Grannie. Our joyful reunion was short-lived, though, shattered by a special-delivery letter Mother received from a friend in Athens. It enclosed a newspaper clipping that I didn't know then would change my life forever.

It was about Ned. He had been practicing night landings without landing lights, in an effort to duplicate conditions he would encounter in the Pacific, and he had crashed and burned. Unknown to him and the private who was sandbagging in the backseat of the plane, there was a bomber parked next to the runway, waiting to take off. Ned's plane, making touch-and-go landings in a crosswind, crashed into it. Later I read the letter his commanding officer wrote following the accident:

MARINE NIGHT FIGHTER SQUADRON
FLEET MARINE FORCE
USMCAS, CHERRY POINT, N.C.

20 January 1943

From: The Commanding Officer
To: The Commanding Officer,
    45th Bombardment Squadron,
    U.S. Marine Corps Air Station, Cherry Point, N.C.
Subject: Commendatory action.

1. The Commanding Officer wishes to express his sincerest appreciation to, and admiration of the below named officers and men of U.S. Army Aircorps [*sic*] 45th Bombardment Squadron for their presence of mind and complete disregard of personal safety in assisting in removing Major E. McC. Hodgson, USMCR, and Private T.M. McAwliffe, USMCR, from Navy

SNC-1 airplane Bureau No. 05190 which was enveloped in flames as the result of an aircraft accident:

ESTES, J.A., 1st Lt., USAAC
EDWARDS, F.W., 2d Lt., USAAC
KIRKPATRICK, G.E., StfSgt., USAAC
THOMAS, H.M., Corp., USAAC
WHEELER, H.S., PFC., USAAC

2. During night flying operations on 13 January 1943 at the U.S. Marine Corps Air Station, Cherry Point, N.C., Major Hodgson's airplane collided on the ground with U.S. Army A29 airplane No. 41-23345 piloted by 1st Lt. J.A. Estes, USAAC. Both airplanes immediately burst into flames. In spite of the shock of collision, the above named officers and men ran to the SNC and released and removed Major Hodgson who was trapped in the burning cockpit. These men then returned to the SNC and removed Private McAwliffe whose foot was caught in the damaged rear cockpit, McAwliffe then being unconscious. The rear cockpit was also in flames.

3. If Major Hodgson and Private McAwliffe recover, their lives will have been saved largely as the result of the above named men's prompt action in the face of danger from fire and possible explosion.

F.H. Schwable

Copies to: Above named men (5) C.O. (2) Commander, Eastern Sea Frontier (1) FILE CMC (1)

That day in Winnetka, Mother said to me in a choked voice, "Marion, why don't you write the dear boy and cheer him up? He may be too badly hurt to know about it, but it will make you feel better."

I left the room in tears to do just that.

3

[Winnetka, Illinois]
January 23, 1943

Dear Ned:

Just about ten minutes ago I heard about your plane crash and your getting burned, and I've just wired you.

There are so many things I want to know, and so when you are all well again, do write me and tell me when it happened (the newspaper clipping didn't tell), how it happened, etc. Was it that old crate you flew the aces around in? You didn't have the accident on your return trip to Cherry Point, did you? Funny, I worried about you.

Golly Pete, Ned, when I think about what a close shave you had, I just go cold all over. It's all right for other people to get hurt or even bumped off in this war, I guess, if that's the way it has to be—but not you!

I'll drop your mother a note tonight [Miss Mary had rushed to his bedside] and maybe she'll have time to let me know how you are . . . . Please be good and do what the doctor tells you to, and remember I'm thinking about you—

Marion

[Chicago, Illinois]
January 26, 1943

Dear Ned:

I just can't stand not knowing anything about your accident any longer. Therefore, I have made out a questionnaire and all you have to do is tell the nurse where to put the check marks. Maybe if your right arm isn't hurt or anything, you could do it yourself, mmmm-m-m-m? Anyway, I hope you find it in your heart to inscribe a little "X" on the place designated for a signature, even if you have to take pen between teeth to do same. Just that little personal touch will help so much. [I did not realize his eyes and hands were bandaged.]

[Chicago, Illinois]
January 27, 1943

Dear Ned:

Well, howdy do! And how are you today? Do you feel better? I sure hope so.

By now the news about Roosevelt and Churchill, announced at 9:00 last night, is old stuff to you, I spose. But everyone is still talking about it around here, since the news is still fresh. At first, when the newspapers and radio stations kept announcing that at 9:00 P.M. on January 26, a world-shaking announcement was to be made and extra editions of newspapers would go into print, I thought they were going to announce that I'd been accepted in the WAFS [Women's Auxiliary Ferrying Squadron, who served before the formation of the WASPs], so nachully the news about Roosevelt and Churchill was sorta anticlimactic tuh me, but it thrilled me right on. [It was announced that Roosevelt and Churchill had concluded a ten-day secret meeting at Casablanca at which they'd agreed that victory would require unconditional surrender of the Axis powers on all fronts.]

Ned, why in the world can't I qualify for the Women's Flying Training Program (I suppose this is the same thing as the WAFS, don't you?) that the Army Air Forces are sponsoring? It seems wasteful for the government to have trained me this far and yet not want to go any farther just because I have only 55 hours instead of around 100. The only applications they are considering right now are those with 100 hours of flying time, even though they say "applications are based only on individual merit." Aint I got no merit?

Like the general public, I did not know then about the power struggle that was going on. Nancy Harkness Love had over a thousand hours in the air and had established an elite corps of experienced women pilots known as WAFS; Jacqueline Cochran, famed aviatrix, wanted the Air Corps to take licensed women pilots with far fewer hours of flying than Nancy's WAFS required and train them the same as male cadets.

As far as the public could tell, Nancy got there first with her WAFS in the Ferry Command, but Jackie's scheme (which had been brewing for a long time) ultimately prevailed. Her WASP organization swallowed up Nancy's original WAFS, with Jackie in charge of all. Nancy remained head of the girls in the Ferry Command.

It was one of the minor miracles of the war that these two women, so totally different in background and approach, were eventually able to serve effectively as leaders under the same umbrella, with Jackie emerging as boss lady. Absolutely the only thing they had in common was their love of flying and a driving ambition to use women pilots in the war effort.

Nancy Love was a stunning, soft-spoken, to-the-manner-born lady who was also high-spirited and adventuresome. While attending Vassar she became the youngest woman ever to earn a commercial pilot's rating, and she got into trouble by buzzing the campus. She left college voluntarily at the end of her sophomore year to fly to her heart's content. In 1936 she married a fellow pilot, Bob Love, a Princeton graduate who eventually formed powerful connections in the Ferry Command and who undoubtedly helped Nancy implement her plans.

Jacqueline Cochran came from an impoverished background and was uneducated and tough. Working in a mill when she was eight years old, Jackie didn't know who her parents were. She later chose her name out of a telephone directory.

She passed her first flight test without knowing how to write, worked her way up from being a hairdresser to a cosmetics magnate, and married a wealthy and influential man who adored her and encouraged her to fly. They moved in circles that included movers and shakers and presidents of the United States. Jackie was pretty, ambitious, ruthless, generous, and totally fearless. When she died in 1980, she held more aviation records than any other pilot of either sex in the world.

In the summer of 1941, Jackie and her husband, Floyd Odlum, had dinner with President Franklin D. Roosevelt and First Lady Eleanor at their Hyde Park home. Jackie told them of the nearly two thousand women pilots in this country and asked once again if they shouldn't be used to release men for combat if we went to war.

The president was interested, and Eleanor suggested that Jackie consult with the Army Air Forces as to whether women pilots would be useful. This she did, and found that Col. Robert Olds had already been approached by Nancy Love. But Gen. H. H. "Hap" Arnold, head of the Air Corps, had stated at the time that there was adequate manpower available.

After Pearl Harbor, in 1942, Jackie recruited and accompanied a small group of American women to England to serve in the Air Transport Auxiliary as ATA-GIRLS. Jackie's service to the ATA has been bitterly disputed. She was an honorary flight captain serving without pay but, according to some, lacking sufficient flight training to meet the qualifications for the ATA.

According to Lettice Curtis, author of *The Forgotten Pilots,* Jackie "had little time for flying. Our main memories of her are of someone who lived at the Savoy Hotel, wore a lush fur coat and arrived [at the air base] in a Rolls Royce, both noticeable because by now we had clothes [rationing] as well as petrol and food rationing."

In any event, Jackie was released from the ATA in July 1942 and remained in England for a while. Her detractors say she stayed to hobnob with nobility; her champions, to study and write a plan for ferrying planes for the 8th Air Force. Whichever—maybe it was both—in September she returned to the United States to lay out her strategy for women to be used as military pilots at home.

When I wrote to Ned in January 1943, my assumption that the WAFS were the same thing as Jackie's Women's Flying Training Program could hardly have been more erroneous. Regardless, I needed more hours in my logbook to qualify for Jackie's program, and there was no hope of buying more flight time. If time in a Piper Cub was six dollars an hour in Georgia, it was sure to be more in Chicago. I was now making $135 a month and receiving regular raises. But nearly every dollar was allocated for rent, meals, transportation, and buying a war bond. My only hope was that flight time requirements would be reduced. I continued my letter to Ned:

The only encouragement I've gotten so far came in a mimeographed letter from Jacqueline Cochran, saying that if the requirements were lessened, I'd be notified. Meanwhile, I'm just beating my life out on this d—- typewriter.

On 28 January I wrote Ned again, complaining that nobody had told me how he was. My next letter, the next day, was an effort to be light and gay.

When I got home last night there was not any news of you from anyone. Why doesn't someone tell me how you are? After all, how is Dr. Stegeman to function without a progress report?

It's snowing again, practically a blizzard.

Here's a pome for you:

It aint no fun
*   To be in baid*
Flat on yore back,
*   Now is it, Naid?*
Yet to have a place
*   To lay yore haid*
Is better than none
*   And better than daid.*

So with that cheery thought, I leave you now. Be good. Love.

M.

I did not know then how near death Ned was, or I might not have been so silly. And then, finally! Early in February, I received news of Ned. I wrote:

Dearest Ned:

I just this minute got your letter and I was so relieved that if I hadn't been such a big girl now, I would have sat right down and cried. You have no idea how worried I've been about you. Your mother was mighty sweet to write all that, and you were mighty sweet to dictate it.

Gosh, it gave me cold chills to read about your accident. I could personally kiss every member of the bomber crew who got you out.

I was so glad to know that your face wasn't seriously burned. I'm awfully thankful that your puss won't be marred because it's such a nice puss. I hope the feet, too, are much better by now and that it doesn't still feel as though someone is giving you a perpetual hot foot.

Saturday I got some good news. I got a letter actually signed by Jacqueline Cochran, saying that the requirements for the Women's Flying Training Program had already been lowered by

25 hours, and that I was to advise the Army Air Forces Flying Training Command at Fort Worth when I had logged a minimum of 75 hours, at which time my name would be assigned to a recruiting officer in this area. Of course what Jackie doesn't realize is that it takes just a little bit of *argent* (as we say in France) to add 20 hours to your flying time, and money is one of the things of which I aint got none. But anyway, it is encouraging to know that they have reduced the requirements once, and if they will only reduce them a similar amount again, I will be eligible, in which case I would go stark, raving mad from sheer joy.

Well, Ned, be a good boy and don't get too impatient about having to stay in bed. Things could be worse, as you well know, so do what the doctor tells you; take it easy, and leave the nurses alone. Remember, you're shy! That's what you told me. Hah! Leave them alone, I say.

My love to your mother, and lots to you, too.

About this time, Ned's mother, who apparently found it difficult to express feelings in person, wrote Ned a note on a Saturday night as she sat by the bedside of her suffering son:

Ned, my dearest, after writing for you that sentence in Hardy's letter about your winning your medals in the battle of Cherry Point, I want to be the first to present some of your medals. I can do this in writing more easily than orally. The first medal is for fortitude. The second medal is for your high spirit. The third is for your infinite patience in big and little things. The fourth is for your unfailing courtesy to all. The fifth is for your uncomplaining attitude and acceptance of your accident, suffering, and "detour" in your career. The sixth is for being such a shining star to me, to keep my sights lifted, and to keep me aware of what is meant by man's being made in the image of God.

These I present with all the love in the world.

Mother

I received more letters from Ned in his mother's handwriting. He was having a rough time with skin grafts and infections, and they were worried about running out of donor sites. Meantime, I kept writing him. On 18 February I wrote the exciting news that I had been accepted for flight training, if I could pass the physical. And on 23 February I did pass the tough Army "64" exam—physical—and was ordered to report for duty in Houston on 24 March.

I gave the Federal Reserve Bank of Chicago notice, borrowed the price of my train ticket to Texas by way of Georgia, and set out to tell my family good-bye. I fervently hoped it was only a temporary good-bye. I fought down a great knot of apprehension and concentrated instead on the incredible opportunity ahead of me to serve my country as a female pilot.

During my stopover in Georgia, I received a telegram from Jacqueline Cochran changing my orders to Sweetwater, Texas. I was sick with disappointment. I did not know the whole training program was being moved, in steps, to the West Texas prairie.

The switch was made to Sweetwater for several reasons. The facilities in Houston were miserably inadequate, with trainees sleeping in rooming houses or tourist courts where single beds and hot water were in short supply. Those things, however, could be corrected. What could not be changed was the unpredictable winter weather at Howard Hughes Field. It had produced enough fog to inspire a song that trainees sang like a dirge as they marched three-quarters of a mile to the mess hall from the flight line:

We get up at six in the morning
   Regardless of where we have been.
But at quarter past eight
   It won't hesitate,
The – fog – rolls – in.

We hurry our eating at lunch time,
   Get out our 'chutes, check the pin

But exactly at two
   We've nothing to do,
For – the – fog – rolls – in.

At dusk when the daylight is waning,
   'Tis then, at the end of the day
That you'll hear us all sigh
   That it's too late to fly,
And – the – fog – rolls – away.

Had I realized how rough things were in Houston, I wouldn't have been so disappointed that my orders now read: Report to Sweetwater's Avenger Field.

But where was Sweetwater, anyway?

4

When I disembarked from the crowded day coach at Sweetwater, I boarded a battered old open-air cab with two other trainees to go to the Blue Bonnet Hotel, center of all activity in the treeless West Texas town. We would learn to love it in spite of its bleak countryside and cruel weather, because of the wonderful people who were so incredibly kind, opening their homes and hearts to us on weekends.

Our first act at the Blue Bonnet was to put a nickel in the Coke machine for the "pause that refreshes." Then it took another nickel to call Avenger Field to tell them the troops had landed. We had to wait until the next morning, when Avenger Field dispatched its infamous "cattle wagon" to pick up the motley group of girls that assembled in the lobby of the hotel. Among them were a Powers model (who washed out), a schoolteacher, a riveter, a nurse, and at least one war widow.

While we milled around the lobby that morning, noisily waiting for our ride, two lieutenants strutted through the room pretending to ignore us as they wound their way toward the drugstore that adjoined the lobby. Just as they passed behind me, I heard one of them snort, "More women pilots! I'd like to give a U to every damn one I ride with. I'm putting in for a transfer."

I sank into a deep leather chair next to a brown-haired trainee who had also heard. "Must be the welcoming committee," I said. "What's a U, anyway?"

"I think it stands for Unsatisfactory. They must be check pilots. But don't let those drips intimidate you." She looked at me in a skilled, penetrating way that made me guess she was a teacher. She seemed older, wiser, wearing sensible shoes and a nondescript suit that hid an excellent figure. "You're from the South, aren't you? What state?"

I confessed to Georgia, and asked her name and hometown. "Marjorie Sanford, but just call me Sandy," she said. "I'm from Peoria, and please don't laugh."

I wasn't laughing. I was just trying to assimilate the fact that there was a terrible lot more to it than just being accepted by Jacqueline Cochran. What I felt must have shown on my face, for Sandy asked if I'd had any trouble getting into the program. I thought back, visualizing my mother on one side of me wringing her hands. On the other side was Grannie, wearing a sic 'em smile. All at once I wondered if Mother had been right and Grannie totally out of her sweet old mind.

Before I could answer Sandy the cattle wagon arrived, a creaking old trailer-like bus with flapping canvas windows and wooden benches, waiting to haul us and our baggage out to Avenger Field. I had thought it was so named in reference to the enemy, but it now appeared to be more the site of the continuing battle between the sexes.

As I climbed into the wagon and sat down with Sandy beside me on the hard wooden bench, I felt my first tinge of identification with the incongruous group of my own gender. As we pitched forward and were off, a sudden high, comic voice broke out with, "Off we go, into the wild blue yonder . . ." In a few seconds everybody was singing it.

"I can see we're going to be one big, happy family," Sandy shouted in my ear, not meaning it. How could we guess that closeness we would someday feel to this noisy, crazy, courageous bunch of females who were to fly everything in the Air Forces' arsenal, from primary trainers to B-29s, including all the fighters?

Thirty-eight of us would be killed doing it, but our record would be slightly better than the men's for the same type of flying. Whatever the Air Corps would let us do, we'd do it, understanding that we had to try harder and gripe less than the men we flew with. The fact that they made more money and had more perks than we did meant less than nothing to most of us then. We were just grateful to have a chance to do something women had never before been allowed to do in our country: fly military airplanes. We ourselves would be on Civil Service status, but for all practical purposes were in the Army: living on Army bases, getting Air Corps training, flying their planes, obeying their rules.

By the end of September 1944, WASPs would deliver more than half of all fighter planes from factories to air bases around the country. Ferrying was all we had expected to do, but Jackie Cochran had bigger ideas. Before it was all over, WASPs towed targets for gunnery officers to shoot at with live ammunition (and sometimes they missed and hit the planes); flew tracking and searchlight missions; did administration and utility flying ("aerial dishwashing"); instructed; performed simulated strafing and test piloting; and did anything else, short of combat, that needed doing.

But all that was beyond our wildest imaginings as we jounced toward Avenger Field, three miles out from the Blue Bonnet Hotel. I could not have dreamed that Sandy, the ex-schoolteacher I was sitting next to, would become a B-26 pilot. Or that she would marry her B-26 squadron commander from New York, who, like the lieutenant in the Blue Bonnet Hotel had initially vowed he was "not going to fly with any goddamn woman" and was going to put in for a transfer. I often wondered if the lieutenant changed his mind, too.

As the bus jerked to a stop at the guard station that protected the entrance to Avenger, the striking model exclaimed, "Look, guards with guns!" At that moment the gravity of being at war hit me full force, and patriotism almost conquered my misgivings and fear.

Waved on by a guard, the bus rattled up a hard dirt road that wound around the bare, semi-desert starkness of Avenger Field. As we swayed with the bus, I admired the swinging, well-brushed blonde hair of the girl in front of us and the darker head of soft waves next to her. A few short months later the two of them, the blonde and the brunette, would disappear from the face of the earth along with their instructor and their airplane, in a pile of wreckage, leaving few clues. And it would happen in a twin-engine trainer that Sandy had been scheduled to fly.

Someone cheered as the bus pulled up in front of the long, one-story wooden administration building. In a pitching spasm, the cattle wagon stopped. We piled out, squinting against the glare. Surrounded by luggage at the base of a tall flagpole, Sandy and I waited with the others as Old Glory whipped straight out, as if in a salute. I pushed back the hair that slapped against my face in the wind that was said to never stop blowing. I saw a plane then, some distance away, high up in the hard blue West Texas sky that swelled with sun-filled clouds. I didn't know one Air Force trainer from another, but this one had its nose up too high, and it was mushing through the air dangerously. Sandy followed my eyes and commented, "Someone's practicing stalls." As we watched, spellbound, the plane fell off to one side and began slowly to spin, plummeting toward earth. It spun around once, twice, winding up faster now, three times . . . then it recovered and flew away.

"And we have to do that solo," Sandy said. I groaned.

An Army officer, tall, attractive, graying prematurely, was waiting for us to quiet down before he welcomed us in a friendly voice. His name was Lieutenant Gerron, and he smiled as he said, "Follow me, please." He led the way inside the building, where he personally fingerprinted each girl. Later he would teach us fancy drill steps, and we would learn to love him. His official title was adjutant.

I was photographed, handed a batch of papers, and told to join the group that was being rounded up on the concrete walk outside the back door. From there we were marched over to Hangar Number Two, to pick up our bedding. We were a disparate group in our civilian clothes as we paraded in an unmilitary fashion, out of step, toward the hangar. I felt like giggling at our ragtag appearance as we passed a neat formation of coverall-clad female trainees in perfect step, the rhythmic cadence of their feet keeping time with the lusty song they were singing. Excitement swept over me at the thought that I'd soon be one of them—sunburned, disciplined, fit, happy, purposeful.

Suddenly we heard masculine voices repeating, "Hup, two, three, four . . ." and there, marching toward us on the hard, sun-bleached earth, was a formation of cadets. No one had told me Avenger was coeducational! A male cadet program was being phased out at the same time we were invading the territory, someone explained.

Before we went inside the hangar we could see the PTs—primary trainers—and they were beautiful, sleek, silver open-cockpit Fairchild monoplanes, shining in the sun. I hadn't realized they'd be so big. I wanted to touch one of them, to look inside the cockpit at all the gadgets, but I didn't dare. I gawked for a moment, then silently fell back into line, as bidden.

"Hurry up and wait. That's the Army way," someone quipped as we stood in line, waiting for sheets and blankets to be issued. I had lost Sandy, the only familiar face (by virtue of a couple of hours). I looked around but couldn't find her. Weighted down with towels and bedding, I staggered back to the rec hall, where we were to meet our commanding officer.

I found Sandy again, and while we were sitting on our stacks of "linen," filling out endless forms, a shapely girl walked over and stood next to Sandy. She was tanned (in March!) and her hair was streaked with blonde. Everything about her was expensive looking, down to the diamond-studded ring on her well-manicured pinkie. She was so pretty, I stared. "This is Shirley Slade," Sandy said. "I've asked her to room with us. There'll be more than two to a bay. That's an Army word I just learned. Bay. It means a room in the barracks. Anyway, we need to grab some nice roommates quick, before somebody else does."

Inwardly I groaned as I looked up at Shirley, *Life*'s future cover girl. I couldn't imagine ever really liking her—she looked rich and snooty. If someone had told me that during the next six months of training she, along with Sandy, would be my closest friend and confidante, I would have laughed scornfully.

"I've already promised four other people I'd room with them," Shirley said. "That's all right, isn't it?"

I opened my mouth to protest. After all, I wanted to have something to say about the females I was going to be locked up with. But before I could speak up, Sandy said, "Sure."

Then she caught my look and said, "It's all right, Scarlett." She had decided to call me Scarlett after finding out I was from Georgia. "There have to be at least six to a bay."

It turned out we had seven. And every last one of them except me was a Yankee. Shirley was from Chicago and Sandy from Peoria. Then there were Hattie, also from Illinois; Jane from Michigan; and Jill and Bertie from New York. "It's a frame-up," I muttered after hearing the various accents falling harshly on my ears. How could one poor little ol' magnolia blossom from Georgia hold her own against six descendants of Sherman?

"Attention!" someone shouted, and we all scrambled to our feet and stood stiffly, waiting for a look at our CO.

We had heard he was a personable bachelor but had absolutely no use for women pilots and was existing only for the day when he'd be ordered to combat duty. Didn't he realize that by having women fill the stateside cockpits he'd get overseas faster? Wasn't that the whole purpose of the WAFS? (Our name had not yet been changed to WASPs.)

"As you were," he said, entering.

There was a military bearing about him, in spite of the slouch cap that set him apart as a pilot. Nonpilot officers left the stiffening in the crowns of their caps.

The smile beneath the trim mustache was weary, the brown hair thinning, and there were lines around the blue eyes from squinting against the Texas sun, but the total effect was one heck of a good-looking guy, oozing sex appeal.

Mesmerized, I was unprepared for his caustic tone of voice when he spoke. It was obvious then that the rumors were true: Major McConnell hated the assignment of CO to a bunch of would-be female pilots. Although his job was to demand the near impossible of us, he made it clear that he, personally, wouldn't be surprised if we all washed out.

He's already decided we're a bunch of sissies, I thought, and felt a tightening of determination within my spirit. I'd show him, by damn! We all would!

He talked for nearly an hour, explaining the offenses that would eliminate us from the program. He went into detail about the process of washing out—the civilian check rides followed by Army checks—and told us sarcastically that when the die was cast, it would do no good to cry or write our congressman.

He dismissed us abruptly, and we were assigned bays. Ours was D-5. My address for the next six months would be Barracks D-5, 318th AAFFTD, Avenger Field, Sweetwater, Texas. AAFFTD was Army Air Forces Flying Training Detachment. I'd have to send my new address to Mother and to Ned, if he was still alive. If he was, he didn't have much to look forward to, from day to day, lying in that hospital bed. I could at least write to him and share this experience.

In D-5 we threw our things on our cots, then went back to Hangar Number Two to pick up flight gear: helmets, goggles, winter flying suits, coveralls. The coveralls looked like mechanics', and they were made for men. They were several sizes too large for most girls and were quickly dubbed zoot suits, the name given to the suits made famous by Harlem men, with voluminous pant legs that tapered at the ankles.

The smaller girls had to roll up their sleeves and pant legs several folds, to be able to function. Zoot suits were what we had to wear all day long, and we each were issued two of them. We washed them by standing in the shower, wearing one, soaping it down, and scrubbing it with a brush.

We turned in our food-ration books (since we were still civilians), long enough for the mess-hall people to buy meat for us as well as sugar. We ate off divided tin trays and sat at long tables on hard benches, but no one complained. And the food was surprisingly good, except for the few times we were fed buffalo and, once, horse meat.

That first night I was really tired and ready for my hard little cot, even though I hadn't finished unpacking. There was just too much stuff to fit into the small metal cabinet each of us had, with a mirror in the door. But they'd said we could keep our extra gear, for awhile anyway, in our foot lockers at the end of our beds.

I wasn't quite sure what to do about undressing. Should I go into the latrine that served thirteen suitemates (occupants of two bays connected by the bath), or would that look too prudish? I decided simply to turn my back and get it over with as quickly as possible.

A low whistle came through the open window, which had no shades. I dropped to the floor, horrified. I had forgotten about the cadets next door! They obviously had been waiting quietly for just this moment.

"Attenntion!" a shrew-like voice screamed. "Prepare for inspection." I snatched the top to my pajamas, pulled it on, and dived under the covers of my newly made cot. The next thing I knew, a mannish-looking upperclassman grabbed me by the arm and yanked me to my feet, while I fumbled at the buttons of my pajama top.

"Come to attention," she ordered. "Chin in, shoulders back,

head erect, arms by the sides, palms cupped, heels together, toes apart."

"Yes ma'am," I said, trying to look military in only my pajama top, with bare feet.

What followed was mild hazing, something we really hadn't expected. "Wipe that smile off your face." "Suck up your gut." "Don't speak unless you're spoken to." "Sit down." "Stand up." And so on.

After the indignities were over, there was a gentle knock at the door, with a pleasant voice inquiring, "May I come in?"

The voice belonged to an equally pleasant face, with friendly sparkling eyes that crinkled at the corners when she smiled. She told us her name was Jane Champlin and she was an upperclassman, and she just wondered if she could help us in any way or answer any questions.

"Yes, what was that, who just left?" I asked.

"Oh, just another upperclassman, having her fun at your expense. She told me what she was going to do, so I thought I'd follow along behind her and reassure you that we're not all like that."

Then Jane sat on the long wooden table in the middle of the room where we were to do our studying and letter-writing and hair-rolling-up, and answered our questions. Later I would always remember her sitting there, swinging her legs, talking and laughing, trying to make us feel at home. She was very reassuring about everything, especially about the safety of the airplanes we were going to fly—and all the time one of them was going to kill her very soon.

5

The next morning it was still black outside when we were awakened by a bugler who was swinging reveille. Nell Carmody had been a band leader and could jazz up reveille until it took the misery out of having to get up before the sun. Then I heard another sound that was to fill the dark air with magic early every morning: airplanes being warmed up—for us! The engines sounded powerful and exciting, beckoning us to come harness their energy and fly off into the sky on silver wings.

On 26 March I wrote a penny postcard to Ned and another one to Mother. She was temporarily staying with my now-married brother in Atlanta, where he was attending medical school at Emory. His wife, Janet, was my oldest and dearest friend.

March 26, 1943

Dearest Assorted Pipples:

Today I went up for my first instruction in a PT 19-A, and it's the sweetest airplane that flies, I'm convinced. Lordy, I love it!

Everything is fine and I'm getting a big kick out of every minute of this.

How are y'all? Please write me. I miss you and love you.

I didn't have time to write the details leading up to the first flight. Thirteen of us in two bays had fallen all over each other in a bathroom that seemed to be built for two, as we tried to brush teeth in one of the two basins and take turns in the two latrines. After that we had to rush back into our own bays to pull on zoot suits, brush hair, and "fall in" outside for breakfast formation.

We hadn't yet learned to line up correctly or march in step, so we were a shambling group as we made our way to the mess hall. One girl marched daintily on her toes, her Achilles tendons apparently shortened from wearing high heels constantly. Some cadets pressed against the screen door to the mess hall as we passed them. There were low whistles and much rolling of the eyes (I was peeking and couldn't help smiling at them) as we "marched" past them. Someone in our group had found time to splash on cologne, and I heard one cadet inhale deeply and say, "They'll *never* be Government Issue!"

After a quick breakfast of French toast we were herded to the flight line, and everything else was blotted from our consciousness. The primary trainers were lined up precisely, shining silver in the sunlight, waiting for us. Four of us were given to each instructor, a civilian. We four had to be somewhere near the same height because of the shortage of parachutes. The trainees with the same instructor had to share the same chute and then leave it in the plane after each dual flight period, without the necessity of adjusting straps each time.

We were assigned to a nice-looking young man, a bashful brunet named Mr. Wade, who was courteous and mild mannered. I heaved a sigh of relief; I had heard about the instructors who yelled and cussed, hated women pilots, and made you cry. I needed patience and understanding, and Mr. Wade seemed like the type to supply such. We gathered around him.

He began by saying, "I don't know much about girls. Er, I mean, I've never taught girls to fly." He shifted uneasily. "I'm used to men. I've been instructing Canadian cadets, which is what we had at this field until the last couple of classes. But British or

Canadian or American, it's all the same. I mean, they're men. Oh, hell, let's go look at the airplanes."

We walked up to one of the PTs. Mr. Wade pulled four sheets of paper out of his pocket and gave us each one. "This is the cockpit procedure. I want you to learn it so thoroughly that you can say it in your sleep. I'll climb into the plane, and two of you get on each wing, and I'll explain things."

He put one foot on the wing and hoisted himself up easily, then slid into the cockpit. "I want you to say your cockpit procedure like this, and I'll show you everything as I go along. Form One checked, right tank full, left tank full, safety belt fastened, gosports connected, seat adjusted, controls unlocked and free, parking brakes set, gas on, switch off, throttle cracked, mixture full rich, flaps up."

The next day I learned I was to go up with Mr. Wade first. The schedule was posted on the big blackboard in the ready room, and my heart thumped happily. I hoisted my seat pack (parachute) up behind me the way I'd been taught and fell into step with Mr. Wade as we walked to our plane. He was wearing goggles and a baseball cap instead of a helmet. We climbed in, me in front, and he leaned over the side and shouted instructions to my fellow student who was going to crank the engine for us.

I went through the cockpit procedure, and Mr. Wade started the engine with a roar. We taxied out and swung into position next to the runway. My goggles were still on top of my helmet when the plane ahead of us checked its engine and blew all the sand in West Texas into my eyes and mouth and down my neck.

"Watch what I do now," said Mr. Wade, not knowing I was blind from tears and grit, as he again demonstrated the cockpit check before takeoff. I felt the earth rushing under us, and we became airborne.

He made a turn to the left in the traffic pattern. Mr. Wade was telling me something through the gosports; it was one-way communication only, like speaking through a hose that was connected to my helmet. I couldn't understand him. The roar of the engine and the howl of the wind muffled his voice. I pressed the gosports to my ears and heard the words, "stalls and spins," so I waited anxiously while he climbed to eight thousand feet above sea level. I had done those things before, in a Cub, so I wasn't really afraid. Not so long as Mr. Wade was doing it.

This was really flying! We were right out there in the elements, which was a lot more fun than being in a closed cockpit. "First we clear the area," he shouted. The plane rolled to the right, and the horizon stood dizzily on end. I had the sensation that there was nothing to hold me in, but Mr. Wade had already told me to check my safety belt, and a nervous glance assured me that it was still fastened.

Then there was a roll to the left. The earth, though thousands of feet away, seemed just off our left wing, in miniature, with a wisp of cloud separating us. Mr. Wade leveled the plane, pulled the throttle back, then lifted the nose of the PT higher and higher into a stall. The engine gasped; we hung motionless for a moment; everything dropped out from under us as the nose fell. He pushed the stick forward, then neutralized it, and we were in a normal flying position again. Mr. Wade could sure fly an airplane. I swallowed and nodded my head for more.

Once again he cut the throttle, lifted the ship's nose, and waited. I waited. The earth waited. I didn't like to think about the earth waiting. There was no sound. Then, with a snap, Mr. Wade brought the stick all the way back into my stomach. With a whine, the ship flipped into a spin, and the earth went around once, twice, and suddenly I could count no more. No Cub had ever spun like this. I wanted to shut my eyes.

Mr. Wade popped the stick forward, throwing my body out of the seat as far as the safety belt would allow it to go.

"Jesus!" Mr. Wade cried. "I mean, dear me! I lost my baseball cap on that spin recovery. Hold tight, and we'll see if we can get it."

He peeled off to the right, dived at the hat, missed, and tried again. On the third try, miraculously, the hat zoomed past my head and caught on the crash bar behind me.

"Grab it!" he shouted as it hung there, glued by the wind. "Bet we couldn't do that again in a million years."

I was afraid to reach out for fear I'd upset the center of gravity, but Mr. Wade's attachment to his baseball cap was such that I knew I'd have to take the chance, if I didn't want to alienate my instructor forever. I had to loosen my safety belt and twist around to reach the crash bar, holding my breath as I snatched for the cap.

And then it was done. I sat on the cap and panted with relief, feeling as if I'd passed the first test.

"Thanks," he said through the gosport. I was learning how to understand him better now. "Now we'll have some fun." He told me to check my safety belt again, then he pointed the nose of the ship down, then up, then lifted a wing, and suddenly we were flying inverted.

I grabbed the steel braces at each side of me. I must not have pulled the safety belt tight enough, I thought, because I was dangling halfway out of the airplane, my feet falling helplessly from the floor toward the earth, while all the dirt and debris from the bottom of the ship flew into my face. There was a moment of complete terror when I wondered if that little old safety belt would hold, and then, in a flash, we were right-side-up again.

"That was a half roll," Mr. Wade explained. "Now let go of the sides of the plane, and put your hands in your lap. Check your belt again, and I'll show you how well it works."

I had already checked it and pulled it so tight it was probably cutting off all the blood to my legs. Before I knew what was happening, we were upside-down again. The engine sputtered. Gravity was suddenly above my head, and my feet fell off the floor. I wanted to grab for the braces but made myself cross my arms instead. My body felt as if it weighed a thousand pounds as it hung against the safety belt. I was so panicky I couldn't get my breath at all. And in spite of the tightened safety belt, my bottom wasn't even touching the seat and I didn't know how long I could go on that way. We were defying all the forces of nature, asking for trouble. But the belt held. Then we were right-side-up again.

Mr. Wade put the plane into a spin to lose altitude quickly, and in a few minutes our wheels found the hard earth at Avenger Field. When Mr. Wade yelled, "Switch off!" and I knew it was all over, I sat bewitched, knowing I'd never be the same again.

"How'd you like it?" he asked, grinning. He was standing on the wing next to me.

"I'm hooked," I said, handing him his cap.

"Thanks," he said. "Next time we'll practice takeoffs and landings. Today we were just separating the men from the boys. I'm glad to say you're a man, Miss Stegeman."

I looked at him and laughed. "Thanks a lot."

Now I really had something to write home about. But after ground school and PT (which we called Physical Torture) I was so exhausted that night that it was all I could do just to write Ned and Mother cards that began, "Today I went up for my first instruction in the PT 19-A." Only Ned would be able to read between the lines.

6

We didn't see Major McConnell, our commanding officer, again until our first formal inspection. I had trouble keeping a straight face, because Shirley stood right across from me at the foot of her cot, and if we both looked ahead as we were supposed to, we looked into each other's eyes. Shirley the society girl had surprised me by being full of humor and devilment.

When the major looked Shirley over as she stood there, rigidly but voluptuously at attention in her zoot suit, not moving a muscle, I felt my mouth twitching. For a horrible moment I thought I was going to giggle. Shirley had a secret crush on the major in spite of his attitude, and it looked as if she was blushing. When he crossed the room and got to me, Shirley made faces behind his back. I thought I'd explode if his scrutiny went on much longer. I was glad when he turned away to rub a white-gloved hand over the bedsprings I'd just dusted. I could hardly believe it when he said, "Two demerits for dust." I realized then how frustrating it must be to be a West Texas housewife. But I didn't plan to be a housewife, in West Texas or anywhere else.

He turned back toward Shirley, walked straight to her locker, and opened it. I waited, holding my breath, because I knew Shirley had put bourbon in her Listerine bottle. The major picked up the bottle, uncapped it, and sniffed. How had he found out?

I'd heard that there were informants among the trainees, but surely no one in D-5. . . .

I shut my eyes and waited. How many demerits would it mean for the whole bay? When I opened my eyes again, the major was recapping the bottle and putting it back in Shirley's locker without changing his expression. When he was gone, Shirley and I collapsed on our cots in a fit of hysterical laughing.

"Why didn't he gig you?" I asked, when I could speak.

"Because mouthwash was in there. I transferred the booze to another bottle this morning."

I thought it was so funny that I wrote Ned about it. I'd been writing him every day, sometimes by the light of an illegal candle after taps. I'd heard a few meager details about his condition from Mother: he had been conscious since the third day following the crash, but if he lived, he'd probably be terribly scarred. The man in the plane with him, Private McAwliffe, was out of the hospital with nothing more serious than a big scar on one leg. No one else was hurt. Ned's family and Red Cross Gray Ladies read to him because his eyes were bandaged. It was his only diversion, and mail was the high point of his day. "Be sure to write often to that darling boy," Mother urged, "even if it means you have to skip writing me. I know you don't have much spare time."

I wondered who would read him the letter about the booze in the Listerine bottle. Not a Baptist, I hoped.

Major McConnell had our windows painted black, to keep the cadets from leering from their nearby barracks windows when we had to change clothes. But in West Texas in late March, it could get hot. And it was always stuffy in our bays, so we had to open the windows. We just tried to remember to walk around crouched down like Groucho Marx when we were in various stages of undress. If we forgot, we were reminded soon enough by wolf whistles.

One night several masculine voices came through the open window of D-5, saying in unison, "Oh, Waffies! Oh, Waffies!"

We ignored them until they insisted that they had something

important to tell us. Shirley took one corner of the window and I took the other, allowing only an eye to show. "What are your names?" they asked. We could see them crowded into the window opposite ours.

Shirley pointed to me and said, "Her name is Scarlett."

I reached over and pinched her, then called out to them that her name was Shirley.

"Let us see your faces," they demanded.

Reaching across and grabbing Shirley, I pushed her face to the window before she could recoil.

"Oh, we know you!" one of them said. "I've had my eye on you for a long time. Who is that other one?"

The spirit of competition filled me, and I allowed my face to be shown. "Oh, boy!" shouted one of them. "That's the big one I've been telling you about."

"What have you been telling them?" I demanded, thinking, I'm not big, I'm just tall.

"That I was going to have a date with you before I left," he said gallantly. "Will you go to the dance with me Friday night?"

"He's six feet one," one of his baymates put in, obligingly.

"We're still confined to the post," I said with regret.

"Haven't they told you? We're leaving next week, and they're letting us have a dance here on the post, and we can fraternize with you WAFS."

Several eavesdroppers in the adjoining bays let out squeals of delight, bringing more cadets to the windows down the line. Invitations were passed out and accepted, and Shirley and Sandy and I had our dates lined up before we knew it. We didn't hear taps blow, so the lights stayed on until the OD (officer of the day) came by and threatened us.

The dance took place and we all had fun, although the cadets seemed terribly young. Before dawn on Sunday morning, a familiar cry came through the window. "Oh, Waffies!"

The cadets again! I turned over and bent the pillow across my ear, but the cry became more insistent. Shirley dragged herself from bed to window and said grouchily, "This is our one morning to sleep. Will you please shut up?"

"Oh, Shir-lee! Oh, Scarlett!" they called.

"What do you want?" I said grumpily, at the window, careful not to show my morning face.

"We're leaving this morning."

"I'm sorry," I said. "Goodnight. I mean, good-bye."

"Please ask Shirley to come back to the window."

Shirley called good-bye from her cot, and Hattie told her to be quiet. The cadets continued to shout, apparently having no intention of letting us sleep when they could not.

I could see from my corner of the window that other lights were flashing on as other girls went to the windows to call hush up or good-bye. Finally at seven, the barracks across the way (that would never be the same again) emptied. We could hear the buses pulling away from the administration building.

The post seemed strangely quiet and lonely. I hadn't realized how much we were going to miss those crazy boys. They seemed to think we were wonderful. And they never let us forget that, although we flew the same airplanes and ate off the same tin trays, underneath the identical zoot suits, there was a difference, and *vive la différence.*

There was something else, too, something I didn't want to think about. These young, eager, goofy, wonderful boys could be some of the very ones we were releasing for combat. I wished I could tell them good-bye all over again, and do it right. They deserved a better farewell than we'd given them.

I punched my pillow to try to make it more comfortable, but there was a hollow feeling in the pit of my stomach, and I couldn't go back to sleep.

In April 1943, news from the Pacific war zone was sparse. Some girls had radios, but we seldom got to see a newspaper. We were quarantined during our first two weeks at Avenger Field, which was standard procedure. We couldn't even go into Sweetwater to see a newsreel at the end of a movie, to find out how our fighting men were faring. Before coming to Avenger we'd known that American forces had completed the occupation of Guadalcanal, but that was all.

On 9 April at eleven o'clock A.M., blissfully unaware of what was going on in the rest of the world, I rushed to the pay phone to call Western Union and send the following slaphappy telegram to Mother:

> JUST ME AND THE PT 19-A. I LOVE YOU.
> IN FACT I LOVE EVERYBODY.

I had actually soloed an Air Corps trainer. I had begun to wonder if I would ever be ready to.

But Grannie had had no doubts. The day before the solo, I'd received an airmail letter from her. Her sweet, spidery handwriting confidently asked the question, "Have you soloed that bomber yet?" Lordy, I hadn't even soloed the PT-19, and here she was still telling her friends that I was going to ferry bombers overseas! I'd have to straighten her out, *again,* gently.

Grannie loved me. I was named for her. She was proud of me. She was the only person who'd been willing to go up with me in a Cub when I got my license, if only we'd had the money. Was she willing because she was in her eighties, in ill health? I preferred to think it was because she had faith in me.

I could see her rocking, hear her gentle voice on a lazy Georgia afternoon after she'd finished her writing for the day. In her heyday she'd been a well-known author listed in *Who's Who*— Marion Foster Washburne, editor of *Mother's Magazine* and author of countless newspaper and magazine articles, essays, novels, and nonfiction books. Now she didn't want to admit that she was unable to keep up the pace after a stroke, heart attack, diabetes, and phlebitis. So, in order to feel productive, she wrote a little bit on her autobiography every day.

Perhaps because her own life had been so exciting, it was hard for her to restrain her imagination where my adventures were concerned. She was totally convinced that her namesake would be flying along on her ferry run to England any day now in her bomber, in spite of my disclaimers. How could I tell her I hadn't even soloed the primary trainer yet?

Well, I had to, somehow, without disappointing her too much. And so I'd begun a letter to her on the morning of my solo flight, indulgently correcting her misconceptions for the umpteenth time. I asked about her health, about Mother's morale, and if their good friends the Hodgsons had given them any recent news of Ned. I hadn't heard from him recently. Did they think he was going to make it, or was it too soon to be sure?

Before I could finish, it was time to go to the flight line, so I stuck the letter in my locker and got out my helmet and goggles. I marched with Flight Two to the flight line, in cadence with my classmates. Occasionally we heard an unnecessary "Hup, two, three, four," from the section leader.

After shooting three warm-up landings with Mr. Wade, I was

shocked when he told me to take up another ship, number 43, alone. I stared at him, horrified, because my landings seemed worse than ever. I wasn't ready, for goodness' sake. I wanted to scream Help! but I just nodded and swallowed.

"Look out for all the solo students in the air today," he cautioned. "As you know, it's thick up there."

"Lawsy me," I moaned, waiting while another trainee cranked the engine of number 43 for me.

She was hardly tall enough to do the job, but the PT coughed to a start. I waved my thanks and began to taxi out. My hand felt clammy on the stick. As I snaked down the ramp in order to see what was ahead of me, Mr. Wade ran wildly toward me, waving his arms.

"Whoa!" I cried to the plane, and managed to get it to a halt in spite of the weakness that had spread to my legs.

Mr. Wade bounced up on the wing and put his face close to mine as he yelled in my ear, "Now shoot three landings, and then taxi back over here. I'll be watching and waiting. If you should do something wrong on the first landing, I'll signal for you to come back here, instead." If I do anything wrong on the first landing, I thought, I won't be able to come back here, Mr. Wade! "But if everything is all right," he continued, "I'll wave you on."

He had told me all that before, and I wondered why he was repeating it. I licked my lips and nodded. "If you are uncertain about anything, I'll take you around once more."

I shook my head, lying like a dog. "Good luck," he said, then jumped down.

When the tower gave me the green light to take off, I shoved the throttle forward, feeling as if I were in a dream. There was an other-world quality to the goings-on, as the wheels gained speed along the hard ground next to the concrete runway, which was saved for larger planes. Before I knew it I was airborne. My mind was a complete blank. I made the first turn in close formation with another solo student who had forgotten to look back, and only then did I realize that my reflexes must be functioning.

The downwind leg was a nightmare. I didn't know where everybody had come from, and they had me hemmed in on both sides. I was afraid to move, so I let the plane do most of the flying, knowing if I left it alone it could do a better job than I could, in my tense condition. We remained in the air, the plane and I, by some phenomenon that I hardly understood. I felt like an observer and not a participant in the miracle of flight.

The base leg was a rat race and the final approach was worse, but between ol' 43 and me, we worked things out. We settled comfortably into a glide, and I refused to give an inch to the airplanes on my right and left and above and behind me, so some of them pulled up and went around. It was every man for himself. By that time I had automatically put on half flaps, amazed that I could remember that function without a single impulse ever consciously reaching my brain. The ground came up gently to meet us.

"Glory, glory to old Georgia," I shouted as we slid on, the airplane and I. I thought of us as a team now. A smoothly coordinated, undefeatable team. This was no wild stallion, after all; it was just a gentle mare, and I was riding her without need of a crop. When we had slowed down, I looked over to the spot where Mr. Wade was supposed to be standing and saw a bunch of people huddled there. Had he fainted? I gave the ship the gun.

Ecstasy shivered through my body, and I was goose-pimply with success. The next two landings were not as great as the first; nevertheless, I got down and walked away from the plane. Everyone agreed this was the only criterion for a good landing.

Mr. Wade met me with a scowl on his face. "Did you faint?" I asked.

"No. We found a rattlesnake on the field. But I was watching you."

I tried not to show any feminine squeamishness about the rattler, but it was unsettling to know they were everywhere, even on the field. One girl had seen one crawling along the wing of her airplane while aloft. She'd banked the plane and the rattlesnake had gone sailing off.

"Was I more interesting than a snake?" I asked him.

"More dangerous than a snake," he snarled. "Miss Stegeman, did you by any chance see any other airplanes up there?"

The criticism came, in torrents. He was positively picayunish about every little mistake I'd made. I'd had no idea he could see so much from the ground. After he was finished with me, Mr. Wade unexpectedly broke into a grin. "Well, anyway, you soloed!" he said, patting me on the back.

I was still slightly numb, and the full realization took a few minutes to hit me. On my way back to the ready room, it registered. "I soloed!" I whooped with glee, so loud that Shirley and Sandy came running toward me. I saw several other familiar faces behind them, all rushing toward me. I was swooped up and carried by my arms and legs, upside down like a Georgia possum.

"Scarlett soloed!" they screamed as they ran with me, leaving the flight line, heading toward the administration building while I twisted and turned and tried to wriggle free. Obviously these goofy females had cooked up something special to mark the auspicious occasion, but before I could figure out what, they shouted, "One, two, three!"

They released me over the water of the wishing well. I splatted on my back into the cool water, and sank among all the pennies and nickels we had tossed in for luck. When I climbed out my zoot suit weighed a ton, and I knew I looked a sight. I tried to run—waddling in slow motion after Shirley and Sandy—back to the flight line where the flight commander waited.

"If you ever leave this flight line again without permission, you'll be grounded for a week."

"*Yes*, sir. Yes, *sir.*" I couldn't stop grinning. Grannie, I've done it, I've soloed! I couldn't wait to write Ned and tell him. But first I'd wire Mother. As the flight commander turned away, I saw the corner of his smile. "You have permission, Miss Stegeman, to leave the line long enough to change your clothes."

I ran all the way, hugging my new warmth to me that no wet zoot suit could quench. I stood naked in the middle of D-5 and filled the empty place with rebel yells, then sang "Glory, Glory to Old Georgia." It was glory that wouldn't rub off that day, and I wasn't sure it would ever rub off. I had brought back a piece of the Texas sky, the feel of flight, in my bones. All alone.

"Just me and the PT-19A," I wired Mother. Then I finished my letter to Grannie, knowing I could never convince her it wasn't a bomber I'd soloed.

8

On 12 April I only had time to send a penny postcard to Mother:

Ground school aint too hard, though you have to keep up day by day or you're lost. Anyone who has less than a 70 average doesn't get to go out on the weekend, so it keeps us on our toes. We have two or three tests in each subject every week. I'm taking Math (!) and navigation. Doing hokay so far.

Math, as everybody in my family knew, was my weakest subject. When I was in second grade I was a poor student, because, the teacher decided, I was bored. She suggested to Mother that perhaps I should skip a grade. That summer when I was seven and my brother John ten, he took it upon himself to teach me the third grade. The principal of my school, after testing me at the end of the summer, decreed that I was ready to enter the fourth grade. The only deficiency that showed up later was my inability to remember my "times tables," a handicap in ground school.

If it hadn't been for Sandy, I never would have made it. But fortunately for me and everybody else in D-5, Sandy the schoolteacher was willing to help us all with our homework. (She also brushed Shirley's and my hair for us every night.)

Our navigation instructor tried hard to teach us what he knew, but he was intimidated by some of the trainees who had hundreds of hours of all kinds of flying behind them. They seemed to know all the answers and didn't hesitate to argue with him. He soon lost control over the class and undoubtedly came to regard us as a tribe of wild women with wings. But he did his best to show those of us who needed to learn how to use aerial maps; plotters called computers (known to us as "confusers"); and various formulas for outsmarting wind drift, gasoline shortage, and things in the ground that made compasses go haywire.

Ground school, a necessary evil, took second place to flying. On 15 April I wrote my family another postcard:

Had my first [civilian] check ride today; passed same. Needless to say, the "mind" is greatly relieved, so maybe I can relax until the next one.

Grannie writes me all the time. Isn't that sweet of her? Her last letter said, "I'm so proud of you for soloing that big *bomber* all alone!" Seems like we just can't get that idea out of her head! [She went to her grave insisting to one and all that "Marion is ferrying bombers to England."] We'll never see a bomber, much less fly one.

Little did I guess then that in just a few short months, Sandy and Shirley would both check out as command pilots on the B-26, the medium bomber some men were refusing to fly because of its reputation for being a flying coffin. Eventually Nancy Love and Betty Gillies would check out as first pilots on the B-17, Boeing's Flying Fortress, and be ordered to deliver one to Prestwick, Scotland. They would get as far as Goose Bay, Labrador, before General Arnold heard about it. He radioed a message to hold the plane and decreed that from then on, women would be permitted to ferry only in domestic service. The two original WAFS were at the end of the runway in their Fortress, waiting for clearance to take off and head for the United Kingdom, when Arnold's orders reached them.

In April of 1943, such an event was hard to imagine. Yet before long, Shirley and Sandy would be towing targets out over the Gulf of Mexico in their Martin Marauders.

In the middle of the month, I wrote my mother:

Weather kept us from flying for several days and so we had to fly on Saturday and Sunday.

Today I soloed snap rolls, half rolls, and slow rolls. More fun! I hate to disillusion you, but there's nothing really dangerous about that stuff. You're up so high that you have plenty of room to make mistakes, so don't worry.

My last check ride was satisfactory and so it looks like I'm going to get through PTs all right.

As soon as weather permits, we go on a cross-country—to and from a place called Harpersville, about 100 miles from here. [That cross-country never materialized.] Reckon I'll get lost? There's one good thing about Texas—there are fields and fields everywhere, in case anyone should want to use one. So, see? Evathing's on our side.

Talked to Jacqueline Cochran for several minutes tuther day, and she's quite nice. She took off for parts unknown in her plane, but will be back some time this week.

I had sat next to Jackie, a well-made-up blonde with beautiful big, brown eyes and a soft, rounded figure, in the rec hall and admired a cigarette case she held in her large, capable hands, hands she detested. The case was made of gold and there were rubies, diamonds, and emeralds on it, showing the route of a Bendix air race. Her husband had given it to her as a memento, for she had been responsible for opening the race to women and had flown in it three times, winning it in 1938. She held speed and altitude records and was the first woman to break the sound barrier.

Floyd Odlum was confined to a wheelchair with severe arthritis, and he lived his life vicariously through Jackie. They were married forty years before he died, and although the war and Jackie's pursuits often separated them, they communicated daily and were great admirers of one another. She brought excitement to his life, and he gave hers stability, wisdom, and security.

I didn't have time to write Ned about chatting with Jackie. In fact, I hadn't heard from him in a while. But Mother, who kept in close touch with his mother, kept me updated. Ned was going to make it! The doctors had been wrapping him in cellophane to preserve the body fluids that he would otherwise have lost. All Athens had rallied to round up cellophane—which at that time was almost impossible to buy—and sent it to the Naval Hospital at Norfolk.

In my next (undated) letter to Mother, I wrote:

I thought maybe you'd like an idea of our daily program, so I'll outline it approximately for you. I'm not supposed to tell the exact schedule.

6:15 — Fall out of bed
7:00 — Fall in for mess
8:00 — Ground school formation (We take two subjects at a time. One hour each.)
10:20 — Drill or calisthenics (sometimes sports in place of the latter) for one hour; alternate days. (We are subject to inspection any time of the day or night!)
12:00 — March to mess
12:50 — Flight line formation. We stay on the flight line for five hours. Each flight period is an hour long, and soon we'll be getting in two or three periods of flying a day.
6:00 — Mess formation. We change from our uniform coveralls to "dress slacks" for this.
8:00 — Study hall for ground school delinquents. Hope I'll never have to go.
10:00 — Taps

A busy chicken, aint I? In all that spare time I have to do a little housework: dusting, sweeping, mopping, making my bed. Then I have to wash out my personal items (things that can't be sent to the destructive laundry in town) and press same, also write a few letters, study my lessons, and keep my hair and fingernails as well groomed as possible.

In addition, it is necessary to fight my way into the shower (since 12 other people use it, too) to keep the body beautiful clean. By the end of the day I'm pretty well whupped and even the board-like Army cot feels good tuh me.

Did you know the Army is spending $30,000 on each one of us to train us? [Later the figure was lowered, and the estimate was $12,000, going only as high as $20,000 for added pursuit or bomber training.] When I think of all that dough being taken out of you poor civilian taxpayers' pockets I feel right obligated.

We fly in the mornings one week, in the afternoons the next. This week, as you can see by the schedule, it's afternoon flying, which we don't like nearly so well. The air is hotter, thus more bumpy.

There is always a strong wind but we are fast getting used to same and learning our tricks in spite of it.

Have I told you my impression of Texans? Maybe it's just the reaction from Chicago, but I've never seen such friendly people. They are just wonderful, and Sweetwater is a cute li'l ole town with everyone striving to please. On the weekends we gals overrun the place and they give us full sway.

Some of the farmers in the area viewed us with suspicion, though, and one girl in the class ahead of me found this out the hard way. Hazel Ah Ying Lee was a boisterous, first-generation Chinese-American and one of the funniest people I'd ever met. She was a wiry, buck-toothed, black-haired clown, with a loud voice and raucous laugh, and an infectious sense of fun. Wherever Ah Ying was, there was laughter.

One day she made a forced landing in a farmer's field and was held at bay by the pitchfork-wielding farmer who yelled, "Are you China-gal or Japanee?" She hastily assured him, "Me China-gal," and pointed to her name tag.

"Some day," she told us afterward, "somebody's going to kill me, thinking I'm Japanese." But what killed her was a collision in 1944 with another P-63 like the one she was ferrying. Her badly burned body lay in a military morgue for more than a year while the AAF tried to locate her husband, who was flying for Chiang Kai-shek in China.

But in 1943, Ah Ying was still making us laugh in Sweetwater. And I was having the time of my life, as my letter dated 24 April showed:

Dearest Mother:

The gods must envy me! This is just too, too to be true! (By now you realize I had a good day as regards flying. Nothing is such a gauge to the spirits as how well or how poorly one has flown.) Where was I? Oh yes—I'm far too happy. The law of compensation must be waiting to catch up with me somewhere. Oh, God, how I love it! Honestly, Mother, you haven't lived until you get way up there—all alone—just you and that big, beautiful plane humming under your control. I just sit there and sing at the top of my lungs while I'm climbing up to 4,000 feet—or however high I want to go. Of course I'm too busy to sing while I'm in the middle of acrobatics—but you ought to hear me let loose when I'm "clearing the area" between maneuvers. (We always clear the area first to make sure there are no planes underneath or close by—safety foist!)

The only thing that I know of that's going to happen that I won't like is that they are changing my instructor some day soon. Mine is going on to the BTs (basic trainers—one step ahead of primary trainers).

You asked for more details about the "nice date" I had last

Sunday. Honey, don't never ask things like that on a post card!! You'll see why, when I explain.

First lemme tell ya I had a nuther date with aforesaid personage Saturday night, and again all day Sunday. We had a wonderful time. Saturday night we went out to a friend of his'n's house and danced and chatted and danced some more. . . . Of course it's always a thorn in my side to have to sign in by 1:00 A.M. (one demerit for every minute you are late) on Saturday night, and 7:00 Sunday P.M. Seven demerits confine you to the post the next week, and 70 demerits wash you out. Needless to say, we get in on time!

Anyway, Sunday we went out to a beautiful little lake near Sweetwater. Shirley and her date were along. Shirley is the only roommate my age and she is a precious gal.

Well, Maw, here's the catch in the date set-up (and you must swear to secrecy): he is an instructor. You know I told you we weren't allowed to date them? The reason for that inconvenient rule is to keep instructors from dating their own students (and reluctantly, I must say I see their point) and so I'll try to obey that much of the rule. Of course if they caught me dating any instructor I'd probably get a pile of demerits and be confined to the post, but they'll never catch me! [Later Jacqueline Cochran lowered the boom and said, "Immediate dismissal if any trainee is caught dating any instructor."]

Well, honey, I gotta get to studying. I want to keep on making good grades because now I have a real incentive to get out on weekends! By the way, all lingering thoughts of Hal have long since vanished. Didn't I tell you they would, soon's I met another cutie? Anyway, I don't want to get serious about nobody again until this war is over!! Keep reminding me of that, will ya? I'm so damn susceptible.

9

We still had no idea what was going on in the war. During the month of May 1943 there was scant news from the Pacific. In the European theater, U.S. and British forces completed the conquest of Tunisia. Jews in the Warsaw ghetto had revolted against the Germans in April, but by May the Nazis had squashed their resistance. We gleaned snatches of current events from heavily censored newsreels whenever we went into Sweetwater to see a movie on "Open Post." I always left the theater feeling tearfully patriotic, proud to be allowed to help out on the home front in such an exciting way.

Soon after I got back to Avenger Field, my world narrowed down again to the goings-on in Class 43-W-5, especially the activities in Barracks D-5.

On 10 May I wrote Mother:

I'm enclosing some snapshots of my baymates, me, and the PT 19-A. We'll take some pictures of us in helmets and goggles and I'll send you those—also some in our "zoot suits" so you can see how we look all day long. Aren't my roommates cute? I love 'em all dearly.

We're having another dust storm today, so all flying has been stopped for this afternoon. I got in a solo period early this morning before they grounded us, though. We're doing chandelles, lazy eights, spins, stalls, eights along the road, slow rolls, half rolls, snap rolls, and a wee bit of inverted flying. 'Tis indeed a funny feeling—hanging upside down with only that safety belt between you and the earth, thousands of feet below. It's great sport. I like it!

Well, sugar, I've done enough raving for one day. I'll see you in the newsreels. Look for me. Hope you haven't missed 'em. They're showing them all over the country. [Camera crews had invaded Avenger.]

Thursday

[To Mother]

The yellow flag is up, which means dual flying only—and since I'm up to schedule on dual and need only solo for a couple of days, I'll grab this chance to exude a little of my happiness all over you.

My civilian check ride comes up last period. I'm not a bit nervous, but I'm due another Army check (having had only one) on PTs before I'm through, and I'll probably have a few butterflies in the stomach before that ride.

Anyway, do you realize how nearly through the primary course your chicken is? We go on a cross-country next week, then we'll be through the PT course! [Once again, the cross-country never materialized.] Praise Allah! But I just can't, by the wildest stretch of the imagination, think of me flying a BT next month. But then I felt the same way about the PTs, and here I am, nearly through. Don't we accomplish a lot in a hurry, though? It amazes me!

Today I feel as though everybody in the world loves me. Colonel Keehn [my old boss] wrote that they (in his office) still did; John Ashford wrote that he always would; Norman wired me to please consider "Stinky" again; Click [the instructor I had dated] smiled at me (when I caught a glimpse of him this morn-

ing) as though he might—all in one morning!! It's too much—
and in Ned Hodgson's last letter he said even if I didn't have
time to write in the future, he'd love me as much as ever.

Enclosed is a picture of my first and all-time favorite instructor, Bill Wade, who is now teaching on the BTs. That plane is
the kind I'll be flying only next month. (450 h.p.) [Actually the
model we flew at Avenger, the Vultee BT-15, had only 400 h.p.
and was notoriously underpowered.]

We were almost through primary training when Bertie unexpectedly resigned. She was a good pilot, so we were dumbfounded.
She packed her bag, kissed us good-bye, and left—tearless,
unemotional, without a backward glance. She had suddenly, mys-
teriously, decided to marry her fiancé, a wealthy older man, before
he went overseas. She'd known all along he was going, so why
did she sign up for Army flight training if she didn't intend to see
it through?

I liked Bertie and I would miss her, but I couldn't understand
her. She was not at all like my other roommates, whom I
described to Mother in an undated letter:

Monday

Dearest Mother,

Enclosed are my ration books for Janet, though I may have to
hastily recall them. The reason I had to have 'em this time was
so's we'uns could go on another picnic, but it rained, so we went
to Abilene again and danced instead; hence the ration books are
status quo, and tell Janet to use all she needs.

The girls and I were having one of our discussions tuther day
and we unanimously agreed that if we had our choice of any
place in the world to be, of anything under the sun to do—that
we'd unhesitatingly choose just this. I wondered if you realized
just exactly how your daughter felt about what she has got herself into.

It really makes it very pleasant to have the other girls (just the ones in our room, I mean—we don't have to go outside our bay for companionship) feel the same way.

Bertie left in order to marry her Lt. Colonel, so she is not included in this. Now that she is gone, we have been able to get Jill back in our room in her place. Jill, you know, started out with us and was moved when they decided that six in a room was suffish. She, by the way, is the next least like us—being sort of tom-boyish. Except for the fact that she snores louder than any man and coughs a lot (cigarettes) during the night, we all like her fine, and she's a good ole gal.

Jane Chapman is the older one (32) with the wonderful sense of humor. Her interests aren't exactly along our lines (meaning that she's not a she-wolf, being married and having a 12-year-old daughter) but she's a picnic. Her only fault is that she's always talking about washing out and has a defeatist attitude, as though she hasn't a prayer of making the grade. Since this isn't good for morale, we try to shush her (about what a lousy flier she thinks she is) as much as possible, and I think maybe her attitude is improving a little.

Sandy, Hattie, Shirley and I are more alike than the others. Hattie's 23 or 24 and Sandy is 28, but really we're all about the same age to all appearances. Sandy taught school before coming here; she's the one who never gives out of jokes, could talk the horns offen a billy goat, and is simply a swell girl. Hattie, too, taught school a couple of years, then worked for her father before coming to Texas. Except for being too picayunish about the condition of the room at times when we have Open Post and don't have to [keep] it spotless, she makes a grand roommate. She is the chubby one whose marriage to a Naval officer in Alaska can't last much longer, in my estimation. She's always in good spirits. . . .

As for Shirley, you've heard all about her. [I had written that, to my astonishment and delight, she had turned out to be a good sport, uninhibited and fun, and a terrific pilot.] Honestly,

Mother, we have the most congenial and happy group in this room in the whole camp! I sure hope we can stick together and none of us washes out.

Enclosed is a snapshot of Jacqueline when she was here, taken with the major (our CO) and our favorite lieutenant, who teaches us drill.

May 29, 1943

[To Mother]

Yesterday Class 43-W-2 (from Houston) graduated here, and you should see the beautiful silver wings we'll have when we get out of this place! [There had been no provision for wings, so Jackie Cochran helped design some for the first seven classes and paid for them out of her own pocket.] We are Class 43-W-5. [43 standing for 1943; W for women; 5 for the fifth class to be graduated.] In only 3½ more months we'll be through! I can't believe it!!

We had an Army band for the occasion and had to march for the visitors. They say it was really a beautiful sight, and out of the hundreds of girls, not one was out of step. We had to stand "at ease" in the broiling sun for two hours, but not one fainted. Men usually do! Guess we're really tough. We have "dress uniforms" now: white shirts, tan slacks, and matching overseas caps [bought at our own expense in Sweetwater].

Latrine rumor has it that we won't begin on the BTs until Wednesday, so we'll really get a good rest between now and then. But we can't go out and raise any hell, because Jacqueline Cochran is clamping down on us (she's here running things now, since the whole school has moved to Sweetwater) and the Army personnel is being moved out en masse and new officers brought in. Jacqueline is furious because we've been dating instructors and Army personnel and so she's having a bunch of old men moved in to direct us, so's we won't get into mischief.

Everyone is either being more careful about dating instructors or stopping completely. Me—I'm doing the latter. I adore Click, but not enough to take a chance on getting kicked out of the one thing that means life itself to me. And this does mean that much to me, Mother. It has really become an obsession with nearly all of us. Oh, we gripe in true Army style—sometimes about the food, more often about not getting Open Post like we used to (no more overnight passes, either, since Jacqueline has clamped down)—or about anything and everything—but the Army expects us to gripe, and surely everyone knows it's only skin deep and that really our whole hearts and souls are in this thing and we'd die if we washed out.

Which reminds me, I got a real compliment this morning. Shirley's instructor on the PTs (we can't have our old instructors on the BTs) told her he was really anxious to get me as a student on the BTs because he liked my attitude and he looked up my flying record and it was good! I'm flattered and encouraged beyond words. But frevingsake, don't mention it on a post card! We're never supposed to know things like that. Mr. Walker (Shirley's ex-instructor) must like lazy girls if he likes my attitude, because he's often remarked that every time he sees me I'm flat on my back (at the flight line) on a bench or a table, or even the ground, and half asleep while waiting for my next flight period. I really do relax! But one just about has to, because if you ever get a case of nerves—out you go!

Time and *Life* will soon be here to take pictures, and their scouts have Shirley's and my names as being photogenic!

Friday

[To Mother]

Well, today I had my first instruction on the BT and I felt as green as though I'd never been in an airplane—almost. But I felt that way on the PT at first, too, and now it's old stuff. The main difference is that there are so dern many instruments on the BT—that and the fact that we're handling hundreds of more horses than we were on the Fairchild. I think it'll really be fun on the Vultee, but the thing that we are all really looking forward to is flying the ATs (advanced trainers) which are supposed to be the sweetest ships on the market. But that's a long time off, and meanwhile, after twenty hours of transition work on the BT, we'll have instrument (under the hood) work, night flying, and lots of cross-country.

Monday

[To Mother]

Had my second BT lesson today; didn't do too well, but I refuse to be discouraged. It sure is a lot trickier to handle than the PT, and I'm a busy bee when I crawl into that cockpit!

Wonder if you know how insane we girls are over airplanes? Every time a strange one flies overhead, we dash outside, shade our eyes, crane our necks and just gape. It's really funny to see how universal the obsession is with us.

Last night a terrible storm broke loose and three BTs from another field had to circle around and decide to land here. It was after taps had been blown, but I wish you could have seen how quickly every bed in camp was emptied when we heard those planes! We all dashed out in our nighties with one robe to every three girls and tore out to the flight line to watch them land. The supervisors (women) had a terrible time trying to make us get back to bed before the pilots (British) could get out of their ships and see our rain-drenched, ill-clad figures standing there, chattering, squealing and giggling excitedly on the flight line. They almost had to twist a couple of girls' arms off before any of us would move, but somehow they got us back in the barracks before the boys got out of the planes. It was really thrilling— lightning flashing, thunder crashing, and huge clouds moving at a terrible rate across the sky.

June 10, 1943

[To Mother]

Flew the BT again today (it'll have to be just every other day until they get enough planes) and at last I can land the d—- thing and am sorta getting the feel of it now. Sure is hard work, though.

Guess you read in the paper about the crash two nights before last. [Jane Champlin, the upperclassman who had been so nice to us our first night at Avenger, was killed with her instructor, night flying near Sweetwater.] I wasn't going to tell you, since I hoped it would stay out of the papers, and I didn't want to worry you unnecessarily, but you've got to expect things like that when you think of all the hundreds training here. We've been lucky so far, and that was the first accident since I've been here. But don't worry about me, honey. I can take care of myself, and I have no qualms about bailing out if anything ever should go wrong. We felt pretty bad about the girl, though, because she was a likeable and popular kid [a vibrant college graduate who had been a good horsewoman, diver, and tennis player, as well as a good pilot], but I repeat: you have to just expect and accept things like that, because they are going to happen. We have the best record here of any school in the country, and really, the chances we take are small compared with what thousands upon thousands face every day all over the world.

June 11, 1943

[To Mother]

Hope you didn't order me a ration book because everyone here was supposed to order her own, which I did. If you get one, too, better send it back so we won't get put in jail.

Today I flew the BT for a change, instead of it flying me. I actually made some good landings, too. I'd solo right now if they'd let me, but I have to have four more hours of instruction before I can. Look for an ecstatic telegram next week, unless weather or lack of planes holds us back.

[12 June 1943]

Mother, darling,

Get set! Prepare yourself! Because here comes another one of those slaphappy, nonsensical, ecstatic letters. Oooooooo, Mom, I'm so happy I could die.

By now you know I've either (1) had a good day at flying or (2) passed a check ride. It just so happens that both are correct!

Honestly, Mater, I was so scared when I climbed into that cockpit to take my first civilian check ride on the BT that I thought I'd "gomit" all over the controls. I had been running to the jonny every ten minutes. One girl, seeing me dash into the jon for the fourth or fifth time (prior to my check ride) said to me, "You are either about to have a check ride or you're going on a cross-country. Which is it?" It seems that it affects all us gals the same way!

Anyway, I gave the check pilot a good ride and he told my instructor he might have an H.P. (Hot Pilot) on his hands. But since the only H.P.s are dead pilots—proved by experience—he got his terminology mixed, but anyway, he meant it as a compliment. Happy day!

[To Mother]

WESTERN UNION

WUK 148 18=WUX SWEETWATER TEX JUN 15 913A

GUESS WHO JUST SOLOED THE BIG BT EXCLAMATION POINT. FIRST ONE IN OUR FLIGHT. OH, HAPPY DAY. LOVE=

10

The same week that Jane Champlin was killed, our roommate Jane Chapman washed out.

Sandy and I were sitting on my cot one morning, unaware of Jane's fate, happily counting money from our kitty—a piggy bank that collected dimes and quarters for cussing: a dime for "damn" or "hell" and a quarter for worse words. Jane Chapman, who was in Flight One, was the major contributor to this cuss pot, which was going to finance our upcoming spree. We were planning three days in Dallas at the end of basic, which would be our first leave since we'd arrived on the post.

Shirley was writing a note to "Bacchus," a Navy pilot in Dallas who was arranging a wild celebration in our honor. "Just think, three whole days in Big D!" Sandy said, her eyes burning in anticipation. "I'm going to party, party, party, and not shut my eyes the entire time."

I stared at Sandy, fascinated. Not only had she overcome air sickness that had nearly washed her out, but there was nothing left of the schoolteacher who had arrived in Sweetwater in a colorless suit and sensible shoes. She had dropped the old demure mannerisms and emerged tan and glowing, ready for anything—everything. Her appetite for freedom and fun was intensifying, just as mine was. Suddenly Shirley looked up from her letter. "Jane! What are you doing here?"

We knew Flight One hadn't yet been dismissed. But Jane didn't speak or look at us. She moved like a zombie toward her cot and fell on it, burying her face in the pillow. Shirley, Sandy, and I flew across the room and hovered awkwardly over her. Bad news from home? A U on a check ride?

Jane sobbed, a dry, strangling sound that was pitiful to hear. I put my hands on her shoulders and was surprised at how frail she felt. Ordinarily there was so much vitality to Jane that one forgot to notice how thin she was. "Jane. What is it?"

"I washed out!"

She hadn't even known she was up for a check ride, but they'd given her three, in rapid-fire succession—and before she knew what was happening, she was scheduled for that final Army washout ride that was just a formality. Her days as a trainee were over.

We sat huddled together in a mass of misery, all of us weeping and protesting. Some day, Jane's whole life would be her grand-children. But I knew that at that moment, life for her was D-5, spins and stalls in the BT, sleeping on a lumpy cot, eating off tin trays, and reaching for a pair of silver wings. I wanted to change it for her by reminding her of the comforts of civilian life—the pri-vate bathroom, plenty of sleep, freedom, and the joy of being reunited with Chappy and their daughter, Ann, for more than just an occasional weekend. But it was no use.

"I can't go back to playing bridge and rolling bandages. I just can't." She was hiccuping now. "And what am I going to write Ann at boarding school? She bragged about me to all her class-mates. She and Chappy were so proud of me. Now I'm nothing but their stupid old wife and mother again."

Something inside me protested. Nothing but a stupid wife and mother? It was her description, not theirs, of course, but I under-stood what she meant. Still, why wasn't it enough for Jane to be a wife and mother, when she loved her husband and child?

Would it be enough for me? For any of us? Could we go back?

Would there be enough waiting for us as mere women, after we'd owned a piece of the sky?

I decided that after the war was won, those of us who could put our silver wings away, wistfully, tenderly, and go back to an uncomplicated concept of a woman's role in life—those would be the happy ones, probably. Those who would bear children and stay home with them while they were little, without feeling trapped or cheated—those would be the lucky ones, they and their children. But I didn't know if I could ever be one of those. Could Jane? I looked at her tear-swollen face and wondered.

Well, if we were tampering with the role nature had intended for us, I reasoned, it was because there was a war on. They needed us, didn't they? If there had to be a war, I wanted to do something more important than sit on my stenographer's seat. But what was going to happen to me—happen to all of us—after the war was over? I could only look at Jane and guess that it was going to be a struggle.

Finally Jane disentangled herself from our arms and stood up. Her breath was still coming in convulsive little gasps, but I could see she'd made up her mind not to cry anymore. She dug into the pocket of her zoot suit. "One of you drips hand me a cigarette," she said in a shaky voice.

When she had lit up, she shouted some cuss words defiantly. "I can cuss all I want to now." She tried to laugh, but at the sight of our faces she turned away. "How can I tell you fools good-bye? I will never have friends like you again."

June 16, 1943

Mother, the most heart-breaking thing has happened. Jane (Chapman), the older roommate, washed out yesterday.

The check pilots said the BT was just too much for her to handle, that it was no reflection on her flying. Four instructors on the PTs washed out on the BTs when they were given a chance to learn to fly them. After ten hours those four still weren't ready to solo, so they were left as primary instructors, at which they are pretty good. Isn't that strange? Some people just aren't capable of handling the faster, heavier ships [it's not a matter of strength, but technique], and still they make good pilots on lighter planes. Poor Jane. . . . I'll sure miss her and her inimitable sense of humor. Poor gal cried for two days, and I cried right along with her most of the time.

After her experience, I don't feel much like blowing off about my solo ride, but I know you'd like to hear about it. My instructor was taking me around a few times to shoot landings, and I had already asked him to let me solo that day, since I was nearing the eight-hour mark. But I thought surely we'd shoot landings for about an hour before he'd climb out, so I was really surprised when he said, "Okay, let me out," after having shot only three landings. I was simply thrilled to death, and not at all afraid the way I was just before I soloed the PT. Well—maybe there was just one fleeting second of terror.

Here is the cockpit procedure. It's too long to tell you all of it, but this is the cockpit check we have to make just before we take off. We're lined up at a 45° angle to the take-off position. First I "rev" it up to 1500 rpm and check each mag (magneto) to be sure it's working all right. If it doesn't lose too many rpms on either mag, I rev it up some more on both mags to see if the engine is clear. (All the while, of course, holding on furiously with the toes on the toe brakes, stick held all the way back.) Then I say, "20 degrees flaps," as I crank down 20 degrees of flaps; "stabilizer zero," as I adjust the elevator tab; "rudder trim tab three degrees right," as I adjust that to correct for the torque of the engine; "gas on reserve," since we always take off and land on the reserve tank; "mixture full rich," as I adjust the mixture control; "prop in low"—we take off, climb, and land with the propeller in low pitch—"carburetor heat full off; oil shutter full open; altimeter set at 2400 feet (elevation of this field); instruments caged (automatic gyro and artificial horizon instruments);

carburetor heat okay; cylinder head temperature okay; fuel and oil pressure okay," and then—*thayun* I'm all set to take off, so I radio in to the tower, saying "FF 81 from 97 (number of my plane for that day) on runway in No. 2 position for takeoff. Over." And the tower comes back: "97, follow 103 for takeoff. Over." And I say, "97. Roger," and follow the other plane off. We also have to radio in on our base leg when we're ready to land, to get permission to land and to get spacing. . . .

The new regime has taken over, and it is definitely a rule that you get kicked out for associating with any instructor, so I can't have another date with Click until I graduate (we have one then).

As I began to build up more solo time in the BT-15, the traffic problem at Avenger Field steadily became worse. It was decided that we should fly from two auxiliary fields some fifteen miles from Avenger, to ease the situation. These fields, imaginatively named Number One and Number Two, were no different from every other flat, grassy rectangular field in that part of Texas, with the exception of a small stage house in the center of each, a wind sock and T. None of it was easily discernible from the air from any distance.

All of us were supposed to know the location of these fields, for we had used them occasionally in primary. The only way I ever found them was by pure luck or coincidence, or by spotting other planes circling the fields or parked thereon. I had never been able to find Easter eggs, either.

Fortunately for me, we usually rode to these auxiliary fields in the creaking old cattle wagon, because only the instructors and first-period students flew the planes over. We arrived armed with ground-school books, stationery, cards, and suntan lotion. Ordinarily we flew just one period out of the four and were permitted to sprawl around on the hot ground with sleeves and pant legs rolled up, a privilege that had been taken away at Avenger.

There were drawbacks, however, to flying from an auxiliary field, no matter how lax the rules. One day, as we jumped from the wooden bus onto the hard ground of Number Two, Sandy said, "Has it ever occurred to you that if one of us cracked up over here, there's no fire truck or meat wagon?"

"I could forgive them for that," I said, "If they'd just put in a Coke machine." The weather was really getting hot.

"How could they? There's no electricity. Be grateful for the ice water in the thermos jugs. Remember when we didn't even have any water? Scarlett! Look out!" Sandy grabbed me by the arm and we ducked as an errant BT zoomed past our heads.

"Someone is practicing 'shooting stages' all by herself," Sandy said.

Sandy and I continued on toward the stage house. Before she could suggest homework, I said, "I've got to write Ned."

"How is he, anyway?"

"Doing better. He has the most amazing spirit. Mother wrote me that the doctors say that's the only thing that has pulled him through."

Inside the little stage house we found an unoccupied bench, and I got out my stationery. Sandy opened up a book. A plane zoomed overhead, so low that we rushed to the door to see what was happening.

"What is wrong with that girl?" I said. I found out the next period, when it was my turn to shoot stages. The exercise consisted of making spot landings on three points, with power-off approaches and no cheating with the flaps, meaning you could use them but you couldn't "milk" them up and down (something I didn't know how to do, anyway).

I felt more empathetic toward the wayward BT driver when it was my turn to try these spot landings solo. Before, when I had practiced, it had seemed comparatively easy. But the wind was acting peculiar now, and the T setting was new to me—diagonally across the field. Not only could I not hit the mark, I couldn't even get the BT down on the field in time to make a running takeoff again. I was humiliated.

Each time I'd make a good approach, put on flaps, and glide in. But then I'd hit a thermal or a gust of wind, and the plane would rise and sail across the field instead of settling down onto it. The man with the flags would wave me on. After a few unsuccessful passes at the field, I detected impatience in the way he threw those flags around. Other people seemed to be getting their ships down. But how did they do it?

For the first time since I'd started training, I had sincere doubts about my ability to make the grade. Always before, in spite of off-moments and bad days, I had felt sure, within myself, that I would get through. Now my confidence was shaken.

On the way home in the cattle wagon later that afternoon, I did not join in the lusty singing. I had always enjoyed belting out the songs with the rest, but now I stared out the window at the barren, windswept West Texas landscape that suddenly was very, very dear to me. If I had to leave it, I simply didn't know what I should do. Go back to work as a secretary? Never! Go home? To a little hick town in Georgia when a big, terrible war was changing the world? Not a chance! Well, what then? And where? I knew now how the girls who had washed out must have felt. I even understood how Jane, with a husband and child, could feel that the bottom had dropped out of everything when she had to go home.

Back in D-5 there was much mail waiting. I read it without interest, even though mail was usually the big event of the day. As dear as my correspondents were, they didn't have a clue as to what our life at Sweetwater was all about.

Then Shirley held up a letter and said, "This one's for you, Scarlett. I don't know how it got in my stack." She handed me a letter from Ned. Well, at least here was one person who talked my language and would understand what was going on. The whole letter was in Ned's own handwriting! I was as thrilled as if I'd accomplished something terrific myself. Some of his determined spirit seemed to penetrate my dejected mood, and my depression lifted. If Ned, in his condition, didn't let things get him down, why should I be defeated by one bad day? By damn, I wouldn't be.

With fresh resolve I went to the flight line the next day, fully expecting to find my name on the board for a check ride. I was determined to give the check pilot a good ride. But my name was simply posted for a solo period.

I spent the hour doing what I'd been told ahead of time to do: practicing chandelles and lazy eights, and doing precision work. I even slipped in a couple of illegal slow rolls, just to keep my hand in. It was foolish, because we were not supposed to fly inverted, solo, because of fires that had broken out in the BTs at a number of training fields when solo students had flown them upside down. Also, spins in the BT were not permissible solo, because of a nasty habit the plane had of winding up and not always responding to recovery efforts. I felt no urge to disobey that rule.

In the PTs it had been a different story. We were encouraged in primary to practice solo spins, and I used to spin down to lose a lot of altitude quickly.

In a few days I was given a chance to repeat shooting stages. This time the wind was straight out of the south and there were no gusts, so I did okay. Now all I had to worry about was cross-country and night flying.

11

[28 June 1943]

Mother, honey—

Although I'm so tired every muscle (and I've really got 'em now!) in my body aches, I know you're dying to hear how my first solo cross-country in a BT came off, so I'll write you before putting my fatigued bones away for the night.

Well, first the buildup: They scheduled me for a solo cross-country hop of 370 miles in all (triangular course) before giving me any dual cross-country. And in a BT at that!! I was horrified.

So after a sleepless night, I set out this morning with a sick stomach and completely empty bowels. I mean to tell you I was scared!

When I first saw my name posted on the board for the solo cross-country, I thought it must be a mistake. I had just over five hours' solo in the BT, with not even five minutes' instruction in the air on cross-country flying. Of course we'd been briefed in ground school, and some of the girls in my flight were already making dual trips with their instructors. But solo?

"There's no mistake," my instructor said, smiling. "I couldn't help you much, anyway. I've only had ten more hours in the BT than you have."

"You're trying to get rid of me," I murmured.

"Don't you know how to plot your course?"

"Well, yes, I think so."

"What's the matter, then?"

"I've never been any farther than the auxiliary fields, and I can hardly find them. How am I going to find Mineral Wells and Wichita Falls?"

I walked between the long lines of basic trainers, looking for number 78. My parachute seemed to weigh a ton, and the heat from the summer sun (it was almost July) boiled up from the asphalt in visible waves. My hot zoot suit was plastered against my back between my shoulder blades, and my hair sagged limp and damp against my neck. I longed to roll up my sleeves and trouser legs but didn't dare. I'd be gigged if I did. It didn't look military, they said. Hah! General MacArthur wouldn't look military in a zoot suit.

I felt the dust clinging to my perspiring face where the telltale triangles of suntan sat upon my cheeks, triangles made by wearing goggles, identifying me as a WAFS trainee even when I wore my best civilian clothes into town. A recent newspaper article had called us "glamorous" and I smiled wryly to myself as I recalled it.

Nearly four hundred miles was a long way, all alone. I wasn't used to the BT yet, and I couldn't help remembering the only cross-country I'd ever taken alone, in a Cub, when I had ended up in that cotton field, blown off course by a crosswind. I swallowed. Well, at least the BT had a radio and they could keep me advised of any change in the weather. It didn't take long in Texas.

Mechanically, I began the cockpit procedure; I had memorized it thoroughly. It began, of course, with the Form One. I picked it up, looked at it, and gulped. A red diagonal! That meant something was wrong with the ship. But underneath the red line the plane had been released for flight, with a mechanic's signature to testify that there was no danger in flying that plane.

Okay. Gas tanks. Safety belt. Headphone. Radio. Rudders. Controls. Brakes. I went through the rest of the check automatically. I was still wondering what the red diagonal meant. Some tech order not complied with, it said, but the TO number meant nothing to me. Oh, well, I "had to trust": Ned's expression.

I made S turns down the ramp toward the runway, lined up at a forty-five-degree angle from takeoff position, and ran the engine up for its pre-takeoff check. The tower cleared me to take off. To take off! On a trip almost four hundred miles long, over parts of Texas I had never seen before, in an airplane I had only a nodding acquaintance with? They must be mad! But I opened the hatch, took a long, dust-filled breath, turned into position, and gave her the gun.

The BT roared down the runway and gave deceitful little indications of wanting to fly. My hand tightened on the stick as I held the nose down, because I knew that if we lifted off too soon we'd mush unsteadily through the air and perhaps squash back to earth. This ship needed more horses.

As the end of the runway rushed nearer I let ol' 78 take the bit in its mouth, and we lumbered upward and onward. We were off! That was something in itself. I sang, "Off we go, into the wild blue yonder. . . ."

I circled the field for altitude and penciled the takeoff time on the patch of adhesive tape stuck to the knee of my zoot suit for that purpose. Turning to my compass heading, I flew on toward Mineral Wells. Soon I had the uncomfortable feeling that I was being watched. Ridiculous! There was no one in the backseat. Still, I sneaked a quick look just to be sure.

I gasped. Immediately off my right wing, close enough to chew a hole in it, was the prop of Shirley's BT, with a grinning Shirley in the cockpit of the plane. She was flying formation with me.

We hadn't yet been instructed in the art of formation flying (and we never were, officially; mostly we just taught ourselves). I tried to edge over a little, but Shirley stuck close and only laughed when I tried to wave her away. She had already been over this course with her instructor, and I suddenly realized it might be nice to have her around. I made motions for her to crank her radio to our "private number."

Ever since we'd soloed the BT, we'd agreed that if we were able to rendezvous anywhere without an instructor spying on us, we'd turn to a certain frequency and talk to each other and per-haps sing a few songs. Being untutored in the mysteries of radio, we thought we could have a private transmitting and receiving frequency by twisting the "coffee grinder" to a different number. We were unaware that our radios were wired to one frequency, tied in with the tower at Avenger. We found out later that when we talked, anyone within range, or any CAA (Civil Aeronautics Administration, forerunner of the FAA) station tuned in to receive our frequency, could hear us. We understood this a week later, when the CAA silenced all of Avenger's radios for a ten-day period as punishment for the foolishness that had gone on between trainees. It had blocked out many of the CAA's incom-ing calls.

But today I cranked to our private number and jabbered to Shirley. "Not so close, old dear, I'm not ready to spin in yet. See that town? That's our first checkpoint. Right on course!"

"What checkpoint? I'm not on a cross-country. I just saw you and thought you might like to hedgehop a few minutes. I'll beat you to that car down there."

She peeled off and dived toward an old car chugging along a farm road. It looked like fun, so I peeled off too. I was close behind Shirley, diving on the car, when I saw it stop and the driver jump out and fling himself face down on the ground as we roared toward him.

We both pulled up at the same time, and I wondered if Shirley was engulfed in the same hot flush of guilt that made my head pound. That poor man might have a heart condition! I banked and looked down, and saw him shake his fist at us as he got up and headed toward the car. I'm sorry, I thought, desperately hoping he had not got the numbers off our planes in order to report us.

"Okay," Shirley said contritely. "Somebody might get hurt that way. No more zooms. Let's just put our props in low pitch [to make as loud a roar as possible] and skim along the tops of trees and houses."

So we did, until Shirley finally waggled her wings in farewell and left me. I regained my altitude and checked my watch to see how much time I'd wasted, and looked at the ground below. I was lost. A few minutes away from Avenger Field, and I was totally lost.

I took up my compass heading anyway, hoping that in a few minutes something below would jibe with my map. I wished for a drink of water. I grabbed the transmitter and cried, "Shirley! Shirley!" but there was no answer. She must have switched her radio back and was winging her way back to Avenger.

Avenger! It usually stood out as if it had been painted on the landscape. I banked the ship, made a circle, and looked for the familiar pattern of smooth earth that meant home, to orient myself. But I couldn't find it. Trimming the ship again, I glanced at the altimeter. At least I was holding my altitude, if that did any good. And I hadn't lost very much time with my stupid horseplay. I'd pick up my heading and proceed.

Wiping my hands on my coveralls, I gasped as a red warning light blinked on. The fuel-pressure warning light! It blinked off just as suddenly, but I was already on the wobble pump, checking the gas selector valve and gas tanks with anxious eyes. What in the world? Automatically I began searching below for a likely field to land in.

The warning light came on again and I switched gas tanks needlessly to see if that would help, and kept my left hand on the wobble pump. I remembered the red diagonal on the Form One, and all kinds of uncomfortable suspicions crowded into my mind.

I wished with all my heart that I had paid more attention in ground school and hadn't relied so heavily on Sandy. I hadn't the faintest notion of what was wrong with my airplane or what to do about it. I held my compass heading and tried to think positive thoughts.

For an eternity I perspired and shivered and tried to swallow but couldn't, because my mouth was too dry. I looked at my map and the ground below, then searched the sky for other airplanes—anybody to lead me to a place to land.

I knew I must be somewhere in the vicinity of Mineral Wells because I could hear the control ship radioing to WAFS trainees who were checking in for landing instructions. I looked around but couldn't see any other BTs. And now I was acutely aware of certain physical disadvantages of being a woman pilot. A man's needs were taken care of by means of a PRT (pilot's relief tube), but all a poor girl could do was wait. Nerves. Just nerves. Forget it.

Then, suddenly, ahead there was an airport, and a disbelieving study of my map showed it to be Mineral Wells. I was on course! I threw back my head and screamed, "Glory hallelujah!" I could hardly believe it! The only thing I had to fear was fear itself. FDR was right. I shouted, "Praise the Lord and pass the ammunition," and radioed in to the control ship on the ground for landing instructions.

Ol' 78 and I plunked down as if there were nothing to it, and I heaved a sigh of relief. Now they could deal with whatever malfunction there was in my BT, and I could catch a ride home with another trainee. There were lots of them, circling and landing. Where had they all come from? I hadn't seen any of them before.

When I told the instructor in the control ship about the blinking red light, he was too busy to be bothered. "Just write it up on the Form One when you get back to Avenger," he said offhandedly. "It's probably just a malfunctioning light."

I gulped. Probably? What if it wasn't? They were trying to kill me! But I couldn't stand there and argue with the distracted instructor. Obviously one trainee more or less meant nothing to him.

"Roger," I said, swallowing. I got a drink of water, used the latrine, and climbed back into my Vultee Vibrator. I sat in the cockpit for a few minutes going over the next leg of the course to Wichita Falls for the umpteenth time, then took off. I saw a group of trainees all heading in that direction, but I was afraid to follow them for fear they didn't know where they were going any more than I did, even though they at least had the advantage of having been over the course with their instructors. But if I was going to be in the Ferry Command, I'd better learn how to navigate by myself, not by following somebody else.

I took up my new compass heading and resolved to hold it. If I had done it once, surely I could do it again. The first checkpoint passed underneath on schedule. But that was the last time anything looked just right.

And my radio went out. Later I wrote Mother:

My transmitter was working [I thought], but not my receiver, so when I got to Wichita Falls (second leg) I radioed in and said I was headed back for Sweetwater. We didn't have to land.

Apparently they didn't hear me, because Sandy, who was in a nearby ship, heard the control ship at Wichita Falls calling the number of my plane over and over, trying to locate me. I couldn't hear them, of course, so I set off for home—fat, dumb and happy. My instructor was sure glad to see me here, having circled WF for half an hour, looking for me.

I flew through rain on part of the trip, and since the visibility was good, it was fun!

When the unmistakable shape of Avenger Field appeared on the horizon, ol' 78 zoomed toward it like a horse returning to its stable.

[Undated]

[To Mother]

You wanted to know if it took a lot of actual physical strength to fly the BT (since I complained about being tired after my first cross-country.) The answer is: heavens, no! Except for acrobatics (which we are through with now) the thing is flown mostly by setting trim tabs and rudder tabs and prop pitch and throttle settings, and on a calm day in order to fly straight and level, you can take your hands and feet off everything completely, and it'll do a better job [of flying] than you can! Of course there aren't many days when the air is that smooth. . . . The only tiring thing about cross-country is having to sit there strapped in your seat for so long. The glute really takes a beating.

Next, you wanted to know about Jane [Chapman]. She's with her husband in Louisiana and is apparently quite happy now, although at times she does get awfully blue, thinking about this place. But mostly she is adjusted, and we are all much relieved about her. We write her letters every couple of days, and she, us. The heartbreaking thing is that many, many other girls have washed out whom this meant everything to, and who had nothing to go back to.

Mother was also still very concerned about the other Jane's—Jane Champlin's—fatal crash. It was hard to answer her natural questions truthfully while giving her the reassurance she, as my parent, needed. I reiterated all the facts and figures, pointing to the good safety record of our training program and added:

After all, hundreds of girls have flown thousands of hours here, month after month—and [there has been] only one accident where anybody was hurt or killed (knock again).

12

Wednesday [Undated]

[To Mother]

I sure don't see why Janet says I'm not mature enough to appreciate Ned Hodgson. I won't argue the point about maturity, but doesn't she realize that I am Ned's greatest admirer, and always have been? I appreciate his fineness, his depth of character, and all his other strong points (I could go on naming them forever) far more than she does, I betcha! But admiring and appreciating a person doesn't necessarily make you fall in love with him, does hit? Nay, things don't work out that conveniently always. And, by the way, I am still writing him faithfully. Never stopped since his accident.

Sandy's mother is here, and last night they were discussing the Army check that Sandy was to have today. Mrs. Sanford said, "Don't worry about it, dear, because it would make me very happy if you washed out!"

We definitely can't date [any] instructors now without being eliminated. [Click and I] have a date for the night I graduate, though, if we're both still so inclined by that time. My fancy shifts so rapidly with circumstances, though, that I'm beginning to wonder about myself. I seem to love 'em all, though I don't let them in on it.

The streaks of ink that keep smearing across't the page are from the wind blowing my paper around. I'm sitting on a blanket on the concrete sidewalk "porch" in front of D-5, since it's too hot inside to live. There's at least a breeze out here.

Norman [an old friend] tried all one night to get me on the phone, but couldn't get through; then this week he wired me to call him, but all the circuits were still busy.

I had begun to appreciate some of the difficulties the rest of the country was enduring. Gasoline rationing, shortages of new cars and rubber tires made private transportation challenging, if not impossible. Buses and trains were always overcrowded, with standing room only being the norm. People formed car pools and often had to double up in houses in big cities. Near military bases couples were lucky to find a room in someone's home, where they often shared the only bath.

Everything was in short supply, from coffee to nylon stockings. There wasn't just gasoline rationing; meat, sugar, and eggs were all in our coupon books. And shoes! No coupons, no shoes. That presented a special problem for WAFS, since we wore our shoes out, marching for the Army.

Government controls over civilian life regulated prices and rents. Factories that formerly had turned out new automobiles, sewing machines, or small appliances had now geared up to produce military equipment. People kept their old cars, refrigerators, and washing machines running, but finding a mechanic or repairman was an experience—and if you found one, he probably couldn't get the parts you needed. Many, accustomed by now to electric refrigerators, went back to using ice boxes when their refrigerators went on the blink. Even then, frequently there was a shortage of ice.

Hoarding, as well as black-marketeering, greed, and exploitation of the wartime situation existed. On a small scale those things were winked at, but on a larger scale they were socially unacceptable and, ultimately, illegal.

The women who stayed home knitted, sewed, baked, rolled bandages, got up Bundles for Britain, and volunteered for the Red Cross. Citizens saved grease (for explosives), tin cans, and foil; had paper drives and war-bond rallies; worked for Civil Defense; planted Victory Gardens; and gave blood.

Women who had never worked before suddenly had to run the family farm or business, while the head of the house went off to war. Women worked in offices and hospitals; drove ambulances, trucks, and streetcars; and some, like me, flew airplanes. Young men and women signed up for military service or tried to get into an essential industry. Older men came out of retirement to join the work force.

Norman, who had rented a room from Mother, was a case in point. He was 4-F, "unfit for military duty," because of an old injury. He was the spoiled darling of a wealthy family, a man with a law degree he had never used, a man who had never worked a day in his life. He went to work in a shipyard and labored for long, grueling hours, yet he certainly didn't consider himself a hero any more than I considered myself a heroine. We both were doing what we could. In my case, I was also doing what I wanted to do more than anything in the world.

My letter to Mother continued:

Honey, I'm so happy that it makes me feel guilty that everyone can't be this way. I keep waiting for the law of compensation or sompin to catch up with me and smack hell out of me, because this really seems too good to be true.

[Undated]

Dearest Mother,

Ned Hodgson sounds very encouraged in his recent letters, and seems to be getting along better all the time, though I'm afraid (from what I've surmised) that he will probably be horribly scarred for life on at least his arms and legs. Isn't that awful? But he sounds so happy lately that I don't think he is worried at all about that part, and I feel so much better about him.

In July, the war in the Pacific went on without Ned. Our forces cleared the Japanese from the central Solomon Islands. In the European theater, Generals Patton and Montgomery led an Allied invasion of Sicily.

July in Sweetwater had brought nearly intolerable heat. Ground-school rooms were stifling, and we didn't have so much as a fan. But Mr. Kreiger, our meteorology instructor, kept things lively. He had done Bugs Bunny cartoons at Warner Brothers, and he used his background as an animator to do chalk illustrations on the blackboard.

We learned about troposphere, stratosphere, ionosphere, air pressure, and body pressure, things that stayed with me long enough to get by on tests. But I probably never would have made it through the aircraft-engines course without Sandy's patient drilling. Because of her I managed to pass, while mentally thanking heaven that aircraft maintenance depended upon trained mechanics and not me.

Those blistering summer days in West Texas nearly got us. Besides the hot, stuffy ground-school rooms, there were the Link Trainers (simulated flying machines) to contend with. We nearly suffocated, closed up in those little boxes with wings and instruments. We called it the Torture Chamber. By the time our scheduled hour in one of them was up, we were dripping with sweat.

Our barracks, one board thick and facing so that we couldn't catch the prevailing wind through the windows, made it much hotter inside than out. We hauled ice in our mop bucket from the mess hall each night so we could make ice water, which we drank by the gallon. We increased the number of salt pills we took daily (in those days they were thought to be helpful), but we still nearly perished from the heat. At bedtime, we wrung out our nightgowns or pajamas in cold water and at intervals took turns sprinkling each other with water. But those measures offered only temporary relief.

We were able to endure the heat, and the fact that we'd had no time off between primary and basic, only because the beautiful North American AT-6 was beckoning, with all its new gadgets, retractable landing gear, and awesome speed. Meanwhile we were trying to master cross-country in the BT. In a letter to Mother I described another solo four-hundred-mile training trip:

[2 July 1943]

It took only 3 hours and 15 minutes. There's only one way to travel, I've decided. Landed at the beautiful airport in Brownwood [at the end of the second leg], but had to take right off again. The visibility on the first leg of the trip was practically nil—it was really awful—but I hit every checkpoint on the nose (though I couldn't see them until I was practically over them)— which was a most satisfying feeling. Then it cleared up, but was bumpy by the time I left Brownwood. Also, I had to disrupt my course home to steer around a danger area, which took a little special navigating. I was right proud of m'self, even if I do say so. Oh, good heavens, I haven't told you the good news yet. I had an Army check yesterday and passed same! Now I'm definitely over the hump, and although one is never actually out of danger as regards washing out, I don't think there is a lot to worry about from here on out.

I made it sound terribly casual about the Army check ride, when actually I had been terrified, because when I'd seen on the board that I was up for the check ride, I'd recognized the name of the pilot. He was the woman-hating lieutenant I'd seen in the lobby of the Blue Bonnet Hotel my first day in Sweetwater, and the poop was that he would wash out a trainee if she so much as smiled.

I found my old friend and former instructor, Mr. Wade, in the ready room, and wailed, "I'm up for a check ride with the ogre."

"You've been doing okay lately," he assured me. "I've kept up with you. This is probably just a spot check."

"Any last-minute advice?"

"Yes. Use lots of rudder for him. Watch out for other planes. Be swivel-headed."

"I woke up with a stiff neck," I moaned.

Mr. Wade gave me a pat of encouragement. "Do the best you can, anyway. Your best is good."

When I met the lieutenant, his lips were pressed together disapprovingly. I matched my steps to his long stride as we headed toward the assigned airplane in hostile silence. He had me take off and head for one of the practice areas, but already he was finding fault with every move I made. I didn't reduce power soon enough. I didn't wait long enough to change the prop pitch. I went out too far before making the first left turn. I used too much rudder on that last turn. Yap, yap, yap. Picky, picky, picky.

I had to sit there and take it while he made sarcastic remarks. This man had the power to make me or break me, and it was obvious which he preferred to do. It wasn't fair! Clenching my teeth, I knew I was too tight on the controls, thus committing a deadly sin, but I couldn't help myself. I could not relax my hold on the stick. Even my feet were tense on the rudder pedals.

If I washed out, how could I ever face the people who had believed in me? Grannie would be indignant. How dare they wash out her namesake? She would silence my mother's relieved sighs with a fiery-eyed look that said she'd go all the way to President Roosevelt if she had to. How could I ever break the news to her? Or to Ned, the silent observer who went along on all my flights.

Ned. He believed in me. He'd be lying there waiting for the mail—right now, probably—waiting for my letters that gave him a chance to fly again, through me. How could I let him down?

Well, I wouldn't, by damn. Not without a fight. But the way to fight now was to relax. Relax. Don't think of the lieutenant. Think of Ned. I loosened my grip on the stick. Center the needle. Center the ball. Watch the airspeed. Needle, ball, airspeed.

"Figure eights," the unpleasant voice grated through the intercom. I nodded and performed. Climbing turns. Stalls. Spins. Forced landing. I did it all, the best I could. I could feel Ned's presence. I felt another invisible passenger, too: Mr. Wade. His words came back to guide me now—sharp words, encouraging words, critical words, words of praise. I heard them now and remembered. Roll into that turn. Dammit, more rudder! Pop that stick forward. Atta girl!

But none of it was good enough for the lieutenant. He would have chosen a different field for the forced landing. I missed the point he'd picked out for my spin recovery. My stalls were sloppy. Everything was wrong. He criticized and swore and criticized some more, and when it was all over, I was trembling with exhaustion and defeat.

At least the landing was good. He'd have to give me credit for that! But he got out of the airplane without speaking, without telling me whether I'd passed or failed, and left me without even a grunt of farewell. As he turned his back on me, I felt tears sting their way into my eyes and I blinked. I will not cry, I resolved, as I walked toward the ready room.

I was sitting on a bench staring at the floor when Mr. Wade sat down beside me. "Well, how did it go?" he asked.

"I think I busted it," I said angrily.

"The grades won't be up until after we leave tonight," he said, "but your instructor will let you know first thing in the morning."

"Thank you, Mr. Wade."

"What did you do wrong?"

"Everything, according to him. I thought I did pretty good."

"Don't worry about it. Come on, I'll buy you a Coke."

After supper that night, Betty Clements, a classmate, offered me her binoculars. She described how you could time it to sneak into the hangar after the watchman had made his rounds, put the binoculars up against the glass door of the instructors' room where the grades were posted, read the results of your check ride, and sneak back before the watchman came by again. A big blue S by my name would mean I'd satisfactorily passed the check.

I decided against it. Why take a chance on getting busted for that, after all I'd gone through to get this far? It was hard to sleep that night. But the next morning when I met my instructor in the ready room, I knew by his smile that the ogre had passed me.

"Hallelujah, I'm still a Waffie!" I exclaimed, when he told me the good news.

The next day I wrote Mother, "I had an Army check yesterday and passed same." Cool.

13

[9 July 1943]

[To Mother]

It thrills me to death to think of [my brother] John in uniform. I'm so proud of that boy and Janet.

I went on my fourth solo cross-country (X-C) yesterday, and a strong wind blew me off course and made me temporarily uncertain. I decided to head out for home anyway, but things started looking wrong, and the checkpoints didn't jibe with my map. I buzzed a couple of towns but couldn't find the names of them anywhere, so I turned around and went back to a town I had just passed over that had an airport. I knew it was either Ballinger or another town north of Ballinger, both of which had Army airports. The roads leading out of each town made a similar pattern and the fields were located in the same place in relation to the towns. So I entered the traffic pattern with a bunch of PTs and landed. The Army cadets and instructors nearly fell out of their planes when they saw a girl taxiing by in a BT! I beamed at them all and got out at a hangar, where I telephoned our squadron commander, after I had found out that it was Ballinger, after all.

While I was waiting for the call to go through, some lieutenant [Bob Moore] came up and said, "You're from Sweetwater?" I said

89

yace, and he went on, "Have you seen Major McConnell?" I said, "No. He's not at Sweetwater anymore." (He was our commanding officer before being transferred.) The lieutenant grinned and said, "I know. He's the CO here, and I bet you knew it all along."

This last remark was untrue, though I had heard that he was at Ballinger, but had forgotten it. He's a young, attractive bachelor, so I don't blame Bob for thinking I had stopped over on purpose. (It turned out that one girl [Jo, from our adjoining bay] had preceded me there by about a half hour, having secretly planned deliberately to stop over and see him. Sh-h-h-h! No one knows).

The [Avenger Field] Sqn. Cmdr.— when I had gotten him on the phone— had told me I had done the right thing and to come on home if I could get clearance to take off from Ballinger. So I sashayed over to Major McConnell's office and got the most cordial greeting I've ever had. He said, "Sure, I'll clear you, but I refuse to do it for a couple of hours." So he took me to the PX (Post Exchange) for Cokes and cigarettes and showed me around the post. He devoted his entire time to me.

I couldn't believe this was the same major I remembered. The mustache was gone, and so was the old sneer and the sarcastic manner. The man was positively jovial. He laughed and said, "I don't have to be mean anymore. And the mustache had served its purpose. I'm sure as hell glad they transferred me out of there because now I can enjoy Avenger. I felt like a muzzled rat in the middle of a pound of cheese while I was there. Now I can go back without my muzzle on."

I was dumbfounded when he added, "I'll fly home with you. I need some BT time. We only have one BT on this field."

Later the major climbed into his BT, which was parked next to mine. I had left my chute in the plane, but when I looked into the front cockpit just prior to climbing in, I saw a strange parachute and an unfamiliar yellow cushion on the seat. For a moment I thought the major had got our planes mixed up. Then I saw that my chute was carefully placed in the seat of the rear cockpit.

"What goes on?" I muttered.

Someone gently nudged past me on the wing and climbed into the front seat without a word. He put on the parachute, fastened the safety belt, adjusted the headset and seat, then turned around and grinned. It was Bob Moore. "Hop in," he invited cordially, waving me into my own BT.

Since I was only a guest at his field, I did as told. I rode all the way back to Sweetwater without touching the controls of my airplane. Indeed, my hands were over my eyes most of the way. I had never been in a dogfight before, and this one lasted all the way home. The major flew so close to us that I could see his expression as he zoomed past, missing our plane by inches. There was a little buzzing, too. Then, to top it off, they took turns doing the tightest formation flying I had ever seen, even in movies.

The flight commander was the only person left on the line when we landed in formation. If he was awed by our traffic pattern or the unorthodox (for Avenger) landing, he showed no signs of it. When I got out of the plane, weak as water, he merely helped me fill out the Form One, then whispered, "You're doing all right. The major! Wow!" and told me I was released from the flight line.

Bob flew back in the major's BT, but first he asked me for a date. I accepted but added, "I know it's only my BT you're after."

I concluded my letter to Mother:

After delivering me here safely, the major's parting words to me were: "Next time, make it late in the afternoon."

My instructor gave me a wonderful compliment today. Every day that we don't go X-C, we do instrument work, and this afternoon, after flying two and a half hours with me under the hood, he said, "For the amount of hood time you've had, you are unusually good. I'm really proud of you." So I'm a happy girl.

Darling, please don't worry about me. I fly well-kept-up planes in a country where no one will shoot me down, so I'm not really brave at all, though you may keep on thinking so if you like.

Night flying, the thing that had done Ned in, was upon us. It was the part of training that we all dreaded most. I was especially apprehensive because my instructor was just one nervous jump ahead of me. Two nights before he took me up for my first night flight, he had almost collided with another trainer in the traffic pattern and had accidentally done a snap roll as he frantically maneuvered to get out of the way, winding up behind a hill just above the ground.

His lights were out of sight of the control tower. They thought he had spun in, until he regained enough composure to answer them on the radio. The near-accident had not been wholly his fault, but it destroyed his confidence and had a disastrous effect on students like me, who quickly absorbed his frightened approach to nocturnal flight.

The first night he took me up, we were just a few feet off the runway when I saw flames shooting back from the engine, and I screamed in horror that we were on fire. Paying no attention to the flames or to me, he seemed too busy to answer. It wasn't until some time later (when I was contemplating going over the side) that he explained that exhaust always looked like that at night.

The second night, not only was my instructor still seemingly frozen on the controls, but he talked nervously on the intercom, nonstop. I was actually only a passenger, not able to practice take-offs, landings, circling in our zone—he was doing it all. How was I supposed to learn?

The third night, I was waiting in the ready room for my instructor's ship to return to the line, so we could go up for what I hoped would be some real dual. He came in for a cup of coffee, bummed a cigarette, drank a few swigs of the coffee, and then said, "I'm too tired to go up again tonight. Suppose you take it up alone."

I thought he was kidding. He had been up with me at night exactly twice. I hadn't really flown the airplane then, but had only shared the controls with him, if you could call it sharing, while he'd had a death grip on the stick and heavy feet on the rudder pedals. But when I indicated that I took his suggestion of my soloing as a joke, he grew irritated.

This was preposterous. The man was serious, and moreover, getting angry about it. So, in disbelief, I walked out to the ship, wondering what to do. It was like being given scuba-diving equipment before being taught how to use it, and then told to go swim with a man-eating shark. What did you do? How did you get back alive?

Feeling a little sick, I climbed into the ship, went through the cockpit procedure, and called the tower. My last hope was that the tower would discover the error in my instructor's judgment and save me. But no.

"Clear to taxi out." Gulp. I S'd my way toward the runway flicking on first one landing light, then the other, as we had been taught to do to keep from running down the battery.

At the edge of the runway I watched two ships come in, bounce, and finally stick to the ground. The exact location of the ground was a dark illusion at night. When the planes turned off the runway, I was cleared into position for takeoff. It couldn't really be true. This wasn't really me. I had no more idea how to fly a BT at night than how to remove a brain tumor.

The tower cleared me for takeoff. I wiped my palms once more on my coveralls, swung into position, and gave the ship the gun.

Flames from the exhaust seemed to lick even closer to the cockpit than on the two previous nights. The green lights at the end of the runway got larger, and when I had to, I let the BT lift off and lumber upward, shuddering like the Vultee Vibrator it was.

I was soon surprised, however, at how easily the ship handled now. I also discovered something less welcome: without the nervous yammering of my instructor, I was picking up a disconcerting feature of my airplane's radio reception at night. It sounded as though the Japanese had set up interference in their own language to jam our frequency. Also, there were snatches of ghostly music. It lent an eery quality to the already frightening business of flying around in total darkness, with nothing but luminous instruments glowing in the cockpit and startling reflections shooting past on the windshield.

I'd been told to fly at night with the hatch open, to cut down on those reflections. But there were still enough of them on the windshield to cause instantaneous and often dangerous reflexes. Now every instinct made me want to veer sharply away from what seemed to be another airplane's lights, but what actually was just one more flash of light from some unidentifiable source, probably a reflection of something on the ground.

Gradually I began to shake off the tight feeling of nerves. The tower directed me to the altitude of the zone called Upper Four to circle. I could hardly believe the difference between flying alone and having my instructor's heavy hand wrapped around the stick. This was fun! In a few minutes, I was singing.

We were supposed to fly by reference to the instruments, not to both instruments and the ground. But I couldn't resist looking out now and then, to assure myself that Avenger Field was right down there where it was supposed to be, with lights clearly outlining the runway we were using. And I liked to see the lights of Sweetwater and its neighbors. How could we stay in the circumference of our zone if we couldn't refer to something on the ground?

Later that week, a trainee lost RPMs on takeoff and crashed through the high tension wires beyond the end of the runway. It plunged the whole area into darkness. She was not hurt. But I could imagine the terror of the trainees flying solo, who suddenly had no reference to the ground except occasional dim headlights from cars driving along country roads. Eventually smudge pots were put out and the girls were brought down safely, but when I heard about it I was very thankful that I hadn't been one of them up there that night.

A few minutes into my first night solo, I heard the tower calling someone in from her zone to land and clearing someone else for takeoff. The knot in my stomach relaxed, because now I knew that someone down there was keeping track of us. The zones were stacked, with a different altitude assigned to each, and the tower cleared the bottom layers first, then the middle, then the top. That way it lessened the odds of our running into each other.

Finally it was my turn to shoot landings. With a thudding heart I managed to find the ground three times in a row without wrecking the airplane. Each time I gave a rebel yell.

I'd conquered the midnight monster! Glory hallelujah! I shared my triumph with Ned, who knew all too well how treacherous night flying could be. To Mother, I wrote: "I soloed at night! And it really wasn't scary at all."

We flew day and night in order to finish basic, and while we were doing it, *Life* magazine paid us a visit. Everywhere we went, we were followed by photographers. Peter Stackpole seemed to be the one in charge. He and other photographers who had preceded him to Avenger took many pictures they didn't use, and it wasn't safe to write a letter, read a book, or brush your teeth without looking around first.

There was one of Alice Lovejoy and me; I was sitting on the concrete sidewalk in front of D-5 in my bathing suit, typing a letter on her typewriter while she looked over my shoulder, like the executive secretary she had been at Scribner's. A year after graduation, Alice was killed in an AT-6 in a midair collision.

With Peter Stackpole around, if you were going to fly solo you had to check the empty seat behind you to be sure he hadn't climbed in with his camera when you weren't looking. We were so exhausted that while we were on the flight line during the daytime, some of us stretched out and slept on the narrow wooden benches, oblivious to the voices around us, the planes zooming overhead, and the *Life* photographers whose flashbulbs were popping even as we slept.

The day Peter Stackpole was leaving Avenger, as he was about to climb into the airplane that came to pick him up, he saw Shirley just getting out of her BT after a solo flight. She was in her zoot suit, hair in pigtails, wearing no makeup. "Hey, wait a minute!" he called to her, getting his camera out. "I want to catch you, just like that." He positioned her on the horizontal stabilizer of the BT—sitting there was a no-no, but Stackpole didn't care; this was the shot he wanted! Then he snapped the picture, thanked her, climbed into the waiting plane, and took off. Neither of them knew it then, but he had just shot the cover of the 19 July 1943 issue of *Life*.

[19 July 1943]

Mother, pet:

We've started "buddy rides." One girl sits in front to observe planes and to check the other girl, who flies under the hood in the back. Do you realize I'm almost through basic training? I've finished all my cross-country, also all my transition, and have only [some more] night flying and instrument work left before I go to advanced. About another week in all.

We got to fly an hour before a storm moved in Friday. It was a front—a huge layer of white solid clouds (which we flew over, in awe of its beauty) with towering peaks in the background, connected by wisps of white streaks. You see the prettiest things from the sky.

14

Rumors kept us in a state of uncertainty. We were aware of the precarious nature of our tenure, half in and half out of the Army, and aware of being a controversial and experimental group. We knew something was going on behind the scenes at the Pentagon and on Capitol Hill that we weren't being told about.

Was there hair-pulling as well as wire-pulling? Nancy Love and Jackie Cochran were in conflicting and overlapping positions of authority over us. We didn't know whose child we were. Miss Cochran had gotten us as far as Sweetwater, but Mrs. Love was in charge of female ferry pilots, and wasn't that what we were training to be? She had formed the original corps of WAFS pilots who had been trained at their own expense and were already serving in the Ferry Command when Cochran publicly entered the picture. It seemed logical to us that Love should be in charge of female ferry pilots.

Nancy Love flew into Avenger one day in July and told us a little of what to expect after we got our wings and became full-fledged WAFS. I hadn't expected such a capable woman to look quite so young and pretty, with big expressive eyes and a pleasing manner. I was relieved, because I disliked women who looked like men and made a brusque display of their competent efficiency, losing their femininity somewhere along the way.

She told us in her soft voice that we would be flying under her command after we went into the Ferrying Division of the ATC (Air Transport Command). We listened and nodded, glad to know at last who our boss was. But within a week, Jacqueline Cochran flew back to Avenger Field and emphatically assured us that she would be in command even after we left training, and that we'd do a heck of a lot more than just ferry planes. And what was more, she'd changed our name to WASP—Women Airforce Service Pilots—which General Arnold himself had approved.

Comparing the two women, I placed my money on Miss Cochran, partly because she threw General Arnold's name around so effortlessly. I realized I was watching a dynamo in action and was awed. She was attractive and trim, better looking than her pictures, and a compelling speaker. But with her forceful personality, she lacked the woman-to-woman warmth I felt emanating from Mrs. Love. Ambition vibrated through every word Cochran spoke, and determination resounded in her speech. Here was an indomitable ego at work, and I knew that this was what propelled the world-famous woman to miracles of accomplishment.

It made me uncomfortable. I had the feeling that she would head toward her goal like the proverbial steam roller, heedless of obstacles in her path and oblivious to squashed forms that lay in her wake. Still, if that was how she achieved her visionary schemes, maybe that was what it took. And I knew it was because of her that I was here at Sweetwater, being given this unprecedented opportunity. It would be downright ungrateful to look my patron saint in the mouth. So I listened and nodded, still not knowing whose child I was. But I was betting on Cochran.

July 23, 1943

Dearest Mother,

I have to fall in for night flying in about ten minutes. This will probably be our last night flight on BTs, and I'm sorta sorry, because it is thrilling. Sure keeps one on her toes!

Had my last check ride on basic yesterday—a civilian [check ride] on instruments. Passed same, so it looks like they just can't wash this chicken out. Unless I do something awfully stupid in advanced, I should be fairly safe from here on out.

Did I tell you the newsreel man ("News of the Day") took close-ups of me saluting the flag at retreat? Look for it.

We are now learning Judo . . . and next we will be taught how to shoot! Also, they have fitted us for oxygen masks, so our possibilities seem to be unlimited. The more opportunity I get, the happier I'll be, so please try to feel the same way. Don't ever worry about our doing "combat flying" (your prize boner) though—because there will never be any likelihood of that!!

It is just hot as hell, and if I weren't so dern busy I'd sure be unhappy about the weather.

I've been riding in the front on buddy rides (since I'm all through instrument work now) and "instructing" buddies for about a week. There are some darn good fliers here, and it's fun to ride with them.

[23 July 1943]

[To Mother]

Offhand I'd say I can't remember ever having been this tired before. But tomorrow I finish basic, and then we'll go two weeks without flying—ground school and PT and drill only—so that the class ahead of us can catch up. And then we'll go on to the ATs—advanced trainers: the AT-6 (North American) and the AT-17 (twin-engine Cessna). I could use a little rest, I'll admit, but I wish we didn't have to go two whole weeks without flying.

The heat, as I have no doubt mentioned, is simply unbelievable. And they all say, "You aint seen nothin' yet. Wait till August!" I can hardly wait. It's just too hot to eat.

I'd give anything for you to be able to see the sight before me now and every night. The bays are so stifling that many have dragged their cots out onto the sandy space between the barracks, and over half the girls sleep outside. D-5 hasn't taken to it yet (the sun is too bright in the mornings) but we all pull our chairs out or lie on blankets until night falls and it's time to turn in. This row between the barracks looks like Shanty Alley—scores of half-clad women flopped down all over the place—radios going—and much chatter and laughter [usually]. Tonight, though, it is comparatively quiet because everyone is too sleepy and exhausted to talk.

Latrine rumor had rippled through Avenger that we were again to be denied any time off between phases of our training. We'd had no time off between primary and basic, and we'd been flying several periods a day, often including nights and weekends. Rumblings of insurrection turned into an ominous roar that even Jacqueline Cochran couldn't ignore. The Army relented. They said we could have Open Post after ground school on Thursday afternoon, and we didn't have to be back until ten o'clock Sunday night.

My letter continued:

We get next weekend off, and I think I told you that all of D-5 and D-6 (the bay that shares our jonny, hence the friendship) plan to go to Dallas and just *raise hell*. . . .

[Late July 1943]

[To Mother]:

Tonight we go to Ballinger for a dance given by the cadets. Most of the cadets, however, are too young—but that's not why I'm going! The Army personnel there is what I'm interested in.

Shirley's fan mail [resulting from her picture on the cover of *Life*] is still pouring in.

Wednesday [Undated]

Darling Mom,

This is really the morning after the night before! But, considering I only had three hours' sleep, I reckon I feel better than would usually be expected under the circumstances.

Yep, 'twas quite a night. Major McConnell (whom I hope you are acquainted with by now) invited our flight over to the cadets' graduation dance at Ballinger last night. So, after going to ground school, we all piled into one of our famous buses (which I have described to you before: no springs, flapping canvas windows, wooden seats) and struck out for Ballinger—a two and a half hour trip. Gosh, were our fannies dead!

About a half hour before we were to arrive at Ballinger I got so hot I went to the back of the bus, opened the wooden door, and sat on the steps, dangling my feet over the pavement. Shirley came and sat on the top step behind me, and there we were, bouncing along, viewing the road and the cars behind us and the landscape rushing by . . . when we heard the droning of airplanes.

We looked up and saw three PTs flying in close formation. We guessed that Major McConnell and Lt. Bob Moore would be in two of the planes, and we were right. The third turned out to be Sandy's date that night.

Remember the name Bob Moore—he's the one you'll be hearing most about.

The planes zoomed down in formation and flew low over the highway behind us, approaching us at a terrific speed (going the same way our bus was, but facing Shirley and me, since we were riding backwards). Just as I was sure I was a goner, they pulled up over the bus, taking a wisp of my now-gray hair with them, and then repeated the performance over and over again. They got so close to us that Bob recognized me! Anyway, you've never been terrified until you've seen a plane dive straight at you. [Was I being paid back for scaring that poor man on the farm road?]

They "escorted" us all the way to Ballinger.

As we clumb out of the bus, hundreds of whistling (wheeeeeee whooooooo) cadet-wolves bunched around us. [Today some would call this sexual harassment, but we thought it was fun.] One cadet—who went to Georgia Tech!—immediately seized me and monopolized me for a few minutes until Bob (Moore) came up and cut in. He took me away, and the cadet couldn't say a thing, because Bob is the guy who washes them out at Ballinger. We went inside the mess hall and drank *quarts* of beer, then ate the best buffet supper I've ever had. The cadets sang at the top of their lungs for us, then we sang with them and for them.

After the dance, we were loaded back into the "cattle wagon," where I slept on the floor of that old wooden bus with dust and feet in my face all the way home. We arrived in Sweetwater at four A.M.

Bob is the one who flew with me back to Sweetwater when I landed at Ballinger that time, Major McConnell in one plane and Bob and I in the other. He's quite good looking and about my height—maybe taller. Cute as hell, I think. Good dancer, good flier, good kid! He'll be a captain next month. When am I going to stop meeting these wonderful men? I love 'em all. ALL!! Do you hear me?

Got wonderful letters from Colonel Keehn [my ex-boss in Chicago], Ned Hodgson, Norman, Dana, and Ben, all on the same day, and I feel too appreciated to be true.

I have to go take a Link Trainer—flight simulator—period now, so g'nite, darlin'.

United States Naval Hospital
Norfolk, Virginia
[Around 19 July 1943]

Dear Marion,

Saw your picture in *Life*, honey . . .

Delighted you are getting in lots of instrument flying. Are they teaching you the 1, 2, 3 (needle, ball, airspeed) system, or the "Attitude" system? I rode with a student who had 10 or 15 hours instrument time and about 150–175 total. He made an instrument takeoff and flew a pattern like this [drawing], varying speed and altitude at each turn. He did a surprising job. He was flying the Attitude system where you control the attitude of the plane by reference to the gyro horizon, same as you control the attitude of your ship "contact" by reference to the real horizon.

Today is another red letter day for me. I seem to have had a series of R.L. days of late. Besides receiving a letter from you as a *cause celebre,* I took my first steps—about three forward and as many back. You know the big shoes clowns sometimes wear so they can lean over and almost touch the ground? Well, picking my feet up and planting them again felt like moving a very long-toed shoe. I didn't "solo" those first steps but I expect to go up for a "check" in a few days and demonstrate my ability to get around alone.

Yesterday and today I had a tub bath, my first time in a tub in [5] months and 16 days. The water cringed so at the sight of me, it parted in the middle like the Red Sea, in its effort to keep from touching me. Weighed in at 112 pounds. My fanny is so skinny and flabby that my tail bone got in the way.

I'm now all out of my cocoon of bandages. However, the only similarity between me and a butterfly is the spots (skin graft spots). The Franciscan monks shave their heads except for a halo of hair, wear sandals and robes, in order to destroy vanity and develop humility. The doctors have given me my "robe of humility" in saving my leg for me. I think I'll be able to wear it happily for the rest of my life, as soon as the colors fade a bit. It will never be a pretty thing, but right now it's so gaudy it's almost revolting.

Have been feeling swell, thanks to a real break. An admiral moved in across the hall from me (routine check-up) and brought his own mess boy. Some friends in Norfolk gave up their ration books and brought me a couple of steaks, and the admiral's mess boy cooked them for me—rare—and it's the first time anything has tasted good since I've been in the hospital. [An old Marine buddy, Chic Young, a supply officer, also worked it out to get steaks to Ned on a regular basis.]

A corpsman told me I was suffering from malnutrition when they transferred me here from the hospital at Cherry Point. The doctors have put me on a high-protein diet and fixed it so that the Admiral's mess boy can cook my meat for me every day while he's here. I know that's why I'm feeling so great. [An article in a Navy medical journal later backed up Ned's hunch.]

I just had time to write Ned and rejoice with him, and to write Mother the following letter:

July 29, 1943

Mother, sugar:

This will be the happiest, craziest, happiest, happiest letter yet!! "They" are letting us off—today—Thursday—until 10 P.M. Sunday!! Boy, we've been cooped up on this post for so long that we are all going to tear the city of Dallas wide open. Yippee!!

Sandy, Shirley, Jo Myers, Hattie and I are all shoving off for Ballinger right after ground school. Bob and Bill and Major McConnell and a date for Hattie are throwing a party for us. We're so excited and thrilled at all the fun ahead, we can't even get our bags packed.

We'll either be at the Adolphus Hotel in Dallas or c/o Frank Myers, 500 S. Storey St., Dallas (Jo's father) if you should have to suddenly get me or anything.

15

[Postmarked 3 August 1943]

Dearest Mother:

Well, Mom, it looks as though I almost could be in love again, for the ten-millionth time! Yep, it's Bob, and if I weren't so deeply convinced that this is no time to get serious, I could sure love him good. Oooooh, Gawd, he's wonderful.

These last four days (ending Sunday) were just about the happiest and most fun days I've ever had. Ten minutes after we were given Open Post on Thursday afternoon, Bays D-5 and D-6 were empty, and there were nine excited girls running for two cars, with luggage bumping along behind us. We ran out to the parking lot behind the mess hall, and I heard the kitchen attendants run to the windows as we tore past. "Good Lawd! Look at them girls! They done packed their bags and is gone already!!"

One car-load of us headed for Ballinger, where Major McConnell and some other lieutenants, as well as Bob, entertained us—cocktails, steak dinner, etc. We stayed there until around four A.M. [when Bob was forced to ask, "Do you crazy gals realize what time it is? We have to go to work tomorrow morning."]

Got to Dallas early (8:30 A.M.) the next morning and immediately checked into our hotel rooms—Shirley and I in one room, and Sandy and Hattie in the other—where we caught up on sleep. That afternoon we were invaded by the Navy—ten or fifteen flight instructors (lieutenants and ensigns who were brought over by a friend of Shirley's).

The Navy set up a bar in our suite and we partied the rest of the afternoon and half the night. We swapped flying stories, we laughed, we compared Army and Navy airplanes and training. We found out about each other's backgrounds and interests, told jokes, and just generally had a fun, crazy celebration of our short-lived freedom. Amazingly—and Hollywood would never buy this today—even with all the hilarity and free-flowing booze that accompanied the partying in Dallas that day and much of the night, there was no pairing off and no talk of war. And I didn't see anybody get drunk.

Without verbalizing it, everyone there was aware of the fact that any day, any one of us could "buy the farm." We had all lost friends stateside, and would lose more. And these men were headed for overseas combat action, sooner or later. God only knew what horrors awaited them. Of course some of them, like Ned, didn't have to go to foreign countries to receive their portion of horrors. All this we understood, and it just made us drink and play that much harder.

We had only two more days of freedom before we had to go back to Cochran's Convent, where we no longer could even have a Coke in the PX with an instructor, and where we had to obey orders and fry in the heat.

The next afternoon, Bob joined us. I wrote about it later to Mother:

He came on time and showered and changed his uniform in our hotel room (tsk!) since he couldn't get a room anywhere in town—emerging simply beautiful in his immaculate uniform and bars and silver wings. I couldn't take my eyes offen him. He took me out to dinner and we went to an outdoor night club where my

Navy flier friends were saving us seats at their reserved tables. But we never could find them. The place was packed. Bob is a superb dancer and an old smoothie. Just before dawn broke, we had breakfast at a Toddle House and rode around in his car with the top down.

When finally we parked, I burst into song, I was feeling so good. "What is it with you crazy girls?" he asked, laughing. "You're all nuts. Why are you so slaphappy?"

"Don't you remember your first taste of freedom when you were in training, old man?"

"Sure, but I didn't know girls acted this way."

"The pressure is off!" I said, gesturing toward the sky affectionately. "It's just such a relief. No responsibility. No fences. No gates. No guards." I started singing again: "Heaven, I'm in heaven. . . ."

Bob soon caught the mood, and by the time we met the others, we were laughing like fools over nothing except the fact that we were alive.

Back at Avenger, Army routine quickly imprisoned me again. The class of 43-W-5 was still grounded, in order to give the upper class the flying time they needed in the AT-6 to graduate on schedule. I looked longingly at those beautiful, silver ships and wondered if I would ever really get to fly them, too. Life was listless and dull for us in W-5 in early August 1943.

Then there was another fatal crash. A North Dakota girl from 43-W-8 named Kathryn Lawrence was killed in a primary trainer. I didn't know her, but her classmates said she was a popular girl who had been a cheerleader in college. She had worked for Boeing Aircraft before joining the WASPs (now our official name, with Cochran as top WASP). Kathryn crashed near Sweetwater on a routine flight while flying solo in a PT-19, and there were no witnesses. We were given no details. I didn't mention the crash in my letters home, hoping that Mother wouldn't read about it in the papers and want explanations. It would be hard to give her reassuring explanations when there were none to give. Kathryn's death sobered us, but life went on. I knew death was a constant possibility, but it was worth the odds to get to fly.

That month brought good news from both the fighting fronts. In the Pacific, American forces were still clearing out Japanese positions in the Solomon Islands. In the European theater, Axis forces were collapsing in Sicily. The Russians began their summer offensive on the eastern front.

On the Sweetwater front, my zoot suit stuck to me in the hundred-plus-degree heat (in the shade, if you could find any shade). Food had no appeal. Five pounds melted off my body, and I had to cinch the belt of my zoot suit even tighter. With no planes to fly and nothing but PT, ground school, and the Torture Chamber to fill our long, incredibly hot days, lethargy settled upon our class. The Army finally took pity on us and hauled us to Sweetwater for a swim in the community pool twice a week, as a substitute for physical training.

We marched at the graduation of Class 43-W-4 as the Midland AAF band played on 7 August, and suddenly we were the upper class. Sandy was selected as group commander, which meant that she had many more jobs to add to her already crowded schedule. She was liaison officer between trainees and supervisors; she had to arrange schedules, meet formations, make announcements, preside over council meetings, and help organize reviews. Section leaders and individual squadron commanders' reports of delinquencies all went through Sandy. Hers was a gigantic job. But the full meaning of it was lost on her roommates. We concentrated happily on just one feature of her new title: she could excuse people from being late to formations and would stand firmly behind any one of us who got into trouble.

The supervisors liked Sandy and the trainees loved her. She granted special privileges to all who asked (if there was any reason at all to grant them) without ever going to the supervisors about the matter. She listened with a sympathetic ear to all the complaints and gripings that came her way, and she did her best to alleviate the sources of unhappiness.

16

On 9 August, I finally climbed into the cockpit of the North American dreamboat, the AT-6, and discovered why I was born. Whereas flying the BT-15 had been work, piloting the Six was ecstasy. The term "user friendly" had not yet been invented, but that's what the Six was, in capital letters. Flying it was like galloping on a sleek, perfectly trained Arabian horse after having ridden nothing but a swaybacked, obstinate nag.

First came the thrill of tucking those wheels up after takeoff. Next came the realization that this plane would respond to my every whim, quickly and smoothly. Finally, there was the stunning knowledge that it was all but impossible to make a bad landing in it.

After three hours of instruction, I soloed. This time there was no fear, just exhilaration and astonishment that even I could fly this plane without any problem. The Six made me feel as if I had just been transformed from a pesky moth into a beautiful butterfly. In fact, I began to suspect that a hot pilot had just been hatched, a heady and potentially fatal illusion.

I said to myself, No wonder the Japanese copied the AT-6, if that rumor was true, and put a more powerful engine in it. Thus they made it into their maneuverable Zero, which they used as a fighter throughout the war.

However, 650 horses under the cowling were plenty for me, and I looked forward to the thirty hours of advanced training in the AT-6. Almost as soon as we'd soloed, we were sent out on cross-country flights, on instrument hops, and buddy rides. In a letter dated 18 August, I wrote to Mother, "I've been going cross-country every other day and 'bracketing the beam' (instrument) on alternate days in the beautiful, wonderful AT-6."

I also wrote a letter to my sister, all about her upcoming Christmastime marriage to her love, Bot Traylor. "It was sure fun to hear from you and to know about your silver, china, etc. I'm getting excited, too! You've been wonderful about writing."

We did a few hours of night flying in the Six, and then suddenly our thirty hours were over. It was a sad moment when the AT-6 and I said good-bye, but I knew it was only a temporary farewell. It was time to tackle the Double-Breasted Cub, the AT-17, the twin-engine Cessna Bobcat advanced trainer with Jacobs engines that had a total of only 450 horsepower, a comedown after the powerful Six.

However, learning to taxi with two engines, instead of with rudder and brake, was a humbling experience. It made me realize I wasn't such a hot pilot after all, as I spent some time going around in circles on the ground before I finally caught on to the technique.

Landing was another problem. After the heavier, faster AT-6, it seemed as if the AT-17 wanted to float endlessly across the field, when I wanted it to land. It simply didn't want to stick, once it was there. Just like my old nemesis, the Cub! Eventually I found out the secret of how to land the Cessna, but the Air Corps never taught it to trainees, as far as I know. The secret was to make a faster wheel landing instead of a three-pointer. Tricycle landing gears later solved the problem.

Its inclination to float, of course, was how the AT-17 (UC-78) got its nickname of Double-Breasted Cub. It had other names too, since it was made of fabric stretched across a frame of plywood: Bamboo Bomber, Woodpecker's Delight, and Flying Boxcar.

My instructor rode with me for three days—three periods of an hour or so each—and I still couldn't make a smooth landing. I bounced him around until finally he couldn't take it anymore, and he sent me up to solo. The way we "soloed" was to go up with another student as copilot. "Might as well kill two birds with one stone," our instructor said cheerily.

I soon discovered that I was not the only rock that had miraculously sprouted wings. My classmates and I rode with each other, laughing and bouncing and laughing some more. We just hoped we wouldn't die laughing. I wrote Mother from the flight line:

[30 August 1943]

Honey, I'm afraid this will have to be a shortie.

First, though, did Grannie get my birthday telegram?

I soloed the twin-engine AT-17 today. We always have to have a copilot on them, so what we do is to put the instructor out, and put another student in his place. Fun!

Bob flew over today, but he arrived just as I took off, and I was gone too long for him to wait. He left a message that he'd be back to see me later this week.

Tuesday [31 August 1943]

Mother, this was to be a short letter, but now something has happened that I must tell you about.

I put my pen down. How could I tell my anxious mother what I must, before she read about it in the newspapers? Where to begin? In my mind, I went back over the previous day's events. I hadn't realized that Peg and Jo, two classmates—one married, one single—were missing until I heard it as we fell in for supper. Word passed quickly through the formation.

Their AT-17, which they were flying with their instructor, Mr. Atwood, had not returned to the flight line. There wasn't much talk or laughter in the mess hall that evening, and I noticed that some of the girls were hardly eating. Peg and Jo were favorites, and each of them had one special friend from whom she was inseparable. I couldn't bear to look at those friends' faces.

I knew Peg better than Jo, because Peg and I had a special bond: we were sorority sisters—Thetas. When Sandy and I went back to D-5 after mess, we passed a little plot of flowers at the end of the barracks that Peg had planted. Every evening she had dug around her morning glories and petunias, watered them, and tried to coax them into blooming. They were covered with buds.

Sandy said, "I'm going to water Peg's flowers for her tonight." I nodded and went into D-5 alone.

It was so hot that I came out again immediately. I folded up a blanket on the concrete sidewalk in front of our bay so I could sit there and lean back against the wall and write a letter to Ned while it was still light. Writing to Ned served a double purpose: it gave him some mail to look forward to, and it was therapy for me. Ned would understand.

The space between the barracks quickly filled up with half-clad women. Tonight it was quiet. Later we pulled our cots outside into the stifling night. Gradually, small stirrings and whispered speculations about what might have happened got to me.

I went inside D-5 to pull on my zoot suit over my shortie pajamas and walked down to the OD's office. I had to know if there was any word. Deatie, the chief supervisor we all loved, sat with red-rimmed eyes next to the OD. The telephone lay between them, silent.

"Nothing," Deatie said before I could ask the question. "Not a word. Tell the girls to go on to bed. We'll let you know if there's any news." There was a catch in her voice and she quickly cleared her throat and looked away.

I got back to my cot, pulled off my zoot suit, and lay down. At that moment Nell Carmody, the bugler, stood at the end of the beds near the flagpole and blew taps. Nell could swing reveille and syncopate mess call. The only thing she always played straight, like a prayer, was taps. Tonight it was heartbreakingly beautiful, each note clear and pure, played heavenward.

There wasn't a sound when it was over. I took a deep breath and closed my eyes. Sand blew across my face, and the breeze was still hot. Sleep was a long time coming.

I awoke before reveille. As I reached for my eye shade, I saw some girls huddled at the end of the long line of sleeping figures in the open space. From their intent attitude I knew they must have heard something, so I hurried over to ask them what they'd found out.

The two best friends of Peg and Jo's turned hollow-eyed faces toward me as I approached. I didn't need to ask any questions. I bit my lip and turned away.

How would I feel if it had been Shirley or Sandy? I walked slowly back to my cot to lie there sleepless until reveille. No one had wakened us in the night as promised, but it was just as well. What could we have done? At least they had told the special friends.

Word of the fatal accident had passed to all the trainees before we assembled for the breakfast formation. It was the quietest formation I could remember. There was no roll call. As we passed the end of the barracks where Peg had planted her flowers, I could scarcely believe what I saw. It seemed that every bud had burst into full bloom.

How could I tell Mother all that? I couldn't. But I had to tell her something, because she was bound to find out anyway. I picked up my pen again and wrote:

You may just as well get used to hearing about these things, Mom, because so long as I'm in the flying racket, they are bound to happen. Two of my classmates and their instructor were killed yesterday afternoon near Big Spring. A farmer boy saw the plane crash but waited until he was through with his chores that night (the accident was about 3:30) before telling anyone about it or going to investigate. No one at the field knew what had happened until after midnight last night, although they sent out a search party of planes until dark yesterday. The word finally got to Avenger by 1:30 A.M., by which time we all feared the worst anyway. The girls were Peggy Seip and (Helen) Jo Severson—both of whom I knew very well and liked a lot. Peggy was the one who had a write-up in the Theta magazine on the same page as mine. I'll enclose it.

Peggy and Jo and Mr. Atwood, their instructor, were all probably killed instantly . . . and the plane didn't burn—so it was no doubt quick and painless, which is always a comfort.

This is no doubt another one of those undetermined causes that brings about crashes, and no one will ever know what it was. Maybe it was one of those rare cases of structural failure—no one knows. It seems likely, since the instructor was in the plane. Or it could have been that the girls were changing seats in midair, and one of them could've grabbed the wheel for support, thus stalling the plane. There are endless possibilities—most of them being things that could have been avoided, as most crashes seem to be.

See, one girl sits in the pilot's seat, the instructor sits in the co-pilot's seat, and another girl observes ("sandbags") from the back seat. Both of these girls were to fly dual with the same instructor, so they may have upset things if they changed seats in the air.

Don't worry about it, though, Mom, because it's very unusual for anything so mysterious to happen (especially here) and they're inspecting all the airplanes before we go up in them again.

As I've told you before, we do take chances, but they are small compared to those that thousands take every day all over the world. And we could fall down in our own bathtubs at home and be killed, or get in a car and meet death. It's just not up to us to say where or when. You believe that, don't you? We'll talk more about it when I get home.

In D-5 we were doing our best to comfort Sandy, who was even more upset than the rest of us, because she had been scheduled to go up in the doomed plane with Mr. Atwood and Peggy Seip. Sandy was already in the plane, ready to taxi out to takeoff position, when someone ran up to the plane and told her she had a phone call from her mother. Phone calls were extremely difficult to get through, and Mr. Atwood urged Sandy to get out and take the call, saying it might be an emergency.

While Sandy was talking to her mother (who only wanted to know why she hadn't written), her place in the airplane had been taken by the next trainee in alphabetical order, Jo Severson. When Sandy returned to the flight line, the plane had already taken off. A mechanic said to her, "Be sure they get that plane checked when they get back down." So apparently something was amiss. At any rate, Sandy felt horribly guilty, believing she was supposed to be in that airplane. Nothing we said to her could snap her out of her depression. She finally had to go to the flight surgeon for counseling before she could be restored to flight status.

17

Ugly rumors about sabotage and various structural failures circulated, especially about ailerons falling off the AT-17s. We wondered aloud if that was what had caused Peg and Jo's fatal crash; the pattern of the strewn wreckage made it look suspicious.

But we flew on. The closed cabin of the AT-17 was hot and stuffy. The air was nearly always bumpy, so we made our cross-countries without much enthusiasm. The cross-countries were old stuff by now, for there was nowhere new to go and still stay within our radius. And everything seemed so simple and easy when there was someone else along as copilot.

Nothing scared me anymore, not even rumors of falling ailerons. When we flew together, Shirley and I continually pulled back the mixture control on each other, thus cutting an engine, both for excitement and to keep our single-engine procedure up to snuff. At least it kept us awake.

We dropped into Ballinger one morning for a late breakfast with the major and Bob. I was still crazy about Bob, partly because he kept me guessing. And the major was definitely interested in Shirley. No one questioned us about our stop there, which we dutifully recorded. We had a feeling we were just marking time until graduation, and nobody was going to wash us out now.

At last something interesting happened to me: I was assigned a newly created job. An undated penny postcard to Mother told about it:

I've just been handed a new job, that of acting as senior squadron commander for the new class [44-W-1] that comes in next week. Just helping them over the rough spots in the beginning. Lots of work and responsibility, but should be worthwhile.

Thanks so much for the swell candy.

It was an unexpected honor to have been chosen for the job, because I had always considered myself a thorn in the side of authority and discipline. How did "they" ever happen to choose me? It left me speechless.

However, I had to recover and actually make a speech, to welcome the new trainees. My job was to help them get oriented, organized, and indoctrinated. When I saw the sea of 151 new faces waiting for me in the hot sun of that August morning, I wondered what on earth I should say to them.

"Welcome to Avenger," I began. My voice quavered and my throat was dry, but I made myself talk. I would try to tell them the things I wished that someone had told me (Jane Champlin had told us some of it before she crashed). I concentrated, remembering. When finally I made eye contact with some of the individuals in the group, I saw something strange there. There was a look of complete faith, trust, and confidence in those fledglings' eyes. Lawsy mercy, they thought I knew what I was doing!

"The upperclassmen want to help you," I croaked, remembering Jane, "so don't be afraid of us. If you have any problems, come to us, come to me, and I'll try to steer you in the right direction. Also, Mrs. Deaton is the best friend you'll ever have. She's on our side. She doesn't understand doodledy-squat about flying, but for some reason she loves us. She'll help you with

everything except your flying, so if you have any serious problems, go to her.

"Don't think negative thoughts. Don't let the check pilots
intimidate you. Listen, the Army is not trying to wash you out, in
spite of the way some of their check pilots act. The Air Corps
needs you! What they are trying to do is to pick out all those girls
who appear to have the ability to learn to fly the Army Air Forces
way. You can be those girls. Make up your mind to it.

"And for gosh sakes, don't let an occasional off-day get you
down, like I once did. Everybody is entitled to an off-day. Just
come on back the next day and double your determination. You
can fly, or you wouldn't be here."

Soon I had the new class divided into flights and sections and
taught them to step out with the left foot first when I shouted
"For-ward, march!" I marched them to the drill field, where I
tried to show them how to assemble neatly and get from one
place to another with a little snap and rhythm. They were quick
to learn, and so eager it broke my heart. I wondered how many
of them would wash out, and I wondered how many of them
would die.

Two were in fatal crashes: Katherine Dussaq and Edith Keene.

There was an undercurrent of excitement in the beginning of
September, because we knew that any day now the list of bases
would be posted on the bulletin board. There were four Ferry
Command bases that took WASPs: New Castle, Delaware;
Romulus, Michigan; Long Beach, California; and Dallas, Texas.

September 3, 1943

Dearest Mother:

I guess I'm about as happy today as I'll ever be, because the
list of bases has been posted, and Sandy, Shirley and I are
together—in Dallas! Just what we've been praying for.

P.S.: How *about* Italy?

I drew a smiling face in the margin. The radio had announced that Allied troops held nearly all of the toe of the boot of Italy. Later, on 8 September, Italy surrendered. Also in September, U.S. and Australian forces took two Japanese bases on New Guinea. Things were looking up! That gave us an added excuse to celebrate.

The night before graduation, Class W-6 gave us a party that they couldn't even attend. We were allowed to invite instructors, drink bootleg whiskey openly, and stay out until two o'clock in the morning. We made history doing all three things with the greatest degree of abandon ever witnessed. As my date, Bob was an enthusiastic participant. We'd always had fun together, but this was the pinnacle. And I was sure I was in love with him.

Even so, I had one last dance with Click. Then I gave him a happy farewell kiss, right smack on the mouth, in full view of the commanding officer, two generals, and Miss Cochran. Until tonight, she'd been under the impression they'd taken away our right to fraternize with instructors.

Not everyone was as uninhibited as I, of course; in fact, many WASPs were teetotalers. And most trainees had never been stupid enough to date instructors. But everybody rejoiced and sang and visited and table-hopped and made a lot of noise, which was necessary, if you wanted to be heard over the pandemonium.

Bob and I danced and reveled and gamboled with the rest of my class as we celebrated 43-W-5's hard-won victory. For six months we'd outwardly obeyed the Army's rules, passed their grueling ground school, done long hours of homework, suffocated in their Link Trainers, sweated through Physical Torture, drilled in horrible heat, inhaled sand and dust, lived in their ol' zoot suits, lined up, counted off, stepped out, march-march-marched everywhere, checked out, signed in, mopped floors, cleaned out latrines, endured inspections, and gotten gigged.

We'd eaten off tin trays, been stuck with needles, run through poison gas, been cussed at, deprived of sleep, given no privacy, and—for what? As I asked myself that question, I grinned and couldn't stop smiling. For what, indeed? For the chance to fly those wonderful Army Air Forces planes! And all the check pilots in hell couldn't wash us out now, because tomorrow we'd get our silver wings.

The habit of punctuality was so ingrained in me after six months, that I found myself within the gates of Avenger Field three minutes before 2:00 A.M. The line in front of the OD's office door was so long with people signing in that Shirley and I had time to frolic across the sand toward the fire bell, which we rang loudly.

After we signed in, we made raids on underclassmen and pitched them out of bed. But I scrupulously avoided going anywhere near my "babies" in 44-W-1.

There was one particular establishment officer (civilian) nobody I knew liked. She was an earlier trainee who had washed out and who now seemed to be taking out her bitterness on us. I don't think I ever saw her smile. We called her Pickle Puss (PP for short) behind her back. She patrolled the barracks trying to stop the frivolity and noise, but it sprang up the minute her back was turned. It came from so many directions at once that it was impossible for her to identify the culprits.

I was in a friend's bay when I heard that Pickle Puss was now counting noses in each room, so I streaked across the sand in my shortie pajamas toward D-5. It was dark, but not quite dark enough. She saw me.

She blocked my path and I reversed my course. My scuff-type slippers impeded my progress, for they would fall off and have to be retrieved before the sprint could continue. I didn't quite know where I was going—just away from PP. I made it to the end of the barracks where there were lattice-work fences adjoining the buildings, and I started up one of the fences, putting my rather large feet into the small, square holes. I pulled one foot out, then the other, and my slippers stayed in the holes.

PP was gaining on me. To hell with the slippers, I thought grandly, and continued up the fence barefooted. Within seconds I was on top of the roof, running away. Pickle Puss gave up and returned to the OD room without ever making my identity certain. Bed checks had been impossible. She had left my slippers in the fence, and I climbed down and retrieved them.

The September sun came up on schedule and blazed hot and bright by midmorning. A telegram of congratulations came from Ned. Cameras clicked and newsreel men worked frantically to get every conceivable shot of the graduation proceedings. They took close-ups of me because I was tall, and of Shirley because she had been on the cover of *Life.*

The band from Big Spring Bombardier Base played. Under-classmen paraded snappily and passed in review. A general spoke. The photographers caught me again when Jacqueline Cochran handed me the pair of silver wings that were a gift from her and that would always be my most cherished material possession.

I had promised to let Bob pin them on me, so I could only hold them in my hand now and gaze at them in awe. Bob would appreciate what they meant. Ned would, too. Only another military pilot could possibly understand what they represented. I wished Bob would hurry. He was flying in, but the field had been closed while the ceremonies were going on. How was he ever going to find me, with all the people milling around? But within the hour, he appeared at my side, smiling and handsome and proud of me. He pinned on my wings and kissed me, and I thought I would die of happiness.

Before I left Avenger Field for the train station, I accidentally ran into Pickle Puss. I smiled fiendishly. She knew she could no longer touch me. I had been waiting for six long, hard months to tell her what I thought of her, waiting for the moment I'd be out from under her bitter control. "I have something to say to you," I told her.

She looked at me defiantly. "Yes?"

My wings were blazing in silver splendor on my heaving bosom, and I saw her glance at them and glance away. The hurt in her eyes cut through the hate I had been storing up.

I paused. "I just wanted to say good-bye," I told her. Then I managed to give her a brief hug, something I never expected to do. As I turned away to leave her and Avenger Field behind, I felt like crying.

18

Shirley, Sandy, and I took the day coach to Dallas and from there flew on the airlines to Chicago. Mother had begged me to take the train instead, insisting "it would be safer." Sandy went on to Peoria and I went to Winnetka, where Mother and Grannie were still at Uncle Carleton's. They were having a family conference to decide where Grannie should spend her last days. (It was decided to move her to Georgia to live with Mother.)

Miraculously we three roommates got seats on a Chicago-bound airliner, and didn't get bumped. Thus began our ten days' leave, days of sleeping late for each of us, of resting and relaxing, being coddled, and eating home-cooked meals. It was wonderful, but unbeknownst to our families, we could hardly wait to get back to Texas and check into Love Field.

My next letter was written from our new base.

> 5th Ferrying Group
> Love Field
> Dallas, Texas
> *September 26, 1943*

Mother dearest:

Oh, honey, I'm so happy! Mother, how can I ever describe this place to you?! It's HEAVEN! Gosh, where to begin—?

Well, Thursday night we stayed at the Adolphus Hotel downtown, and "Bacchus" brought along a friend for me—a Naval lieutenant who is now taking flight training—and Sandy had a date with an Englishman we met on the train (RAF). We had a wonderful shrimp cocktail and steak dinner and fine time afterwards.

Friday morning we wrenched open our eyes and reported to the base at eight o'clock A.M. We were assigned rooms in the BOQ (Bachelor Officers' Quarters) which are nothing more, really, than barracks. But we have a room of our own. Our barracks are so new that the sheetrock isn't even put up in my room; it looks like Tate [our mountain cabin], though, so I don't mind. We are only furnished a cot (much worse, even, than the one at Sweetwater, but who cares?) and a wooden "closet"—sort of a wardrobe affair that doesn't even close. I'll hang a curtain in front of it to match the window curtains I shall someday buy, and I'll purchase a scatter rug and a bright bedspread, so it should be cheery as soon as I have time and money to fix it up. Also, I'll have to get a desk. Sandy and I have adjoining rooms, and Shirley is two steps across the hall. [There was a communal bathroom on the first floor, with no shower curtains on the shower stalls and basins lined up in a row.]

We are to be on duty every day from eight to five, and the rest of the time is our own. We are treated as officers, and no one cares where we sleep or when we go to bed, which is quite a treat after Sweetwater. But as soon as we get started flying, naturally we have enough sense to get plenty of rest—and I guess they know that.

We were released early on Friday to go into town and buy uniforms. I bought two more shirts and another pair of pants, which should last me until our official uniforms are issued. We wear the Air Corps insignia on our arms and officers' braid on our overseas caps.

We have been issued leather jackets, sweaters, helmets, goggles, navigators' kits, brief cases, luggage, and parachutes—all Air Corps equipment and most of it brand new. We feel very official, and also swanky with the beautiful traveling bag [B-4 bag] which has each WASP's name and base stamped on it. Our chutes were fitted on us and we have cases for them, too. All these above-mentioned items are khaki colored.

There are hundreds (literally) of men ferry pilots here, and most of them very attractive. Say, guess who is based here! Ben Juhan . . . from Athens! We nearly fainted when we saw each other. Neither knew the other flew.

We will be given check rides some time this week, first in the BT and then in the PT (the smaller plane last because they realize how hard it is to jump from heavy planes which we have been flying to the lighter ones). We'll start ferrying in a couple of weeks.

Everyone agrees that Dallas is the best base in the whole wide world. Everyone is so friendly, and we have gotten such a warm welcome—even from the C.O. himself—that it's hard to believe that at some bases the WASPs are resented.

Last night there was a huge party at the Officers' Club (we are members) and I hadn't planned to go since I had a date with Bruce and felt punk anyway from a typhoid shot—but the spirit got me, so I had Bruce come out here to the dance.

We had a wonderful steak dinner, complete with an orchestra and the best floor show I've ever seen anywhere, and a dance afterwards. Sandy and I were having so much fun that once when the band left for their 15-minute intermission, she sat down at the piano and I at the drums—and played. People actually danced to it and applauded, so you can see how happy everyone must have been.

The Officers' Club is simply beautiful—horsehair-covered chairs at the bar, and murals. It adjoins the Officers' Mess, which is where we WASPs eat. Incidentally, the food is simply wonderful and there is a wide variety. We eat cafeteria-style, and it certainly is pleasing to the appetite to have good looking men eating at the tables all around you, and often even with you at your table, if they are feeling bold. . . .

Immediately we began several months of ground-school courses, required when we were not flying: safeguarding military information, military courtesy and customs, how to pack a parachute, navigation courses, weather courses, and instruction classes on filling out forms, forms, forms. There were courses on the automatic pilot, flight regulations, aircraft maintenance, flight logs, CAA and Ferry Command rules, military law, defense against chemical attack, fuel systems and carburetion, radio range stations, radio compasses, weights and balances, and more. Occasionally we marched, mixed in with the men, but it was simply marching, not the fancy drill maneuvers we had executed so snappily at Sweetwater. I kind of missed that.

We learned (they thought) how to take apart and put together a .45. We were required to strap the pistol on our hip when ferrying certain types of planes that had the secret Norden bombsight on them.

On 27 September, I wrote Mother:

This post is like a little city. We have a movie, a post office, a bank, a prison, a PX (Post Exchange), a hospital, men, men, men, and—oh, yes!—airplanes galore. All the airliners have stations here, and all sorts of bombers, pursuits, and trainers are continually landing here as well as the airliners.

There is a darling "Ferry-Go-Round" which is an open bus that makes the rounds of the post every 20 minutes. [I drew a picture of an open trailer with poles to hang on to, pulled by a truck cab.] It never stops but goes about five miles an hour, driven by an Army man. If one wants to go from one end of the post to another, he hops on the Ferry-Go-Round while it drives past and then jumps off whenever he wants to. It's always loaded with Army officers and presents another way of meeting them, since you almost invariably fall in their laps when you jump on. They love it. We do, too.

Tuesday

The weather is bad today, so it looks like I'll have to wait a little longer before my first trip. The only good thing about above-mentioned weather is that Bob and Mac [Major McConnell] can't leave until it clears up. They came over yesterday afternoon, and we went to the Golden Pheasant (restaurant) where I saw Robert Taylor. He looks exactly like he does on the screen, except that he's quite short in real life—about Ned Hodgson's height.

We had a gas mask drill yesterday and it was the funniest thing I've ever seen. Next week we have to run through tents filled with poison gas with our masks on, which should be exciting.

Sandy, Shirley and I are up for check rides this morning in a BT-13, but so far the weather is too bad for us to go up. I'll sure be glad to have it over with.

The first week in October I got a letter from Ned, from the Naval Hospital in Norfolk.

October 4, 1943

My dear Marion,

On the off chance that you should decide to change your mind and write me a letter, I want you to know that I've changed my address. I'm going home! Jefferson Road [Athens, Georgia], here I come, to go to bed early, sleep late, take lots of exercise, get away from some of this liquor, and be handy man around the farm!

For another thing I find myself to be peculiarly susceptible to the female of the genus Mammalia, species: Homo sapiens. The cut-out photograph of your beautiful, smiling face, that I have on my dresser keeps me constantly reminded of you. [Ned had asked me for a picture of myself and I had sent him one.] Perhaps it's because I've been away from everything for awhile;

ordinarily I hardly notice a picture, but things being as they are, I'm not going to lay myself open to the chance of falling in love with the photograph of a gal who isn't interested enough to write me a letter.

Mother wrote me that your mother and Grannie are moving back to Athens, so I'll be there should you get home at Christmas. Give me a jingle; and we'll go out to dinner or a bicycle ride—whatever you say.

I think you are terribly sweet, Marion. I trust you won't think I'm trying to be offensive, for God knows that isn't my intent. I hope I couldn't be so ungrateful. Good night, Miss Pretty.

N

He enclosed my picture in the letter. I sent it back to him and wrote him a long letter, telling him that Joanna was getting married at Christmastime, and I was hoping to get a leave and come home to be her maid of honor. They had canceled all leaves, but if they would make an exception for a sister's wedding, I'd see him in Athens during the holidays. I was thrilled that he was well enough to travel to Georgia on sick leave and recuperate at home for a few weeks. He was going to take therapy in the swimming pool at the university, ride his bicycle, and build up his strength. What a long way he had come!

19

On 5 October 1943 I wrote Mother:

Already I've had my ATC [Air Transport Command] check ride on BTs. Somehow I passed, although I gave the check pilot a lousy ride (not having been in a plane for three weeks, much less a BT!!). I must've been unusually lucky, because at least one-third of the girls flunked their rides. Three of the girls who graduated from Sweetwater have already washed out! [They were transferred out of the Ferry Command.] Unbelievable, isn't it? We thought we were past all that sort of thing when we got our wings, but apparently Nancy Love has decided there is a deficiency in the training at Sweetwater and this is the only way the ATC can prove it to Jacqueline.

Bob and the major came over Saturday afternoon, and Shirley and I took a day off our annual leave on Sunday so that we could see as much of them as possible, since there's no telling when we can get together again. From now on we'll never know in advance where we'll be or when we'll be there.

Say, Mother, remember I told you not to worry about my flying bombers any time in the near future? Well, I may have been wrong. There's a rumor going around to the effect that some girls out of our class (those over 5'6") will be taken out of the

Ferrying Division of the ATC and put on special assignment. This would mean learning to fly twin-engine and four-engine bombers.

Friday

Dearest Mother,

I got a darling letter from Grannie today.

Today we ran through poison gases—without gas masks!—until we were able to identify the odor of each: mustard gas, phosgene, lewisite, chloropicrin. Then as a finis we ran through tear gas, which burned our faces and necks as well as putting our eyes out, but we're all O.K. now.

I had to take a checkout ride in a Stearman primary trainer, a 210-horsepower, open-cockpit biplane the Army called the PT-13 and the Navy called the Yellow Peril. The checkout pilot I was assigned to was a tall, jovial, good-looking bomber pilot just back from England, where he'd been flying B-17s for the Eighth Air Force. He was surprised and delighted to know that girls were flying for the AAF.

He laughingly told me that it had been so long since he'd flown anything but a bomber, he didn't know if he could fly the lightweight Stearman or not, much less teach me how. "But I'm supposed to check you out, so hop in, and we'll see what happens," he said, grinning.

We had to take off and land in a crosswind. I had an uneasy feeling. Something in the back of my memory rang a warning bell. Crosswind. Narrow landing gear. Ground loop. *Ned.* Ned had been trying to land in a crosswind, in a plane with a narrow landing gear, when he'd crashed.

We were on our final approach, windward wings slightly low as prescribed, but still the uneasiness persisted. Had Ned felt any apprehension before the fiery hell nearly consumed him? I could feel the captain's predicament—our predicament—in the soles of my feet, touching the rudders, feel it in the stick moving ever so slightly in my hand as I followed through on the captain's motions, feel it in the seat of my pants, see it in our attitude as we crabbed sideways, taste it in the wind that slapped across my dry lips like a whip. This was trouble.

And there was nothing I could do to help. *If* I knew what to do! How much rudder was too much in a plane like this? How slight a touch of the brake was too much brake as you fought to hold this plane straight on the runway? The captain was used to bombers he could control by advancing windward throttles. How could he be expected to remember the vagaries of a matchbox?

Ned, were you afraid like I am now? I felt the captain holding us off, using power, and then we were committed. We straightened just the instant before our wheels touched the runway and we were rolling, shuddering, fighting the wind.

It happened so quickly I could hardly believe it. The plane spun crazily into the wind, and a wingtip crunched with a sickening sound. Then it was all over and we sat still. It was quiet for a minute. Then the air was blue with curses. The captain turned to look at me, his face beet red as he grimaced in self-condemnation.

Well, we were still right side up and alive, and only the wingtip was damaged. I smiled sickly and the captain managed a sheepish grin, shaking his head. Slowly, cautiously, he taxied the plane back to the line. We got out and I had that limp spaghetti feeling in my legs again.

"Well, consider yourself checked out," he said, mopping his forehead with a handkerchief. "There'll be no more flying that ship today. You go on; I'll take care of the details. Wait! How about dinner tonight?"

I was giddy with relief, light-headed, happy to accept the captain's invitation, and blissfully unaware that I had just received the only instruction I'd ever get in the type of plane I'd fly on my first ferry trip, which would take me over desert and mountains.

Before I got my orders, however, Shirley and Sandy were ordered to Dodge City, Kansas, to B-26 school. So the rumors had been true! All three of us were in shock, and the thought of losing my two best friends devastated me. On 15 October I wrote my mother about it:

Luckily, today of all days, I got sent out on my first trip. Sandy and Shirley were to leave on the 1:15 P.M. plane from Dallas to Dodge City, and I got my orders a couple of hours before they left, so we didn't have time for a painful good-bye—we were all so busy throwing clothes in our B-4 bags.

Yesterday when we found out they were to report to Dodge City and leave me behind, we all nearly died. I cried my eyes out all afternoon, because I don't know when I'll ever see either of them again.

I'm writing this in Wichita, Kansas. Got my orders at 10:30 this morning, and at 11:00 I was on TARFU Airlines [TARFU and SNAFU were Love Field's own private airliners for ferry pilots, the initials standing for Things Are Really Fouled Up; and Situation Normal, All Fouled Up], which was filled with men and a handful of WASPs. The plane we were on was a converted Douglas (same as used by American Airlines) with the seats taken out. There is a small aluminum bench on each side where one can sit, but many of us sat on our parachutes on the floor and played poker.

We were all ordered to pick up PT-13Ds here [at the Boeing factory] in Wichita and deliver them to Glendale, Arizona. They're fun to fly but feel so light after the powerful babies we've been flying more recently that it's like sitting in a matchbox floating around in the breeze.

The wind was too strong to take off this afternoon, so we'll leave tomorrow morning. The Army furnishes our transportation from the field into town and back again; also they made our reservations here at the hotel for us, so we're all set. Can't wait to get started! I'm really anxious to spend some time flying again.

I can't even talk about Sandy and Shirley without choking up. We've lived together so intimately for so long—sharing the same anguish, uncertainty, triumphs and above all, the same interests and goal—that it's like losing my right arm to see them go. Living with those two people 24 hours a day for seven months is a real test of friendship, and we have camaraderie that is rare indeed and hard to equal. I don't know, really, how I can stand it without them—but of course I will.

Your nice letter came at the height of my misery yesterday, and it helped to hear from you. I'm so glad Grannie is doing so well. Tell her I'm proud of her for being so independent these days. Tell the darling I love her.

Well, I must take a shower now and get cleaned up for dinner. These B-4 bags are wonderful: hold dresses, shoes, and everything we need. I'm a civilian tonight.

Our group only got as far as Abilene in our Yellow Perils the next day. Landing the PT-13D was a snap when there was no cross-wind. We were weathered in for three days. We WASPs stayed at the WACs' BOQ, but there were no WACs on the post. There were only countless lonesome bachelor officers among whom to divide our attention. But nevertheless, I planned to call Bob in nearby Ballinger.

Then I met Danny, a Navy lieutenant who had engine trouble with his dive bomber and was waiting at the AAF base for a new part to be flown in. Danny looked like Robert Taylor, only taller. I had seen the real Robert Taylor in Dallas several more times, and he was simply gorgeous in his Navy uniform with wings of gold. Each time I'd seen him he'd stared me down, because I was in a man's Air Corps uniform and he obviously couldn't figure out what in the world I was. Now here was his double in Abilene! I had a Freudian lapse of memory and completely forgot to call Bob. A postcard written to Mother said:

> We are still grounded here in Abilene. Last night a Navy [lieutenant] and I went over to Sweetwater to see my old friends who are still there. The place sure seemed dull, and I'm certainly glad to be out of there!!

On the soggy morning of 20 October, the weather lifted enough for us to be cleared to Midland. Miles and miles of desolate sandy waste stretched below us as we flew west. We refueled at Pecos and flew on through Guadalupe Pass to El Paso, where we RON'd (remained overnight) and filled our gas tanks. The next day we flew to Deming, New Mexico, only an hour away, to refuel once more. We wanted all possible gas before facing the mountains between us and Tucson.

I strained my little Stearman for every foot of altitude it could handle after we passed over the San Pedro River. The air was turbulent and I knew it would be even more unpredictable over the higher mountains ahead. I could almost hear the plane gasping for breath as it staggered at 9,000 feet, but every time I looked at the forbidding terrain below, I tried to push it higher.

The turbulence tossed the PT around like a toy, and I thought, Wow! If I had to make a forced landing on those rocky mountains below, it would be curtains for me. Even if I jumped I'd be killed, or else they'd never find me. So I tried to force the struggling little plane even higher, lest a violent downdraft on the leeward side of a mountain slam me into the rocks that seemed to be waiting.

I looked around at my flight companions. They were all at exactly the same altitude I was, so I knew we had come to the same frightening conclusion and were leaving plenty of room between us and the death trap below.

And then we were over the last of the mountains, and there ahead, stretched out below, lay a green Garden of Eden—Tucson.

Its unexpected lush beauty took my breath away. I peeled off as soon as I could, shouting "Wheeeeeeee," in a carefree burst of relief.

It was too late to push on to Glendale, our final destination just outside Phoenix, so we landed at Tucson and checked into a hotel there. By some miracle I was able to get a private room, and I treated myself to the long-lost luxury of a leisurely, relaxing bubble bath. I almost fell asleep in the warm tub. I had promised to meet another WASP for dinner, so I climbed out and forced myself back into the rumpled khaki shirt and trousers. I had brought along a dress but had worn it four nights in a row and was too tired to iron it, anyway. The best I could do was wear a necktie and shine my loafers so I wouldn't look quite so disreputable.

I met my friend in the coffee shop. I discovered I was ravenous and ate with gusto, feeling curious eyes upon us. However, I'd already ascertained that they weren't Clark Gable's or Robert Taylor's, so I kept my eyes demurely on my plate or on my companion's face.

"Wonder where the boys from our group are?" she said, looking around shyly.

"Probably doing the town," I guessed. "They never wear down." We had gone our separate ways since the first night at Abilene.

I'd hardly gotten back upstairs to my room when the telephone rang. A man's unfamiliar voice said thickly, "I bribed the room clerk and got the number of your room. May I come up?" He sounded drunk.

"What?" I said stupidly. Then, "You have the wrong room." I hung up and sat staring at the phone as if it were a snake. I jumped when it jangled again.

"You're a WASP, aren't you?" he asked this time.

"Yes I am. What do you want?"

"If you're a WASP, you ought to know what I want," he said in an oily voice.

I slammed down the receiver. His insinuating words hung in the air like poison gas, and I wanted to throw open the windows and ventilate the room. I got up and checked the door instead, to be sure it was locked and bolted. I was trembling with outrage.

I had started to undress when a soft, suggestive knock went tap, tap, tap at the door, like a lover who knew he was expected. I could imagine the bleary-eyed creep on the other side, leering with anticipation. What tramp had caused him to believe WASPs were all hussies? Shaking, I yelled, "You get away from there or I'll call the house detective."

"This is me," the startled WASP's voice cried.

I unbolted the door to let her in, and sagged against the wall in a fit of relieved laughter.

"What in the world?" she said. "Who did you think I was?" I told her about the drunk caller.

"I just wanted to see if you were ready to swap reading material," she told me, holding out two magazines.

On 22 October we delivered our planes to the Army Air Field in Glendale, Arizona. I did it! I thought, as my wheels bounced once, then stuck to the runway. I parked the Stearman, turned in the papers that went with it, and got a receipt for the airplane. In Phoenix, I wrote Mother a postcard.

Here el chickeno is, in Phoenix, having delivered the ship safe 'n' sound to Thunderbird Field [near] here. Certainly is a grand feeling to have got it across the country without a scratch.

At the municipal airport in Phoenix, I made out my first government TR (transportation request), which served as a ticket on the train back to my base. Details of the trip came in a letter written the next day to Mother, which concluded:

The trip was a long, cold one. I caught a cold (my first, since I entered training. I was beginning to think I was immune to the things).

Last night was an uneventful one on the train. (Our airliner priority has been taken away. Some senator was put off and got mad.) Tonight was, too, except that a group of pilots just back from the Aleutians have been hanging around Baby, trying to make time, much to my delight.

One night in October I was sound asleep at Love Field on my sagging cot in T-11 (WASP barracks) when I was awakened, more by an awareness of being watched than by any sound. I opened my eyes. A man was standing in the doorway, silhouetted against the dim light in the hallway.

I was the only person that night sleeping on the second floor of the big, nearly empty barracks. I froze with horror. I wanted to scream, but my vocal cords were paralyzed like the rest of me. The man loomed there, not moving, looking in, while I watched in soundless terror. Every newspaper headline I had ever read about psychos and rape seared through my brain while my heart pumped its alarm.

The form took a step toward me and I screamed, the sound tearing from my body while I jumped out of bed and backed toward the window. If he came a step closer I'd jump, right through the screen of the open window. A two-story drop wouldn't kill me, and he might.

"Well, I'll be damned," a deep voice said. "Excuse me. I thought this was T-11." The form reached over to pick up a B-4 bag outlined in the doorway (that I hadn't seen) and the man's footsteps went down the hall toward the stairway.

My breath was coming so fast, I couldn't say anything. I realized now that this man was a ferry pilot returning from a very long trip. He was unaware that his quarters had been moved to another building in his absence, and that T-11 had been taken over by women—two WACs and the rest, WASPs.

"Good grief," was all I could say, as I crawled back between the sheets, still shaking. I couldn't go back to sleep. I lay there listening to the sound of a DC-3 overhead, its engines slightly out of synchronization. It was probably bringing a load of weary ferry pilots home for a few hours' sleep, and I hoped some WASPs were among them so I'd have company on the second floor of T-11.

I wasn't afraid anymore, but I was "shook." Finally, my heart quieted down. It was just that I was so—alone. The cotton pillowcase felt coarse against my sun- and wind-burned face. I tried to fluff up the pillow, but it remained lumpy and hot.

I thought back over the day's mail. I was glad my sister was finally going to marry her beloved Bot, and I sure hoped I could go home for the December wedding. I could imagine Mother and Grannie's nervous excitement, and Jeffie's joy in the kitchen. She would stuff a big turkey with oysters and roll out biscuits for the occasion. Jeffie. She had been part of my joy-filled childhood as far back as I could remember, during those happy years before my father's death. Since then, she still came back to our house for special occasions.

I could imagine her satiny brown face breaking into a million wrinkles of delight when I'd burst through the front door (if I could wangle that leave). "The baby's home!" she would shout, and we'd rush toward each other. Since I was the youngest child I was still "the baby" to Jeffie, even if I was a college graduate and an Army Air Forces pilot. I could just hear her crooning little sounds of happiness; I could almost inhale her warm scent, the smell that meant home. Sweet, faithful, sometimes crabby, wonderful old Jeffie.

I smiled. I could see her grumbling through housework, talking to herself over the stove, chanting weird primitive church songs over the ironing board, trying to shoo us "chilluns" out of the kitchen where we always gathered. I would tease her by pulling up her uniform and exposing the big brown mole on one knee that had fascinated me since early childhood, and she would flap her apron down over it and scold me, but I'd know she wasn't really mad.

I felt a hot tear roll down my cheek. I didn't feel like a big, brave Air Force pilot. I felt like Jeffie's baby, and I was homesick.

Okay. Think about something else. There had been a letter from Bob. He wanted to drive up and see me, but how would I ever again know where I'd be, or when, on any particular day or night? I was a gypsy. Well okay, this is what you wanted, gypsy.

I hadn't wanted a war, for goodness' sake—who had? But since it was there, to be lived through one way or another, I was glad to be part of it. An exciting part. So why was I feeling so sad? I'd won my wings and I had the job I wanted. Why then this restless, nameless, longing, yearning, lingering in my spirit on this warm Texas night? I was where the action was, where the fun was, where the danger was, where the men were—and that was what I wanted. Wasn't it? I turned over, and the bed I'd made for myself creaked. Sometimes I thought I didn't know what I wanted.

Did I still want Click and Bob, or did I want that cute lieutenant I'd met on the last trip? Each of them attracted me, especially Bob, of course, but I wanted them all—yet I didn't want any of them permanently. Well, okay, so who was asking for anything permanent? What do you want, Scarlett O'Hara?

I know. I know one thing I want. I want Ned to get well, to walk again, to wear his proud Marine uniform again, to have bright, shining eyes again, full of health and vitality. I wished I had kissed Ned. Another tear wiggled down my cheek, and I let it fall into the pillowcase and leave a wet blot. I think I'll have a good cry. Over Ned.

I had one, and then I fell asleep.

20

During that month of October 1943, the Germans began deporting Roman Jews to Auschwitz. The Russians advanced all the way to the Dnieper River. American planes attacked the Japanese base at Rabaul in heavy air raids.

On the home front, life in the Ferry Command continued at full throttle. WASPs picked up airplanes at factories, "bought" them for the AAF, filled out countless forms, and navigated from one end of the country to the other in order to deliver the planes safely to air bases or points of embarkation. We knew our services were desperately needed, and it made us feel good. I was still terribly lonely for Shirley and Sandy, but the opportunity for romance was everywhere, at every stop. I was never bored. On 25 October I wrote to Mother:

I was amused at your saying how wonderful it was for me to fly that strange ship. Honey, it was nothing but a li'l ole PT (Stearman), and I didn't need to go up in it more than once to catch on (I, or anyone else, of course)! [They're] very maneuverable, and sorta fun to play around in, but tiring to ferry, because they're so little and slow.

You guessed right about one thing: I had romantic experiences the whole way across the country. The best reception of all, though, was in Phoenix, where we had to stay two nights. Perfectly sober men kept coming up to me in the cocktail lounge of the hotel where we were staying to say, "Pardon me, please, for being so bold, but you are the most beautiful girl I have ever seen," or something unbelievable like that. I've never gotten so many compliments in my life. They must not have any women at all out there.

I had never been especially popular with boys in high school or college, always being much younger than my classmates and being late to "develop," so all this sudden attention was heady stuff to a twenty-one-year-old girl who considered herself too tall, with feet to match and unimpressive measurements. But none of that seemed to matter if you were a WASP.

WASPs were different, and men were curious to find out what made us tick. It was obvious that we loved to fly, loved being allowed to help with the war effort in such a significant way. Also, pilots had a reputation for being daring and adventurous, and the fact that we were girls doing a man's job seemed to evoke admiration in all but the most insecure types, who sometimes openly resented us. I thought about all that, then picked up my pen to finish my letter.

Is Grannie over the bad time with her heart? I surely hope so. . . . Give her a smacker for me.

I'll be able to pay you back *completely* in a very few months. [I had borrowed money to get to Sweetwater, where we made $150 a month as trainees. Now, however, we were making $250 a month—good pay! Also, the WASPs got $6 a day per diem when we were on a ferry trip, a dollar a day less than the men got, but I thought nothing of the inequality.] Isn't that swell? I'll forward another check in about ten days or two weeks. I've paid the bank back *in full*, and it's sure a load off my mind.

Oh! I haven't told you about Shirley and Sandy, have I? The

news is very exciting. They have been sent to Dodge City to fly B-26s—the fastest bomber in the world!

I'm not likely, at this late date [to go to bomber school]. I wish I had been sent with Shirley and Sandy, though. It's so bewildering to be without them. I still can't believe it.

On 29 October, I wrote Mother from San Antonio:

I came over here to San Antone today in a BT-13, which is for lend-lease to Mexico. Makes me feel right neighborly.

But Bob flew over to Dallas to see me today. No sooner did he get there than I was sent out on orders. Looks like we just can't get together.

TARFU is coming to pick us up around midnight. I'm a-gettin' sleepy, and wish it would hurry.

This trip to San Antonio was made with one second lieutenant and four other WASPs. One of the WASPs was Mary Trebing, who had been in the class ahead of me at Sweetwater. She was a pretty, shy Oklahoma girl with a sweet smile, who had been a student law apprentice and court stenographer before joining the WASPs.

Nine days after we delivered our planes to San Antonio, Mary was dead, with a broken neck, killed while ferrying a PT-19.

November 2, 1943

[To Mother]

I'm on a PT-19 trip. We were flown over to Stamford on TARFU yesterday to pick up the planes, and checked out on them there. We're going to Jackson, Mississippi, tomorrow.

At refueling stops, I kept running into boys from Georgia who were as surprised to see me as I was them. The war had flung us far and wide, and I got a lump in my throat when I wondered how many were headed overseas to get shot at, and whether they'd make it home again. That November, in the Pacific alone there were three thousand casualties when U.S. forces invaded the Gilbert Islands.

In the early part of November, my letter home reflected one of the changes that was taking place at Sweetwater.

Just a hasty note before this tired pigeon folds her wings for the night.

I'm the only girl on a trip with 16 men! We picked up Stearmans in Camden, Arkansas, and are delivering them to Sweetwater, where they will be used from now on, instead of the PT-19s (Fairchilds).

From there we'll take a load of 19s to Jackson, Miss., again.

One guy in our flight nosed over in a strong wind and we're waiting for them to repair the broken prop—the only damage. (He wasn't scratched.)

It was strange to land at Avenger Field and not recognize a single girl's face. I was, however, an object of curiosity to those who noticed me as I walked through the ready room with my chest fully expanded, displaying my wings to the greatest advantage. But the only people I recognized were a couple of instructors from Flight One.

The girls looked like a bunch of ragamuffins in their ill-fitting zoot suits. Had we really looked that tacky? It all seemed so long ago. I had visited there only once, and that had been at night.

I suddenly realized that I didn't belong there at Avenger at all anymore. It gave me a homesick, lost feeling, a sadness that people experience when they go back to a place out of the past, expecting to find it waiting eagerly for them, unchanged. And it never is. I felt cheated. Life was going on there without me, never having paused, not even noticing I'd left.

My flight captain—an eager beaver—was hurrying me up so we could get going. I wanted to linger and talk to the girls, but he had visions of pushing all the way to Shreveport that day, so all I could do was take one last wistful look around, and then head on out.

There was no way I could express to Mother the bittersweet longing that I felt when I returned to Sweetwater, so I continued simply to write about the kind of thing that gave her a vicarious thrill:

Another lieutenant axed me to marry him last night!! I've known him exactly two days. Very amusing, and nice to me—but he doesn't interest me at all.

I didn't kid myself that it was my charm and personality that caused so many proposals. It was the war! Boys wanted to get married before they went overseas, wanted an anchor, wanted something to come home to. I understood that, but it didn't keep me from being flattered.

And it was hard not to count the proposals if you were a refugee from Athens, Georgia, and could count all your previous proposals on one finger. Still, it was the very memory of that lone previous proposal that kept me from ever wanting to hurt anyone again, so I tried to keep things light.

It was hard, though, because these boys were pitifully eager for love and marriage before they went overseas. They weren't sure—and I wasn't sure—they'd be coming back. It made me want to kiss them all good-bye, the way I'd never had the chance to kiss Ned. And now maybe I never would. But I kept on writing him.

And I kept writing Mother. On 12 November I wrote:

I'm on my way to California! Here I am in Camden, Arkansas, again, ready to pick up another Stearman, which I'll deliver to Tulare, California. I'm tired of these open ships, but the trip should be fun, and I love the thought of going to the West Coast.

I'm on orders with a bunch of WASPs, but some lieutenants are going as far as Arizona with us, so it shouldn't be dull (as though it would, anyway)!

We were brought up here on TARFU, a C-47 [DC-3]. The trips on TARFU are always a laugh, with people sleeping all over the floor or playing blackjack or just generally cutting up. Somehow, everyone always seems to be in high spirits.

We had to learn to sleep on the airlines, because sometimes the trip back to our base gave us our only opportunity for sleep before we were ordered out again the next day (even though it wasn't supposed to work that way).

The other night, coming back from Jackson, Mississippi, [the airliner] left at 11 P.M. and was loaded up with ferry pilots (about 14 men and six girls). We had to put the people originally scheduled for the flight off the plane. [Our priority on the airlines had been promptly restored, because the airplanes headed for overseas shipment stacked up alarmingly.] Well, ennawho, at 11:10, every light in the plane was out, and every single person on the ship was not only sound asleep but snoring.

Whenever we're riding on the airlines or TARFU, everyone always presses his nose against the window on the takeoff and landing, as though we'd never been up before. Needless to say, though, we're a critical crew riding back there, and the poor pilots up front are in a nervous sweat for fear they'll do something not quite perfect—for they know the cracks that are going on between the ferry pilots, and often the men scream remarks loud enough for the pilot and co-pilot to hear. Fehwies is de cwaziest people.

[15 November 1943]

Mother, dear,

Here I am, still in Abilene. The starter on my plane locked and the ship is now in sub depot awaiting new parts to be sent in. I guess my trip to California will have to come later, since I have to report back to Dallas for other orders today.

November 17, 1943

Mom, dollin',

On my way to Fort Sumner, New Mexico, in a UC78B—a twin-engine Cessna like the ones we were trained on in Sweetwater. I'm solo, but there are others on the same trip and we all had dinner together and palled around Amarillo for a spell before turning in for *la nuit.*

November 19, 1943

Dearest Mother,

Here I yam in Kansas again, ready to pick up another C-78 at the factory and deliver it to Fort Sumner, N.M., once more.

We got back to Dallas at 8 A.M. today (after riding the bus and airliner all afternoon and night) and I was sent right out again.

November 23, 1943

Dearest Mother,

I'm in Wichita, Kansas, waiting to pick up another C-78, which I'll deliver to Marfa, Texas. I was supposed to be with a group of people, but the oil temperature gauge on my plane didn't work, so although there was no danger in taking off with it inoperative, Dallas would've raised hell with me if I'd taken off with a new plane that wasn't perfect.

Is Joanna's wedding December 23rd? I'm pretty sure they'll give me a leave without pay, even though they cancelled all our leaves a couple of months ago.

Day after Thanksgiving

[To Mother]

Weathered in at Big Spring! This has been the longest trip to be so short. I picked up another C-78 at Wichita and haven't got it to Marfa yet. We stayed in Dallas overnight and they used our ships there for transition time, releasing them to us late in the afternoon. So we only got as far as Abilene day before yesterday (where the fun began) and Big Spring yesterday. We were on our way to Midland, flying the beam, and called in at the Big Spring radio control to ask the weather, since it didn't look so good. They told us the ceiling was 1,000 feet, which is 500 feet below the Ferry Command minimum, so we got permission to land here at the Big Spring army base. It's a bombardier school and ordinarily ferry pilots don't stop here.

Helen Anne Turner and I are staying together as much as possible. She's a nice girl who lives right across the hall from me at Love, whose best and inseparable friend was sent to B-17 school at Columbus, Ohio. So, since we were both in the same boat as regards lost friends, we've sorta clung to each other for companionship.

We were sent to Wichita, Kansas, at the same time on "detached orders," meaning we'd keep reporting back there instead of to Love Field until further notice. There were a lot of twin-engine Cessnas to be ferried—solo—all over the country. Then, if we were lucky, we might graduate to the twin-engine Beechcrafts, which were also manufactured in Wichita.

We got adjoining rooms at the Allis Hotel. Helen and I enjoyed each other's company, although we were opposite types. She wouldn't take even one drink and seemed very old-fashioned. One day as the two of us waited endlessly for the overworked elevator to arrive and take us downstairs, I broke into a tap routine and was startled when Helen fell into step beside me. I would have been less surprised if she'd begun doing the minuet. She just didn't look like a tap dancer any more than she looked like the proficient pursuit pilot she became, in P-51s and other fighters. My letter describing her to mother continued:

She's good company and she's nice.

I applied for my leave while I was in Dallas, and our squadron commander approved it. So now if it goes through Personnel okay, I'm all set. Has Joanna sent my dress yet? And have you found my silver slippers?

Mother, how can I ever be content after this war? I'm spoiled rotten—getting free rides on airliners everywhere, staying in the best hotels, eating the best food, almost always being received royally and made a lot over, etc., far into the night. I could never be satisfied with the average woman's lot after this.

"How ya gonna get them back on the farm, after they've seen Paree?"

My love to Joanna and Grannie. Tell Grannie I'm so proud of her and her book and the way she's being so independent these days. . . . I loves you all.

—Maddion

On 5 December I wrote Mother about having to strap on a .45 while ferrying one of the planes I picked up in Wichita, because of the top-secret Norden bombsight that was installed in it. Of course I didn't tell her the name of the bombsight and had actually never been told it myself, but we all knew. The plane would be used for bombardier and navigator training. "There's secret equipment in my twin-engine plane," the letter told, "and Baby has to wear a gun. Sure feels crazy."

I failed to mention to her that there were two red buttons above the instrument panel with printed instructions to push the buttons if a landing had to be made "over enemy territory." They fascinated me, and during the whole flight my eyes were drawn to them. My fingers itched to punch them, just to see what would happen. Someone suggested maybe it would only ring a bell back at Love Field. I later discovered that pushing the buttons would have made the bombsight self-destruct.

Whenever I RON'd, the base was thrown into confusion when I requested—as ordered—a special guard for my plane. Nevertheless, some sleepy-eyed GI was always standing there when I appeared at takeoff time the next morning.

It was thrilling to be trusted with something that would really make a difference in the war. I could not guess at that time that the Norden bombsight would be credited with playing a big part in the Allied victory, but I knew it had to be something important. It gave me a tremendous sense of satisfaction to be entrusted with its safe delivery at AAF bases, and it made navigating super easy, because when I set the bombsight to where I wanted to go, it acted as an automatic pilot and steered me straight to my destination.

There were problems, though, caused by my having a .45 on my hip and being dressed in the same uniform shirt and pants that officers in the Air Corps wore. This was before our own blue uniforms were issued, although I had already been fitted for one. Military Police frequently didn't know what I was, with the Air Forces patch on my shoulder, wings on my chest, and dog tags around my neck, so it was no wonder they challenged me, suspecting me of impersonating an officer.

I'd produce my ID card as ordered, and they'd study it incredulously. When one MP was rude about asking for my ID, I stretched to my full height and, producing the card, said, "Say 'sir' when you address me." Since I was wearing a long bob and bright red lipstick, he didn't know whether to laugh or not. But when he returned the card he saluted, tentatively. At least I didn't get thrown in the brig, like three WASPs who spent the night in jail for "impersonating an officer" in Americus, Georgia.

Once in a while I felt insulted when I was in uniform and some snooty maître d' at a hotel icily refused to seat me in the dining room because they didn't "allow women in slacks." If I was exhausted and half-starved after a day of long, hard piloting, this rudeness burned me up. Wearily, if my ID card failed to convince him, I'd ask for the manager. But I always got fed—in the dining room!

On 9 December I wrote Mother:

Seems like every time I get a dream trip to either the east or west coast, the plane or I break(s) down. Right now, it's the *flus*, but I'm in bed, being taken good care of, so don't worry. Thank gosh I'm sick now and not at the wedding.

December 13, 1943

Mother, dear,

I'm out of the hospital now. One day and a half there was all I could stand.

Everything they say about Army hospitals is true! Now I'm "confined to quarters" and feeding on sulfa drugs to cure my sore throat. Flu seems to be gone—no fever—though I still don't feel too sharp. So I'm taking it easy and drinking lots of juices and won't fly again until after I see you.

They took me over to the hospital on a stretcher tuther night. [My temperature was] 102, and when I went downstairs to the jonny, I couldn't get back up the steps. Awful feeling! I'd start to pass out every time I'd try . . . so the girls called the ambulance. I sure wanted my mommy about then! But I'm feeling okay now.

When I was notified that my leave had been granted, I couldn't quite believe it. I rushed to the lone telephone in the hall at T-11, armed with nickels and dimes and quarters, so I could call home. But all the circuits were busy, as usual, and I had to settle for a jubilant telegram instead.

Author Marion Stegeman in the old WASP uniform (same as men's Air Corps) that caused Military Police to challenge her for "impersonating an officer."

The author, a civilian for a few hours, standing in front of Barracks D-5, Avenger Field, Sweetwater, Texas, during Open Post

The PT-19A Fairchild primary trainer

Nancy Harkness Love, commander of the original WAFS (Women's Auxiliary Ferrying Squadron). She later merged with the WASPs, at which time she became WASP Executive for the Ferrying Division of the Air Transport Command. (Special Collections, Texas Woman's University)

The five "survivors" left in Barracks D-5. From left: Jill McCormick, Shirley Slade, Marion "Scarlett" Stegeman, Marjorie "Sandy" Sanford, and Harriet "Hattie" MacLane

Opposite page
Top: The author in front of the PT-19A Fairchild primary trainer after her first solo flight. The patch over her right knee was used as a "note pad" for takeoff and landings times.

Bottom: Helen Anne Turner, Class 43-W-5, in front of the P-51 Mustang pursuit (fighter) she was ferrying

Dora Dougherty climbing out of an A-25 Curtis Helldiver. By the toss of a coin, she was the first WASP to be checked out as pilot in command of the B-29 Superfortress. Dorothea Moorman qualified the same day.

Jacqueline Cochran in post-WASP days, in a Super Starfighter. When Cochran died she held more world aviation records than any other flyer, male or female.

gcon
Regard
od Wishes
ochran

LOCKHEED
F-104G
SUPER
STARFIGHTER

Barracks at Avenger Field

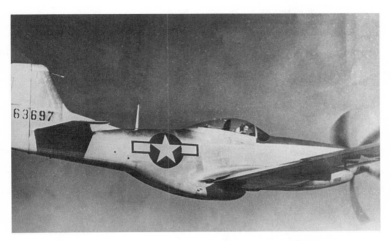

Snapped by a Navy pilot flying alongside, Helen Anne Turner ferries her
P-51 from the North American factory to an Air Corps base

Marjorie "Sandy" Sanford, Class 43-W-5, one of the first WASPs to fly as command pilot of the B-26 Martin Marauder medium bomber, called the Flying Coffin (among other things)
(Special Collections, Texas Woman's University)

Glider being towed by a WASP in a C-60 Lockheed Lodestar
(Special Collections, Texas Woman's University)

WASP trainees climb aboard a twin-engine Cessna UC-78 advanced trainer

PT (Physical Torture) at Avenger Field. Author is in front right corner.
Barracks in background. (Special Collections, Texas Woman's University)

Lila Chapman, Class 43-W-2, in front of flight board at Houston
Municipal Airport, before entire WASP training program was moved to
Sweetwater. (*D* means dual flying; *S* indicates solo.)
(Special Collections, Texas Woman's University)

Jacqueline Cochran, head WASP, in the new Santiago blue uniform (Special Collections, Texas Woman's University)

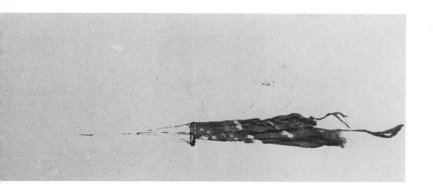

Laurine Nielsen, flying a Douglas Dauntless A-24, tows targets for green gunnery officers to shoot at with live ammunition. Sometimes the tow planes landed with bullet holes in them.
(Special Collections, Texas Woman's University)

WASP trainees at Avenger Field plot course for upcoming cross-country flight (Special Collections, Texas Woman's University)

Louisa Thompson in front of the Lockheed P-38 she was ferrying (Special Collections, Texas Woman's University)

Marion Stegeman, 601st Squadron, 5th Ferrying Group, Love Field, Dallas, Texas. From the Love Field yearbook.

Major Edward "Ned" Hodgson, USMCR, before his crash

Jacqueline Cochran (in dress) with Lieutenant Gerron, Adjutant at Avenger Field, and WASP trainees in Sunday uniform (white shirt, tan slacks, overseas cap) at an early graduation ceremony

Shirley Slade, future B-26 pilot, cover girl for *Life* magazine (Photo by Peter Stackpole; Time-Life Inc.)

Trainees in front of the administration building at Avenger Field.
Overhead is Walt Disney's Fifinella, the female gremlin mascot of the
WASPs.

The author in "zoot suit," lugging parachute, at Avenger Field

Marion and Ned Hodgson, pronounced "man and wife" on June 1, 1944. (The bride has kicked off one high-heeled shoe for the wedding pictures.)

21

A few days before Christmas I caught a ride in a B-24, bound for Atlanta. The pilot let me fly part of the way. He purposely cut an engine while I was piloting, in order to teach me the procedure when you lost an engine on the B-24. I had never so much as feathered a prop, much less flown a four-engine bomber, so I was eager to learn all I could.

What I learned was that you can't always restart an engine once you've cut it. The pilot seemed unconcerned, shrugging and saying, "Three is plenty," as he kept working on the engine. He never could get it going again, so we limped into Birmingham and sat down there for repairs, then flew on to Atlanta.

From there I caught a bus to Athens, still in my uniform, which caused an MP to challenge me at the bus station. He had never even heard of the WASPs. I had to explain quickly what we were and show him my ID, so he'd let me board the crowded bus.

Wartime buses were always filled to overflowing, and at Christmastime it was worse than ever. But men nearly always yielded their seats to women in those days (in the South, anyway), and I gratefully accepted a seat from a fresh-faced young soldier. He was so young and vulnerable, it broke my heart to think about where he might be headed, eventually. But today, a few days before Christmas, he was headed home, just like me. Home and Ned!

In Athens I took a ten-cent taxi (an Athens phenomenon), which I shared with the soldier and two other people. It took me to the big old brown-shingled house on South Lumpkin Street, which held so many happy childhood memories. I was greeted by squeals of delight from Jeffie. She dropped the broom she was wielding on the front porch and ran to me, and we hugged and cried. Hysterical embraces with Mother and Joanna and Grannie followed.

I walked into a house that was bursting with flowers and wedding presents. The wedding had been set for 23 December, and the atmosphere was so charged with excitement and nervousness that I didn't think any of us could possibly survive until then. After things calmed down somewhat, Mother told me, "Ned is coming over on Christmas Eve, to see you and to take you to the midnight service at his church. He said to go ahead and wear your uniform. He wants to see you in it. I think maybe he's thinking of the flat heels."

"Can he walk?" I cried, delighted that he'd called.

"Yes, dear, quite well. Without crutches."

As eager as I was to see Ned, I temporarily forgot about him amid all the wildness of prenuptial festivities. Joanna's Bot (who had just gotten his medical degree) had many friends, as did Joanna, who wanted to give them parties.

I was paired at these parties with Bot's best man, Allen, since I was maid of honor. Allen was a flight surgeon in the Air Corps, good-looking and unattached. We were greatly attracted to one another, and by the time the rehearsal dinner was over, we were a twosome by our own choice. The elation of having a leave during wartime, of being part of a romantic wedding, of being home again and celebrating Christmas, plus being paired with a tall, dashing doctor, all made a combustible situation in my immature heart. It felt like love—yet again!

The night of the wedding was a blur of happy emotions.

Joanna was a stunning bride, and Bot was beaming with pride. The church was jammed with lifelong friends and for that one magic evening, the war ceased to exist.

Ned was there, but I didn't even see him. Allen and I made plans to see each other again, in Atlanta, where he would be visiting his family. I'd meet him there after Christmas, when I passed through on my way back to Dallas. He left on Christmas Eve, his heart in his eyes, and I hated to see him go.

But Ned moved in quickly. He called soon after Allen had left, to confirm our date for church. Church! The last place I wanted to be! But his voice sounded warm and familiar.

When the doorbell rang that night and I knew it was Ned, I nearly tripped over my own feet getting there. I pulled open the heavy wooden door and threw open the screen door, and there he was, smiling in the light that had been turned on for him. His chestnut eyes were shining with pleasure and they were so bright they dazzled me. He just stood there, his sweet warm mouth smiling and his eyes shining, and neither of us spoke for a moment.

Since he made no move to come in, I went out to greet him with a hug. I was startled at the stiffness of his back. Had I offended him, or was he in a brace? Later I found out it was neither. He was standing straight because the Marine Corps taught him to, and he was unbending because he was afraid he might topple over on his unsteady legs.

He limped into the house, into the wild, confused atmosphere of the bride's (now former) home. The telephone kept interrupting all our attempts at conversation with Mother, attempts that were difficult at best because of her deafness. So we went into Grannie's room, visited a minute, then kissed her goodnight, and left.

We parked at a drive-in and ordered setups, and sat side by side, talking. Every time Ned turned to look at me, I was struck anew by the impact of his sparkling eyes. The car seemed to pulsate with magnetic waves that he generated. This is silly, I thought. I've known him all my life. There's never been anything between us but friendship. He's not even as tall as I am. But I could not deny the electric current that was shaking me to the soles of my rationed shoes. I thought, if he so much as holds my hand, I'll faint.

He didn't. He never made any move toward me. He never had! I thought, if he doesn't at least hold my hand, I'll die. I had waited for months to talk to him, and now I hardly listened to his words. I was glad when it was time to go to church, to ease the strain. Did he feel it too?

"You'll be a sensation in that uniform," Ned told me. A sensation, in officers' pants and shirt? "Nobody around here has ever seen anything like it. Do you have a cap or anything to cover your head?"

Not being an Episcopalian, I had completely forgotten that I shouldn't go into his church bareheaded. I held back as Ned urged me toward the door. "It doesn't matter. This is wartime!" He laughed, pulling me by the hand. We were already late, and so we sneaked in and sat in the back row. A few heads turned furtively for a surprised look, but I didn't see anyone I knew and was glad.

We left early, while members were taking communion. As we walked out the swinging doors into the vestibule, I could hear church bells down the street chiming through the clear December night air. Before we got to the front door of the church, Ned stopped me and said, "Merry Christmas," and kissed me.

His mouth was even nicer than I'd imagined. I wondered at the shock that passed between our lips. Ned felt it too, and said, "Must have been the carpet." He took my arm, smiling. Suddenly every church bell in town seemed to be ringing and my head was spinning.

This is ridiculous, I thought. You've been kissed before, much more thoroughly. Why do you feel as if it's the first time?

And then we were in the car, driving toward my home on South Lumpkin Street, not talking. The tension building between us could no longer be ignored. Ned spoke first, suggesting that we stop along the way and check to see whether static electricity had caused the phenomenon of our electric kiss, or had the sparks between us been caused by something else?

After several stops in the name of science, it was determined that it was definitely something else. I was as light-headed as if I'd taken a whiff of some heavenly anesthesia that made my body as weightless as a cloud, only there was lightning in this cloud, about to rend it asunder. By the time we reached the door to my house, I felt woozy and thoroughly confused. How could I react like this if I loved Bob—or was it Allen? Good grief, what was wrong with me? Why was I so shallow and fickle?

We said goodnight at the door. We were afraid to kiss again. I staggered into the house on legs that wouldn't work at all. I think I'm coming down with something, I thought. Surely I'm not coming down with flu again! Shouldn't I be immune for a while? No, I didn't ache that way. This was different. This fever, too, was different, if I had a fever. I put my hand to my forehead. I couldn't tell whether my temperature was normal or not. I couldn't tell anything except that I felt very strange.

I went into the bathroom and turned on the light and stood swaying in front of the mirror exactly as if I were drunk. I had never been drunk, but I was sure this must be how it felt. A stranger with a flushed face and crazy eyes and wild hair and no lipstick stared back at me, half smiling like a nitwit.

Is this *love?* Is *this* what it feels like, after all these years of wondering—this sick, weak, feverish, out-of-this-world feeling, just like in all the corny love stories? I shook my head to clear it and pushed back my unruly hair. No, no, no, *no,* I can't really, truly fall in love now. It would be impossible. I can't fall in love until the war's over. I can't, I can't, I can't.

I sat down on the edge of the tub and put my face in my hands. I had thought I was in love before: Hal in Chicago, Click at Avenger, Bob at Ballinger, and—most recently—Allen. Just today I thought it was Allen! It hadn't been anything like this, yet it was enough to make me think I was in love. And always I had proved faithless. Fickle. Susceptible to other men. How did I know it would be any different this time, even if this was more intense than anything I'd ever felt before? I didn't know. I couldn't know. And I couldn't hurt Ned. He was the finest boy I'd ever known, and I just couldn't hurt him.

The next day I came down with a relapse of flu, which meant I had to stay over in Athens, taking sick leave. They'd never believe, back at Love Field, that I was really sick, it being Christmas and all. I had the doctor wire my squadron CO, and I stayed in bed with fever for several days. Ned came to sit by my bedside every day. I pulled the sheet up over my face because I looked so awful: red nose, swollen eyes, no makeup, stringy hair. So our visits took place without our being able to see each other. Even so, there was stardust in the atmosphere, which bewildered me.

A few days later I was well enough to plan my trip back to Love Field. Ned took me out for my last night in Athens. "I leave in the morning," I told him, as we sat under a streetlight in his little coupe.

"I know. I wish you could stay longer, Missy."

"I wish so, too."

"You can add me to your list of conquests," he said, halfway smiling. I was turned toward him, looking at his wonderful mouth, and I didn't feel the sting of his words for a moment.

"What?"

"I said you can add my name to the long list of fellows who'd like to marry you."

"Thanks." Mother must have told him my secrets. I wanted to cry, but I tried to smile. Oh, dear Lord, what should I do?

"How are you going to get to the bus tomorrow?" he asked.

"In a cab. Nobody around here has any gas."

"Well, I have a little. May I drive you to the bus station?"

"All right. Thanks."

And so he drove me to the station in the unflattering light of early morning, when my eyes were still puffy and my heart ached with indecision. He kissed me lightly before I got on the bus and I felt nothing. I wanted to laugh aloud with relief—and shame. It was nothing. It was gone. It had only been a snare and a delusion—magic on Christmas Eve that melted in the harsh light of day.

Why, then, as I waved to him from the bus window and watched him form the word "good-bye" with his lips, then turn and limp off, why did I want to scream "Stop!" to the driver and jump off the bus and run to him, throw myself at him, never let him go? I pushed my knuckles against my teeth and tasted the salty tears that I was helpless to stop.

22

During the month of January 1944, our air and naval forces in the Pacific raided the Marshall Islands in anticipation of an invasion. At the same time in Europe, Soviet forces broke the blockade of Leningrad. In Italy, Americans secured a beachhead at Anzio behind German lines.

On 5 January I was headed back to Texas. The next day I wrote Mother the following letter:

Hotel Texas
Fort Worth, Texas

Well, here I is—back in Texas. I caught a ride yesterday afternoon—all the way from Atlanta to Fort Worth—with a captain who was coming here in a C-43 (small cabin Beechcraft) for a meeting of Directors of Flying Safety. There were two other passengers, a lieutenant and another captain, and the little plane cruised at 180 mph, so we had a nice trip. We spent last night in Barksdale, a huge Army Air Forces base at Shreveport, Louisiana, and then we arrived here this morning. I still have a cold and know it wouldn't be safe for me to fly [in an open cockpit plane], so I've gotten myself a hotel room here and am gonna rest the remainder of the day and get a good 12 hours sleep tonight—then catch a bus to Dallas tomorrow. Do you approve?

How are you, darling? I hope you're beginning to get your pep back now. [She also had come down with flu.] How are Aunt Heluiz and Grannie? No flu, I'm trusting. Give them both my love.

The colonel [Allen, with whom I kept the date in Atlanta] was darling. We had dinner with his family, then stepped out at the Paradise Room at the Henry Grady. He thinks he is in love and insists he wants to marry me, but he's crazy.

I could've cried when I had to tell Ned good-bye at the bus station. He is so precious, and I'll miss him so.

Back at Love Field I was grounded, so I mailed a postcard to Mother.

[Saturday, 8 January 1944]

It's snowing here, but I'm grounded (because of my cold) anyway, so I don't mind. How is it there, and how are you?

Have you seen Ned since I left? Give him my love if you do. I wish he'd let me write him!

January 13, 1944

Dearest Mom,

You were sweet to write me in such detail about Ned. You knew I'd want every word, didn't you? Nice that he has been going to see you.

My cold and cough are better, though this freezing weather has kept me from shaking them completely.

Allen wrote me a darling letter. He may be sent to Kansas for 2½ months before going overseas. Don't know when I'll get to see Bob again. The weather prevents his flying up, and they are way behind schedule, anyway. I'll be interested to see how I react to him now, after Allen and Ned.

They are making us go to ground school all day long now and

are cracking down on us so much that I'm going to avoid Dallas as much as possible from now on, while on trips. If [anybody gets] weathered in here, [he has] to sit in the Operations office all day—doing nothing. We're all terribly disgusted.

Wonderful about Ned's foot! I'm so glad. Sounds now as though he may fly again.

January 13, 1944

[From Ned]

Miss Lovely,

I got your letter today and was very glad to hear from you despite my request that you not write.

As far as your loving me "in the strangest way" is concerned, I think we all have a very special love for several very special people, but I'm afraid that neither you nor I are sufficiently developed emotionally to really love another in the highest sense of the word. I regret to say this and think it's equally bad if not worse in your case, but neither of us seems to know any emotion much beyond lust. The thing that really worries me is that I'd feel perfectly awful if I had any part in awakening such an emotion in you, and perhaps I did. You spoke of being a wolfess. There aint no such thing! A wolf is a man. A patient wolf is a gentleman. A wolfess is properly termed a "bitch wolf." I'll be damned if I'll have you known as the bitch wolf of Love Field, if I have to come down there and make an emotionally honest woman of you, myself.

I have a tremendous admiration and respect for you and I believe probably the nearest I've ever come to achieving the true sense of the word *love,* but you raise such a hell of a lust within me that it's hard for me to identify the finer feelings.

I don't mean this as a confessional but I feel that you are one of the few women to the memory of whose real love and affection I could be completely faithful. I know I do not inspire that in you, but some man will, and for God's sake, latch on to him even if he's in the damned Army Air Corps.

The worst competitor that any man will have with you is your love of aviation and distaste for the "domestic" side of living. The war will begin to end with the spring, and by 1945 the horrible shake-up of things beginning to fall back into place will be well underway. The man with the wife and family will have to be considered first, for on the family all the good things of life are based. In the meantime, have your fling, see the world and its people.

I love to hear from you but I'd just as soon you didn't write. I might get to looking for letters that don't come. Besides, I'm still suffering from "hospitalization" and am inclined to read into letters thoughts and meanings that are not there.

I believe in whiskey, Saddy night, and woo pitching for boys and girls, and in loving anybody you really *love* 'til you ache all over, but remember, you're a lady and there is a double standard, despite the pants; and if I hear it rumored that you're known as the "wolfess" or, to be more precise, the "bitch wolf of Love Field," I'll come down there and personally administer a spanking.

I trust you know that I wouldn't go to the trouble of giving you hell if you hadn't wormed your way into a special niche in my heart. For another thing, don't ever worry about hurting me, 'cause I've been hanging around for a long time and my heart is calloused enough on the surface so that it would take a pretty hard blow to break it.

That's 30 for now, little one.

By the time I finished reading his letter, I was boiling mad. Here I had been feeling all warm and admiring and loving toward him and all the time he thought it was just lust! I had never had anyone speak to me that way. How dare he! I was particularly incensed at his use of the words *bitch wolf*. A wolfess, yes, but *bitch* wolf? I fired off a letter to him unlike anything I had ever written, and I was so furious that I mailed it without even reading it over.

January 21, 1944

[From Ned]

Honey, to say that your letter, which I just received, knocked the hell out of me—made me sick all over, is a gross understatement.

I have a guest [named Sally] but hope I'll find time to write you before I leave Tuesday A.M. [to return to the hospital at Cherry Point].

My job kept me busy while I tried to decide what to do about Ned.

January 22, 1944

Dearest Mother,

Just delivered another UC-78—this time to Pampa, Texas. I'm still on detached service at Wichita, which suits me fine. I'm waiting now for the airliner to take me back there.

Got a letter from Joanna, and she sounded so happy!

Did I tell you I bought you something in Mexico?

January 24, 1944

[From Ned]

Dear Marion,

The trouble with letters is the interpretation of the recipient. I suppose one should confine one's letters to news or not write at all. We have a hell of a time seeing ourselves as others see us, but I can assure you that it was not my intention to be mean—to scold and chide you, yes, but not to be mean. [He had scolded me about not sending my mother a RON when I left Athens, which I found ludicrous, considering my job. Did he expect me to send her a telegram telling her where I was staying every night?] At present I'm sorry, terribly sorry, I ever felt interested enough in you to scold you. I guess I don't know you very well. Your vitriolic reply is evidence that I know you a hell of a lot less well than I thought I did. You evidently are not accustomed to having anyone scold you, else you would not have gotten so hot under the collar. Perhaps instead of giving up, I should continue, but it's evident it would be wasted effort.

I read your letter and put it away like something I was afraid of.

I hate to bring the thing up again, damn it to hell, writing will never get us anywhere, I fear, except to a worse impasse. [The next sentences were scratched out several times, but I could decipher through the angry scratches what had been written: "I'll take this much from your letter—you tell me you're a party gal, you like many men, you don't intend to settle down soon, you have a special feeling for me but you don't love me, except in a special way, I make you feel selfish."] Skip it. I've put my foot in it and I can't say what I want to say 'cause I haven't got time to write my thoughts so they won't be misunderstood, but baby, you are not a "vicious, lust-consumed moron." I think you are one of the sweetest, finest, highest-principled ladies it has ever been my good fortune to know. As for my saying the feeling I have for you is lust, that's true, but it's a part truth. If that will square that item, it won't be necessary for me to destroy my camouflage.

If you have anything to write, confine your comments to news and gossip. Don't ever feel that you have to answer my letters, in which I'll endeavor to likewise confine myself. I loved being with you, but I sho fo God hate this drivel. You're a "dog in the manger" and I'm a "lascivious ole bastard." If I ever see you again, it would be swell. At that time perhaps I can tell you a thing or two and we can slug it out verbally, but to hell with this stuff.

You're practical and I am, too (about some things); you (at one time) loved me (in a special way) and I love you in a special way. I think you're pretty and spoiled. You probably think I'm interesting enough and spoiled, too. You make me mad as hell sometimes. You say I make you mad. So!! What the hell, skip it all until you see me again, hunh?

                                Your lascivious ole bastard

Wichita, Kansas
January 23, 1944

Ned, dear,

I haven't been back to Dallas since writing you That Letter—so I don't know what your reply was, if any. But I wanted to write you again, anyway, to tell you I didn't mean to sound so harsh; I was just mad, that's all. I'm so confused about you that I simply don't know what to do.

I'm so afraid of saying or doing something that will "lead you on" that I'm scared to open my mouth. Yet, at the same time, I want to lead you on! What to do? Don't let this scare you away, but of all the men I've ever known (and some whom I've loved for awhile)—If I had my choice right now and had to marry one of them, guess whom I'd choose! But, I repeat, don't let that scare you, because you know how ridiculous it would be for me to think of marriage at this point—and you also know how changeable I am. It's really disheartening, even to me, to know how susceptible I am to attractive men—yet there's only one that I really want to hold on to, and that is the addressee. Isn't that selfish? I know I shouldn't want to encourage you, yet I can't help it, because I admire your spirit and your ideals so much, and when I'm around you, I feel a better person because of it. Really, I believe it is catching.

In spite of what you say about how tough your heart is, I know that it is not. It would kill me if I were the one to break that heart—yet if I let you go, I might break my own. Gawd, where do I go from here?

When I think how there are wonderful girls around like Sally who would marry you in a minute and make you a really fine wife, then I'm ashamed for hanging on, because if you wait too long, then someone else is going to grab Sally. And I have no idea how I'll feel toward you in a year or two, so what right have I to stake my claim? Please, Ned, figure this out and tell me what to do.

I want so, with all my heart, to be fair and honest with you and to avoid messing up your life.

> U.S. Marine Corps Air Station
> Cherry Point, N.C.
> *January 29, 1944*

Miss Lovely,

I'm glad you were dateless or bored or something on the 23rd, if that prompted your letter. If you want to be a "dog in the manger" or lead me on, that's a woman's prerogative. You've been wonderfully sweet about telling me just how things are so your tactics won't break my heart—I tell you it's pretty hard to break, though. Hang on, shake it like a dog's rag doll, be "selfish" if you like. I think I understand pretty well your position.

Thinking of you acts as a deterrent to "smooching" and that is the thing that really bothers me—I'm inclined to be faithful to a memory of you and that never happened before with anyone.

You're sweet to be so honest. My suggestion is that you string me along, mess up my life and break my heart if you can, 'cause you've certainly given me fair warning.

In the Navy they hoist the flags Sail Hypo William, which means "cease present operations." The flags are hoisted and it's time I quit, so adios for the nonce, my dear.

> Your lascivious ole bastard

I flew on. The last day in January, I piloted a twin-engine UC-78 Bamboo Bomber over the water at the edge of New York City on my way to Fort Dix, New Jersey, where I was to deliver the airplane for overseas shipment. I had never imagined New York like this. As I looked down I saw a tiny finger-like island glimmering in the sunlight with solid-packed miniature buildings, surrounded by the bluest water I'd ever seen. I was up above all the noise and excitement, the traffic and frenzy and frustrations, cruising along peacefully, looking down on the Statue of Liberty and millions of invisible mortals below, most of whom didn't dream of the beauty and serenity that was possible from the cockpit of a small airplane in a clear blue sky. It was a magic moment.

But reality set in when I got back to Wichita.

Allis Hotel
February 1, 1944

Ned, honey,

Someone just forwarded me the letter you wrote in answer to that hot-under-the-collar job I sent you after you had scolded me. Ned, please let's not misunderstand each other any more. I really can't stand it.

Honey . . . haven't I made it plain how I feel about you? Damn it all to hell, Ned; I didn't want to say this—but I do love you. And not just in that "special way," either. You've just ruined me for every other man I've been with since I was with you. I didn't want to come out and say it, because you know how afraid I am of myself and also of love. And I want—more than anything in the world—to keep from ever, ever breaking your heart. You know how fickle I've been in the past. It leaves me so unsure about anything—I don't even have any faith in myself anymore along those lines. Yet, I've never felt this way about anyone— ever—and this may be It. But how can I ask you to wait while time assures me of that? I can't and I won't. It wouldn't be fair and I might keep you from marrying someone like Sally—some- one who would really make a splendid wife.

Honey, now that I've said it, shall I tell you how I really feel about you? Well, remember when you showed me your legs? All I could think of when I looked at them was, "Oh, darling, you've been through so much, and it makes me love you so very much more for it," and there was no feeling at all of disappointment that your legs weren't beautiful. I'm not sure it would matter if you didn't have any at all. Oh, Ned, why am I telling you all this? I'm risking hurting you some day and I know it, but I love you so damn much that if I keep it inside me any more I'll burst. I just have to tell you. I think you're the finest, most sincere, most lovable—and lustworthy!—person I've ever known. I look at that little picture I have of you all the time and I don't know how I can stand it until I see you again. But, honey, promise me something? Don't count on me, because I can't count on myself, although my heart sure does feel cleaner and more honest this time. That's your influence!

Please tear this letter up because, believe it or not, it's the nearest thing I've ever written to a love letter and it scares hell out of me. I've never written "I love you" before to anyone, and I probably shouldn't be doing it now. But, darling, I do love you—so terribly that it hurts all over—and I just pray that this time it's the kind that will last.

23

Ned, dear,

Looks like I may be stuck here for a day or so, according to the weather man.

I want so much to know how you are getting along and whether you have any idea [if] you'll be flying again soon or not. Mother wrote me about your being able to push up on the foot that was so stiff, and I was as proud as though I had accomplished the feat myself. Honey, you are so brave and uncomplaining that I never cease wondering at you. You are truly to be admired but I'm afraid admiration isn't the sole feeling I have for you, darn it. I don't want to love you like I do because it is likely to come to an unhappy ending. . . .

We flew through some horrible glub today. The ceiling was supposed to be 2,000 feet and the visibility was reported at 7 to 8 miles. Actually I had to fly right off the ground and even lost sight of the plane off my wing at one time—most disconcerting. If my radio had gone out I would've been sunk. [We navigated by "bracketing the beam"—using radio signals.] Instrument flying isn't in my line, especially over an unfamiliar route when it's getting near sunset, so I hope I won't run into anything like that again. I'm a nervous wreck. However, as you can see, I got here all right.

The phone has been ringing all night—restless wolves who have been weathered in here for days (trying to get east) have offered us many forms of entertainment. Ruth Lindley (we're on the same orders) and I finally consented to one drink with a colonel and his co-pilot, but they were singularly uninteresting, so we came home early. Speaking of colonels, I saw Allen, the flight surgeon, last night while I was in KC and had a lot of fun with him, though I spent most of the evening telling him I loved you. I probably shouldn't tell you that, since I'm like I am, but since I've already confessed to you, I may as well get it off my chest periodically. I don't know what's wrong with me—this isn't like me at all. And I don't like it, seeeeee?!? Do you think it can last? I wish I knew.

Cherry Point, N.C.
February 4, 1944

[From Ned]

Miss Lovely,

Yesterday was certainly a wonderful day. Got a flight with a friend to act as a safety pilot, and while I was officially a passenger, I flew. Made two takeoffs and landings. Felt very much at home and at ease; had no trouble taxiing, and found I could make the plane do what I wanted to pretty accurately. My landings were smooth but hot, 'cause that's the easiest way to be smooth. Lord, I was so happy I could yell.

Came to the BOQ and a friend told me I'd been selected for promotion. I knew I couldn't accept it but was glad to know I hadn't been "passed over."

I wish it were as easy to be selected for promotion on your team as it is in the MC.

The gas situation is acute, but I plan to go [to the hospital at] Norfolk Sat. or Sun. Can wait 'til Sun. but am trying to argue myself out of a drunken Sat. night here. My ex-roommate is leaving for the So. Pacific, so I want to stay for that reason, but my best judgment tells me to leave.

I think my flying yesterday is certainly evidence that one never forgets how to fly. I couldn't have made a good three-point landing and might have had trouble in an emergency and was probably much "raggeder" than I realized, but the fundamentals were there and now I have a talking point if the Drs. want to ground me. "I have done it" is a much stronger argument than "I think I can do it."

Read a confidential letter that backed me up completely on the type of practice I was doing the night of my accident. I mean to show it to the friend of mine who wrote my accident report. [Ned's eyes and hands having been bandaged, he'd been unable to write his own report.] Instrument takeoffs, climbs and approaches, I contended, were essential in night fighter training, and instrument landings were extremely valuable. I can't write what the RAF report said, but I think it should back up my contentions.

Returning to SOQ [Sick Officers Quarters], Naval Hosp., NOQ [Naval Officers Quarters], Norfolk. Keep your fingers crossed, and if you ever pray, ask that whatever will be best for my future development and happiness be the outcome of the workings of the Survey Board. Maybe it's time I had to make a living by my few unexercised brains rather than the sweat of my brow at a pleasurable enterprise. Who knows?

Your lascivious ole bastard

Hotel Antlers
Indianapolis, Indiana
February 5, 1944

Ned, dear,

Sat out in Operations all day, hoping the weather would clear up. Actually the weather is all right, but the wind is too strong and gusty, and there's too much turbulence for us to fly over them mountings on the way to Pittsburgh in our Bamboo

Bombers. The wings would fall right off if we flew in really rough air—and that aint for Baby.

> [Pittsburgh, Pa., postcard
> *postmarked 2 February 1944]*

[To Mother]

Hello, darling—here I am with Uncle Geb [Stegeman] and Aunt Mid in their beautiful home. They are being just wonderful to Ruth and me, and it's good to see them again! Both are looking fine. We've spent an enjoyable evening over soup, sandwiches and coffee, catching up on family news and listening to Unk play the piano. Love U.

> Marion

Actually, only my aunt was "looking fine," but since they were mailing the postcard for me, I didn't dare say how shocked I was at the appearance of my father's younger brother. I knew he had been working long, brutal hours, doing some super-secret scientific work in laboratories of the University of Pittsburgh, where he was a chemistry professor. But I wasn't prepared for the dark, drawn look around his eyes. I didn't know until much later, after his death from a heart attack like my father's, that he had been working on the Manhattan Project, which culminated in the atom bomb.

He himself didn't know what his highly classified part in the project was at the time, and he never knew whether his small role had actually played any significant part in the bomb's development. But he grieved over the possibility until he died. He knew the bomb had hastened the war's end, that its use was necessary, and that it had saved countless American lives, but still he mourned the necessity for such a terrible instrument of death.

That night as he played the piano for me, his strong Dutch face reminded me so poignantly of my father: the same honest blue eyes and sensitive mouth, with humor always ready at the corners, the square jaw, the same powerful shoulders and big, square-tipped fingers.

These brothers had been two of five boys who'd come off the family farm in Holland, Michigan, to go off to college in home-made suits and very few dollars in their pockets, to work their way through school. My father entered the world with a master's degree, and the others had either a master's, a Ph.D., or a medical degree. Each of them took a year out of college to go home and help on the farm, then returned to work his way through to a graduate degree. They became legends along the way, with their tall good looks, athletic prowess, and high good humor. They were men's men.

The thing I remembered most about my father, however, was not his masculinity, strength or size, or the admiration and respect he engendered, but his humor and his gentleness. I felt his presence in the room now, while his brother's big hands—looking so much like my father's—moved across the dwarfed keyboard with startling sensitivity.

There weren't many gentle men being bred anymore, I thought sadly. Maybe the war had something—or everything—to do with it, but I couldn't think of many boys of my generation who combined the manliness of my father and his brothers with their gentleness. My brother John did, of course, since he emulated my father, but who else?

Well, there was one. Ned. I smiled, remembering that someone had told me that Ned was referred to in the Marine Corps "as the last gentleman."

Golly, gee, gosh almighty, the world needed more men like my father and Ned, and look what had happened: my father dead at forty-eight after a year of hell, and Ned struggling back from a nearly fatal crash. I thought of him limping on those scarred legs, with the painfully shattered ankle joint. I thought of my father's once-magnificent body wasting away on a hospital bed that last year, before a final heart attack released him. And I wondered for the millionth time why, why, why does it always seem to happen to the finest ones? My eyes stung with tears, and I turned away so Ruth and my aunt wouldn't see them while we listened to Unk play.

On 8 February, Ruth took off from Pittsburgh ahead of me. I wanted to catch up with her, so I skipped the preflight visual check that I was routinely supposed to give every plane I flew. I climbed into the twin-engine UC-78 I was ferrying, very much aware of the people who were lined up behind the airport fence, gawking.

As I taxied past them, I fluffed my hair out around my shoulders so they would be sure to notice I was a girl. It had the desired effect. People stared in amazement, pointed, craned their necks. I wasn't just self-conscious, I was puffed up with pride. I revved the engines up one at a time, checked everything; then, after the tower cleared me for takeoff, I swung out onto the runway and pushed the throttles forward. It was going to be difficult to make a hot-pilot takeoff in a Bamboo Bomber, but I was going to give it my best shot.

As the plane rolled down the runway gaining speed, I was still full of self-importance, very much aware of being watched. I felt the UC-78 wanting to lift off, so I forcibly held it on the ground and glanced at the airspeed. It indicated only forty miles per hour. I frowned. The end of the runway was looming closer, and the marker lights were rushing past so fast that I knew the reading had to be wrong.

It was too late to cut the throttles and apply brakes. I was already committed to the takeoff. Forgotten now were the curious faces that lined the airport, watching the girl pilot. Forgotten was everything except the fact that I had to take off and climb *now*. The end of the runway was at hand, and the airspeed still wavered at around forty.

So I lifted off cautiously, in a shallow climb, to be sure I didn't stall out. I called the tower and told them my predicament. They immediately granted emergency landing privileges, and I made a wary climbing circle around the field, waiting for instructions.

The tower cleared me to land on the shortest runway. I have never figured out why, since wind was negligible. Did they hate women pilots?

I could see the "meat wagon" and fire truck racing out to stand by. I circled, lined up with the runway, which looked shorter by the minute, then started down. I was afraid to trust "the seat of my pants." I could hear my heartbeat in the headphones.

By now I had guessed what was wrong. The Pitot tube (air intake tube that measures airspeed) must still be covered. The mechanic must have forgotten to remove the cover, and I had been in too big a hurry to check it.

I pointed the nose down steeper. I'd rather fly it into the ground than stall out! Well, at least I had finally learned how to make a smooth wheel landing in the UC-78, but then I had never had to make an approach without knowing my airspeed, so it might not be possible this time. I had to come in hot, too fast, and too steep to be sure I didn't stall out.

Wham! I hit the runway. Bounce, bounce, bounce. I had so much speed, I had to force the plane to stay on the ground. The runway turned out to be long enough. When finally I had slowed down enough to turn off, I knew I had to taxi directly in front of the spectators I had planned to wow. My face was in flames. I had disgraced the sisterhood. I quickly tucked my long hair underneath my collar and wiped my lipstick off on the back of my hand so maybe the bystanders couldn't tell for sure that I was the same girl who had taxied by with her nose in the air a few minutes before.

It was a long time before I tried to show off again. And I never, ever again forgot to give my plane a preflight check.

24

In February, U.S. fighting forces in the Pacific captured Kwajalein and Eniwetok atolls and cleaned out the Japanese on the Marshall Islands. In the European war zone, American forces held the Anzio beachhead in spite of fierce German counterattacks.

In Norfolk, Virginia, at the Naval Hospital, Ned was still taking therapy, and our correspondence continued.

February 11, 1944

Miss Glamazon:

You are certainly an artist with your double talk.

With all the "restless wolves" about, and your many devotees, you are certainly welcome to use me as a defense. I will consider it an honor, but if it's purely a service, that's okay, too. A gal in your shoes needs to be able to have some defense against amorous advances, and the name of some other man is far and away the most diplomatic method and the most effective "stick." Be it sincere, or a defense, is of little consequence. If I'm rendering you a service, I love it.

Your wish that I "get what I want" means a lot. Paradoxically, honey, perhaps it's better if I don't get what I want. A man would be just a plain, unadulterated fool not to want you. Of course I want you, but I'm not a big enough man, and I doubt that you are a big enough woman, to happily surmount the physical gap between us.

Now that you are running the mail to NYC, haven't you ever heard of Norfolk, Virginia? Can't some good wind blow you this way? We have notorious weather. There's rarely a ferry pilot who gets to Norfolk but that he's weathered in for a couple of days.

Went down for some Xrays yesterday. The Dr. didn't, or wouldn't, order the Xray shots that show the trouble in my ankle, so perhaps [the board] will look at them and say I can get back on duty. The exec. officer of the station (Cherry Point) called me to say that they would work a deal, to hold my promotion 'til I could get on duty, if the Drs. would clear me here, in short order.

The latest word is that, come what may, they won't retire any aviator who has had any experience, or if they do retire him, they order him back to duty; so that much is settled.

The chow hounds are gathering, so I'll join them. Bye, little "dog in the manger." I love you good.

Wichita, Kansas
February 10, 1944

Mother, dear,

Got back last night and may be here a day or so because it's a-snowing outside. I've been promised another trip—same place—in a C-45 (a beautiful plane—twin-engine Beechcraft, a dream to fly) as soon as I'm checked out in it.

Darling, if you're not a fatalist already, you may just as well become one as of now. I have been, since Tuesday night. We, Ruth and I, were to take the airliner out of LaGuardia Field in New York (TWA) at 1:00 A.M. There were 19 ferry pilots (we were the only girls) and two civilians aboard. On the take-off one engine went out at 300 feet, but the pilot was able to climb to 1300 feet on the other engine, although it coughed and sputtered all the way, and finally went out, too. We were over [a heavily populated area] and I really decided, "This is it!" There was no place to land, except maybe the bay. I really expected to get killed. I've always wondered if I'd suddenly "get religion" at a time like that (it lasted 14 minutes) but I regret to say that God or life-after-death never even occurred to me. Absolutely all I could think of was: "Poor Mother! My poor, darling Mother!" and wondered if you'd realize, even in your grief, that if I had my vocation to choose all over again (from a selfish viewpoint, I suppose) I'd do exactly the same thing—even if I knew what lay ahead. I've been just that happy! Not cheated at all, but almost feeling justified at being killed. Silly, aint it?

Anyway, honey, the point is that never could anything more dangerous happen in an airplane (outside of combat, which we won't have to worry about!) and that airline pilot got the plane back into the field without a scratch! I'll never know how he did it—we just cleared the high tension wires [wheels up], and he made the steepest turn I've ever seen—but we made it! [Gear down, just before landing, and we didn't roll twenty feet.]

When we got a new ship, the pilot let me fly part of the way to Chicago, since I couldn't sleep, and asked me to eat breakfast with him there. He says if I'll let him know next time I'm coming to New York, he'll arrange to be there and show me the town! He's only 25, been flying since he was 15, and is darn nice looking. Big and dark and powerful looking—just the type you'd like to feel indebted to for your life. He's going to let me know when they find out what caused both engines to fail. It's almost unheard of. [One aviation expert called a double-engine failure a ten-million-to-one chance. An investigation showed probable sabotage: neoprene in the gas tanks.]

By the way, would you like to know how I felt inside, when I thought the end was inevitable? Scared! Simply scared silly!! A reaction really set in when we got back on the ground. My teeth chattered and my hands shook like I had the DTs. I rushed into the cafeteria to have a cup of coffee, where I met the pilot (having several cups!) and that's where our friendship began. He said his responsibility suddenly overcame him after he had us all down safely, and he could hardly walk, his reaction was so terrific. He was very modest about his feat, and quite humble at his great responsibility. I admire him, not only for his ability but for his attitude.

P.S. I'm in love with Ned! What's more, I done told him so.

Wichita, Kansas
February 11, 1944

Ned, dearest,

Just got your letter forwarded up here, saying that you flew! I'm so glad, honey! I couldn't even finish your letter until I mopped out my happy eyes.

Whether that means you can fly for the Marines [again] or not, it means a great triumph, anyway! Oh, darling, you are so wonderful the way you can do almost anything, in the face of such terrific odds and with such admirable determination and spirit. I've never known anyone who could equal your stature.

I got checked out on a C-45 (twin-engine Beechcraft) late this afternoon, and learned, for the first time, how to use the automatic pilot and radio compass. Also, oil bypass and cowl flaps and de-icers were new gadgets. We flew back here tonight from Amarillo, Texas, and the first star came out while we were flying toward Wichita. I made my first night landing since Sweetwater and naturally I had to say, "Star light, star bright," etc., and make a wish. The wish was a half-prayer (the nearest an agnostic like me gets to praying) and of course it was for you.

It's grand that you were selected for promotion [to lieutenant colonel]. Was it because of your accident that you couldn't accept it? Won't that [RAF] confidential letter show you weren't out of line? I for one am completely convinced that the kind of practice you were doing would be valuable, not only for night fighter training, but for many other kinds of wartime aviation. It certainly seems sound enough—the idea of instrument training at night—because surely that's what a large percentage of pilots in this war will have to rely on some day.

In one of his letters, Ned cautioned me to familiarize myself with the cockpit of any new plane I was ordered to ferry, so thoroughly that I could sit blindfolded in the plane and touch and name every instrument. "It may save your life some day," he said.

I hurried over that portion of the letter, my eyes racing ahead to the part that told me what progress he was making. He was steadily improving. Glory!

Later, the second week in February, I remembered Ned's advice when I was ordered to ferry a twin-engine Beechcraft, a C-45, to Fort Dix, New Jersey, for overseas shipment. I would be all by my lonesome.

Gulp. I'd been checked out in the plane, along with some other ferry pilots who were being checked out at the same time, and I'd made several landings in it, including the one at night, but I had never been up in the C-45 alone. I was very nervous because the weather was miserable everywhere, and I was going to have to navigate over a route I had never flown before—the northern route to New Jersey, the only one open.

Remembering Ned's advice, I sat in the C-45 with the tech-order manual propped open in my lap. The weather had been below minimums that morning, but I had plotted my course and packed my B-4 so I'd be ready if it cleared.

I tried closing my eyes and touching the instruments as I said the cockpit procedure, but I had to peek almost immediately. I'll never be able to do it, I thought; there are too many of them. For nearly two hours, I sat huddled in the cold airplane. I studied the location of each new gadget and read about it in the tech manual.

I memorized the takeoff and landing speed, the stalling speed, the throttle setting for cruising, and I tried to repeat the cockpit procedure but couldn't without cheating. I looked at my watch and saw that it was past time to check the new weather reports. To my alarm, the weather had lifted above minimums. I wrote out the clearance with shaky fingers, thinking, Ned, I tried to do what you told me to, but there just wasn't time.

I climbed back into the plane and took off. The sky was gray and threatening all the way to Kansas City. I had to use heat to melt the carburetor ice that formed, a situation that always unnerved me. On final approach, as I let down right over the city, I wondered at the strange location of the airport—at the edge of downtown. The approach had to be steep, while I was frantically trying to recall each item on the checklist. What had I forgotten? My eyes swept across the instrument panel. Cowl flaps. I'd forgotten them. I corrected my oversight and hoped there was nothing else new that I'd forgotten, because now it was too late to do anything about it. I was about to make my first solo landing in a C-45, at an airport I'd never seen before.

I didn't know—and the tower didn't tell me—that the runways were coated with a thin film of ice. Almost as soon as the plane touched the runway, I felt it sliding sideways. I manipulated the throttles but couldn't control the skidding. I didn't dare use brakes. When the plane finally came to a stop, I had slipped sideways nearly fifty feet off the runway. I was breathing heavily and perspiring in spite of the subfreezing outside temperature. But I was down. Safe. No harm done—just a few more gray hairs.

There was a pilot's report of icing conditions at five thousand feet, which was above the overcast, where I couldn't fly anyway on VFR (visual flight rules). So I filed my flight plan to take off again after refueling. Then, while I was waiting for the tower's permission to take off, an airliner came in covered with ice. I went back to the ramp and canceled my flight plan, although the weatherman was still reporting clear weather on my route. But a little while after I left my plane, it started snowing and sleeting, so I was glad I had heeded my better judgment.

25

[To Marion]

Honey, I don't know where to begin, now that I've tried to let the cold wind blow my mind clear.

I wrote you a letter from Cherry Point, telling you to string me along and break my heart and I'd love it.

Your picture haunted me, as I told you, so I sent it back. I was falling in love with a "mask," I feared.

Paradoxically, that which you cannot have, you want, so long ago, I decided in order not to run the emotional gamut of ecstasy and despondency, that life would hold fewer disappointments if I'd school myself not to want what I figured I couldn't have. That kills a lot of joy—the joy of expectancy, but it saves a lot of disappointments. What I'm getting around to is that I decided I couldn't have you and reasoned that you weren't meant for me, to make it easier. I still can't have you and I know that, so your letters really leave me confused.

Darlin', life holds too much for you. You are the darling of so many and the secret sorrow of so many more.

A man in uniform who has been banged up provokes the love and sympathy of most fine people in a way that some poor sucker in civilian clothes never does.

There is the matter of Approach #7. Approach number 7 is the most insidious of approaches, a big brother act that worms into the confidence of the victim. This, combined with Approach we'll call #5, which is a dastardly approach and usually used by women, is a matter of getting a little wedge into the heart of the victim, then playing "hard to get" until opportunity permits the driving of the wedge a little deeper.

The ground work is laid. The military semi-cripple used #7 for a long time. You have been proposed to at every turn. Most men fall in love with you and that puts you on the defensive, because you are a lovely person, with a kind heart, who has too much conscience to hurt anyone.

To go way back, I told you I had prepared myself against letting you break my heart, a hell of a long time ago. All right, Approach #7 had been in operation for some time. I tried to avoid confessing any love for you because I had already decided you were out of my reach. So Approach #5 was underway without any conscious effort! I wanted an excuse to write you and scolded you (perhaps a bit unreasonably). This was a departure from the way other men had acted, so Approach #5 was hitting on all cylinders.

Approach #8 is not listed because that's the Real McCoy.

Now think hard, darling, review all the background and see if you aren't probably the victim of the unpremeditated use of Approach #7 combined with #5. Are you sure you love me or have a little sympathy, combination of approaches, a very flattering little picture, and a vivid imagination, along with boring layovers in strange cities. . . . Fine, beautiful, wonderful ladies don't fall in love with me. Baby, I'll probably never be in a financial position to give you the things you deserve.

People who have been as fortunate as you and I, owe a

tremendous debt to society—we have, as you say, been particularly fortunate in our choice of parents. Who, in God's name,
could a man ask for, eugenically or otherwise, who would be better for a life partner than you?

You don't trust your own emotions. I don't trust mine. You're
afraid of love and I'm afraid of marriage.

If after all this, you still think you love me, can tolerate a little
man, the thought of being poor and a few other unattractive
thoughts, please keep on thinking you love me—see if it's real
with the test of time. Leave my picture some place for a while.
Who knows, perhaps I'll develop into the kind of man to be
deserving of you??

If I want to hold on to you, and I do (without any strings, I
mean), I can't afford to tell you what you mean to me or I would
lose you (what little I have). Remember Approach #5? (Lordy,
but this reads like hell!) Honey, you're too far away! I'm trying to
help that "Is it love or aint it; will it last or won't it; and what
about my flying," thinking that's running through your mind.
Uncertainty and no attachments bother hell out of women—
hang on to me, I love it, and you, damn it, damn it to hell, there
goes Approach #5.

While Ned and I wrote back and forth, Grannie entered the fray,
writing to Ned and trying to explain me to him, while champi-
oning her namesake's cause. I was touched to learn she had written him, when she herself was so frail. Meanwhile, Ned wrote
again on 14 February:

I have the most wonderful news. I'm just bursting to tell it, to
shout it from the housetops, but I'm so afraid it may be a mistake . . . but I can't keep it to myself any longer.

I saw my Dr. and asked him what were the possibilities of my
case coming up at Tuesday's meeting. He said, "I want to talk to
you about that," and drew me a picture and retold me my trouble

[about my ankle] for the Nth time. Then he said there probably should be an operation, "but you don't seem to have much pain from the joint, and in your high shoes your joint is pretty well aligned, and anyway, it's a year old, so I am gonna order you back to your station."

"For limited duty, sir?"

"Hell, no, that requires too much paperwork. I'm gonna recommend discharge [from the hospital] and FULL DUTY!" Aint that marvelous news. Full duty! I can consider myself a man again!

Ned's news had not caught up with me yet, so he'd had no reply from me when he wrote again on 17 February:

Hello, darling,

You mentioned a little prayer for me, an agnostic's prayer. I'd rather have just a thought of yours for me than the prayers of the Pope. You said you didn't feel you were too clever "on instruments." You don't understand how they work, and I don't either. You don't know what is back of the force that makes the compass needle point to mag. north but you know that it does, and you are willing to have faith in your compass. (If you ever fly over water, you'll become particularly conscious of the faith you have in a compass—you aint got nothing else.) Your prayer says you recognize some force that is beyond man's comprehension.

When I used to go to the operating room, I'd say a prayer, asking God to guide and direct the hands of the doctors and to give me strength to put up with whatever discomfort was attached. It didn't make it hurt any less, but it sorta contributed to a feeling of confidence, that if the Power that governs the universe saw fit, I'd come out okay.

I don't think you are any more agnostic than I am. In fact, I think you are a religious person and just don't recognize the symptoms.

There's no space left to do more than say goodnight, darling, and wish I could have a goodnight kiss from the most kissable gal in the world, but I wasn't gonna think about that any more.

[18 February 1944]

Ned, my darling,

Four letters from you waiting for me today when I got back to Dallas! After two sleepless nights on the airliner (layover in Chicago) your letters got me so thrilled and happy that I could no more go to sleep today when I lay down than I could go to bed now without writing you first.

Grannie wrote me, too, and speaking of you and us, she said: "To love him is right, whether you ultimately marry him or not. Love, in whatever degree or kind, passing through you blesses you and the one to whom it is directed. You don't need to be cautious, or stint yourself, or warn that there are others, and that you may prove changeable. . . . When love visits you, don't ask how long it is going to stay. Treat it hospitably. Only you'll have to accept the consequences and responsibilities, and the use of your good brain is to put them clearly before you.

"I think you've held back too hard, dear, in your effort not to encourage him too much. You don't have to proclaim your changeability and act so as to scare him to death; your hesitancy has been almost entirely because of your unwillingness to mislead or hurt him." (She doesn't know I finally weakened and told you how much I love you.) To go on quoting from her letter (how did she find out so much??): "You have no more right to misinterpret yourself to your own disadvantage than to your credit. You have shown your true nobility without boasting in your letter about your narrow escape. It's much more religious to think of your mother and her grief when death seems at hand than to pray for God's protection for yourself. Love is true religion itself. It wrongs a fine boy like Ned not to let him have reason to believe that the girl he loves is worth loving."

I can't imagine how she knows so much about us. I haven't even told Mother that much.

Now that she (Grannie) has made me feel justified in letting you see how much I care, I'll "bless" you, to whom my "love is directed" by saying again, I love you! I love you! Oh . . . I'd be so happy if I could just kiss you goodnight tonight!

[Naval Hospital, Norfolk]
February 19, 1944

[To Marion]

Darling,

All I do is write you letters, think about you and know you aint for me, call you darling, mush over you in daydreams and in general, conduct myself like a lovesick pup.

I'm using anything as an excuse for a letter. My doctor was wrong the other day—'member I said he told me he was gonna rush me through and send me back to duty and I was delighted but skeptical. Well, this morning he said he was wrong, and I'd have to appear before the board Tuesday. At least that much is settled. If they will all agree, it shouldn't take very long to get the papers out—about a week. Anyway, once the papers leave here, I can probably get away, so let me know where you're gonna be "weathered in" after about the 24th. I'll have to kill a minimum of about three weeks before I can get my orders back from Hqs. Washington (possibly can get some leave).

The longer the doctor stays around here, the more contaminated his thinking becomes—the more red-tape-conscious. Hope I can get my case settled before he quits bucking red tape, and while he'll still argue to get me back on duty. If it doesn't come soon, I'm afraid the thought of operating on my ankle will have more and more appeal.

I think you were very damn smart on the weather deal. In

general, never trust weather forecasts very far, especially service weather. CAA a little farther, and airline, farthest, but even they make godawful mistakes.

February 19, 1944

[From Ned to Marion]
Guess I'm in for another restless night. If I could only keep track of you, I could phone you, but hell, I never know where you are, but where you were. I doubt that you very often know where you will be long enough to get the information to me. It would sho be a lot simpler if you were an old-fashioned, home-loving, damsel—instead of a modern, wayfaring, "Old Fashioned" [cocktail]-loving pilot.

February 19, 1944

Mother, dear,
Just a note to tell you about Ned and me. I'm really very much in love with him! So far, the test of "time away from him and with other men" has worked in his favor. We've been writing each other regularly and I can't, for the life of me, make any other man stand up to him in comparison. Bob, Allen, Bill—all of them still attract me, but not to the degree Ned does. And as for the steady flow of passing fancies—well, we won't even consider them! Ned remains strong in my heart so far. Will it stay that way, Mother?

February 20, 1944

[To Ned]
I'm afraid I'll be on the West Coast, come the 24th, but if I should be anywhere near you and you can get a leave, you know I'll let you know.
Sat up all night on the train and I'm so tired I'm sick, so I gotta catch some shut-eye now (it's past midnight).

26

[Naval Hospital, Norfolk]
February 21, 1944

[To Marion]

Darling,

I have just received your letter about the near accident while on TWA. You were certainly a fortunate group. To lose one engine and then the second is an extremely rare occurrence indeed. I don't know, but I imagine had the pilot not had a lot of time and been very familiar with everything, you might well have been on your last ride. Honey, you have no idea how delighted I am that you thought, "Poor Mother," instead of "God save me." You're the most wonderful gal in the world.

I got hell from a lot of people because I used to chop one throttle on training hops just after takeoff (the ship would be lightly loaded for a safety factor) to make the fellow remember to get some speed instead of climbing away with just a few knots above stalling, as so many are wont to do. Then, too, to teach them that they had to have their procedure down cold, so they wouldn't waste any time when time could mean so much. (We'd practice the routine hand motions on the ground and go through many procedures aloft before doing anything just after takeoff.) To my knowledge none of the fellows actually lost an engine, but

I think the practice would have served them well had they done so. The CAA and airlines are very strict about it—for that I think you can be happy, in light of your recent experience.

February 23, 1944

[From Grannie, who was dying]

Darling Marion:

Your letter about Ned made me weep for joy, not only because I so thoroughly approve your choice, and rejoice for you and for Ned, but because you said my letter helped you to trust your own outgoing affection.

Hotel Adams
Phoenix, Arizona
February 23, 1944

Mother, dear,

How's my darlin'? I found a pretty white blouse for you today here in Phoenix and sent you same. Also, did you get the Evening-in-Paris soap I sent you from Wichita? [I was finally out of debt, never to get in it again.]

Your chicken really worked yesterday. Flew all the way from Dallas to Phoenix, and if you think that's not a long way in a UC-78, then take a gander at a map. Ruth and I are on orders together again [each flying her own plane], and we really flew over some rugged country. Those mountains between El Paso and Tucson are really somepin. We had to go to 11,000 feet to get over them safely, and even then, it was turbulent. Actually, it isn't necessary to go quite so high, but it's safer that way, because often there are terrific down-drafts on the lee side of high mountains.

Last night we were both completely exhausted, but two Army fliers insisted on taking us out to a sumptuous steak dinner, even on the condition that we were to leave immediately thereafter for our beds (Ruth and I alone, I mean!). So we got to said beds by eight o'clock and really rested up. Flying all day is hard work.

February 24, 1944

[From Ned to Marion]

My darling,

Your grandmother is a sagacious old lady. She wrote me a letter about you. I don't think you are perfect 'cause I know you couldn't be. You do some things I don't wholly approve of. We don't see eye to eye on a number of things, I'm sure—probably more things than I realize—but that doesn't mean you aren't all the things I love 'cause damn it, you are.

Maybe it's just as well I can't be with you all the time 'cause I'd probably get cancer of the lip from kissing you all day—if such a thing were possible. You are sho-for-God doing a good job, intentionally or otherwise, of driving this l.o.b. wild.

[Hotel Adams
Phoenix, Arizona]
February 25, 1944

Ned, dear,

Can't wait to hear about the Board's decision!

Last night I went out with a very nice Air Corps major (a 6'4" giant! Nice looking, too) and about halfway through the evening, he said, "All right, who is it?" Playing innocent, I asked him what he was talking about, and he said, "The man in your life. It's fairly obvious, you know." So I told him a little bit about you, and he wanted to know if I planned on marrying you.

I explained that we were giving each other free rein and not deciding anything along those lines yet. He thought that idea sounded smart, though dangerous, and we began talking about marriage as a generality. He wanted to know what kind of qualities I had been looking for that I apparently had found in you.

That was sort of a hard question, but finally I came forth with six or seven qualities that I consider necessary for a happy marriage. Said major immediately wanted to know if there was a man alive who had all those qualities, and suddenly I realized that by listing them, I was describing you! So I had a good answer for him, and he said I'd better grab you while I could get you! The list, incidentally, was composed of the following: capacity for love; liveable-with personality (including disposition and sense of humor); strength of character; range of interests; breeding; mental and spiritual broad-mindedness and awakeness; and physical attraction. Quite a list, what? And, darling, you make 100 on the whole works. So you must be the man for me!

WESTERN UNION TELEGRAM

WUC1227 10 NORFOLK VIR FEB 22 445P

MISS MARION STEGEMAN WASP
5TH FERRYING GROUP LOVEFIELD

BOARD RECOMMENDED FULL DUTY EXPECT ORDERS WITHIN A MONTH LOVE

NED

27

Hotel Lassen
Wichita, Kansas
February 29, 1944

Ned, my darling,

To think that a ten-word telegram could mean so much! Oh, Ned, I'm so happy for you! I was passing through Dallas last night and had enough time between airliners to rush over and get my mail. The telegram was there in the box, and of course I knew whom it was from and what it would be about. But I was afraid to open it, afraid to hope, afraid to think. But finally, when I read the message, I went into near hysteria. Darling, it just killed me that I wasn't there to get your message the day it was sent, so I could share the triumph with my honey. I wired you last night just as soon as I heard. Hope you got the message.

Do you think your orders will say "Report back to Cherry Point?" Will you be in a position to accept your well-deserved promotion now? Are you as happy as I am?

Had a beautiful trip to California. On the stretch between Blythe and San Bernardino I flew between sugar-coated mountains backed up against the deepest blue sky I've ever seen. There were clouds as white and delicious as whipped cream, some of them hiding in crevices of the huge mountains. Down below, in the valley, orchards and towns were laid out neatly in all shades of green and brown. I really love California! Shall we live there some day?

Honey, this is leap year!! This is The Day. If only there were no war still going on and I had no job to finish, I'd sure as hell ask you to marry me! D'ya think I'll be forced to wait until next leap year? That's too long.

Well, my love, sorry I missed a few days, but we've been up three nights in a row, riding the airliner back from California and having lay-overs consistently en route because of the weather. We got here at 4:30 this morning and I got to sleep in a real bed at last. But I thought about you before I closed my eyes, and even woke up a couple of times this morning, long enough to repeat to myself, "Board recommended full duty," and smile, and then go back to sleep.

Patterson Field
March 3, 1944

Ned, honey,

Seems like muh little scheme for getting to see you wouldn't work out for hell this time. [I was trying to route a trip through Richmond, so I could sneak over to Norfolk and see him.] First of all, you are out of town and I don't know where you are, and they wouldn't tell me at Cherry Point. Besides that, the weather this way looked better, and the control officer practically insisted that I come the northern route this time.

Honey, how long is this damn war going to last? Do you realize that I have been in this thing for a year now? It seems like all my life! Of course I enjoy much of it and am gratified to be able to *do* something, but I'd hate to think of having to live this kind of a life for, say, years to come. And I imagine there are several thousand boys who would like to come home, don't you?

A few days later I wrote to my mother about a trip to New York City, during which I visited my grandmother's eighty-six-year-old first cousin Mary and her son, Ned Sheldon. (Another Ned!) He'd once held the community called Broadway in the palm of his hand. Wealthy, blue-blooded, handsome, and talented, he had been an overnight success as a playwright. Now he lay in his penthouse immobile and blind, crippled by an especially virulent and brutal form of arthritis. Even so, he was still a powerful force in theatrical circles.

March 6, 1944

Dearest Mother:

D'ya want details of muh New York trip?

We made record time, because of a beautiful tail wind. Our ground speed was 200 miles an hour, so we (Ruth and I) delivered our planes the day after we picked them up here. The minute we got to Fort Dix, they rushed us out of there on "SNAFU" (Army airlines) to Roosevelt Field in New York City, where we picked up some more pilots, and from there to LaGuardia, where we were to take the 10 P.M. TWA out of NYC for Wichita again. But luck was with us, and TWA had to cancel the flight because of a low pressure area extending all the way from Montana to Delaware. Well, we couldn't get out all the next day because of the weather, so we actually spent a day and two nights in the Big City.

We called our friend, Gil (the one who saved our lives that night when both engines quit on the takeoff) and he took both Ruth and me out that night. He was perfectly swell to us, and certainly knows how to handle two women at once. [The next] afternoon I called Cousin Mary [Grannie's cousin] and she told me to come right over.

We had tea in her living room, and you never heard such incessant chattering in all your life as went on between us females.

At 6:00 I went up to see Cousin Ned. When I first walked into his room, I felt very awkward and inadequate to meet the situation, because it is hard (I thought then) to know what to say to a distant cousin whom you've never seen and who is lying motionless in bed with a bandage over his eyes. But I didn't know Cousin Ned! In five minutes I was perfectly at ease and talking away as though I had known him all my life. I even found myself telling him [all] about my Ned, and 45 minutes went by without my knowing it. His humor and spirit simply captivated me, and I probably surprised him by kissing him good-bye. He is really remarkable, isn't he?

[The next night] Ruth and I had another date with Gil and he proceeded to entertain us until the wee hours. The next morning (yesterday) our airliner finally left, and we rode it all day back here.

Don't know whether I've described Gil to you or not. He's about six feet, very dark and nice looking. He's coming to Wichita this week, but I'll probably be out on a trip. Anyway, he says he wants to spend his vacation (coming up soon) with me in Dallas, if I'll be there. But I more than likely won't be there, and besides, I'm really not interested. Ned really has me!

[Love Field, Texas]
March 6, 1944

Ned, darling,

I just got THAT letter from you saying "good-bye until we meet again." This DAMN letter writing business is going to tear us apart yet. We just can't let it, Ned!! What did I say in the letter you were answering that was different from what I've always said and thought you understood? "After the war"? Was that it?

Darling, how could we possibly marry before then—when I'm bound by obligations more [binding] than the enforced ones of the Army, to see this insignificant job of mine through. It is insignificant, I know, since I'm only one person; and the war wouldn't be over a day later if I resigned. But how could I quit? You, above all people, should understand the moral obligations of something like this. Not only the tens of thousands of dollars of training, but the future of hundreds of girls are to be considered. If a noticeable number of WASPs resign, then the whole training program will close with a bang. And when I think what that could mean to some girls who have spent every cent they own to get 35 hours of flying time to become eligible—well, I just couldn't!

It's not a contest between you and the man in the sky. Honey, you'd win, hands down. This job is just temporary (and the sooner it's over, the better it'll suit me) and the job with you would be permanent. I love you so much that I can't ask you to wait if you'll be unhappy waiting—because I know at last what it is to love someone so much that his happiness is more important than my own. So don't consider yourself as "waiting" if you don't want to, honey, but just remember: I'll be around when the war is over. Look me up, 'cause I have a strange feeling I'll still be your girl.

Ned, my darling, you have the power to make me so happy or so miserable. Right now I could die. It's bad enough to miss you so that I'm lonely even when I'm with a crowd or on a date, but to know that I can't write to you or hear from you will just about finish me.

But you're the boss. You're the man I love, and I'll do what you say.

LATER:

Damn if I will! I won't do what you say! I'm going to keep on writing to you, and you're going to keep on writing to me—until we can see each other and get all this mess straightened out. I'm sure this means as much to you as it does to me. Ned, I love you with all my heart and I'm not going to let letters or miles or airplanes or anything come between us. I would if I thought you'd be happier without me, but I don't. I can't imagine how I was ever weak-minded enough to say I'd sit back and suffer in silence if you really didn't think we should write each other. I will write to you! I will! I will! You can't make me stop! And I'm going to get a trip your way and RON there if it kills me. Then we can talk to each other and really get things straight.

I have a sign on me, too, apparently, saying "TOOK!" Of course wolves don't exactly stop at that, but they at least keep their distance after they've made sure they read the sign right.

[4 March 1944]

[To Marion]

Honey,

Yes, "after the war" is what I meant!! I had no idea the Army had any strings tied on you any more than they have on the WACs, etc. I don't remember your ever explaining your set-up to me. I do know one gal in training resigned to marry a guy, but I thought that was required only while in training.

March 7, 1944

[To Marion]

Morning, darling,

I'm not doing so well by not writing you.

It is certainly wonderful to be able to say I love you. I only said it to one other person, and it seemed so hard to say; sorta stilted, but it comes too easy as far as you are concerned.

I'm awfully selfish about you. I'm always dreaming up a good wreck or some ailment that will stop you from flying—in other words, to get rid of my biggest competition.

March 9, 1944

Marion, baby,

'Member a long time ago I wrote you that I wouldn't embarrass you by proposing to you ('cause you led me to believe that you were not interested in matrimony)? You have never intimated to me that your lack of interest was due to anything other than something within you.

I don't think your job is insignificant! It's a damned sight more significant than mine!

I think I could easily understand any feeling of moral obligation you may have. God knows, if you had no such sense, you couldn't be what you are.

As things stand right now, we have life's normal roles reversed. Rather an unusual situation, what? *C'est la guerre!*

Now, marriage is out of the question, you say. I have felt that it was, all along, purely and simply because, as I said in my last letter, aviation has set you free.

Time is my greatest enemy. You will see so many men that you'll begin to wonder, perhaps. I'd like to catch you while I seem to have you well fooled.

March 7, 1944

Mother, dear:

Got a nice, long letter and some cards from you today. I'm here in Dallas for several hours between airliners, and at last got to get some clean clothes and my mail.

Got a perfectly lovely letter from Bob, in answer to mine telling him about Ned. He wants to keep on seeing me even so, but says if my Ned is "sure enough," then he'll back out gracefully when the time comes. I'd like to see him again, just to prove a few things to myself. But there's not much doubt.

Delivered another twin-engine Beechcraft to San Marcos, Texas, today. I'm still in love with it (but I'm more in love with Ned)!

Too tired to write more. Just wanted to say I love you *deely.*

One day later that month, I went to the North American plant at Grand Prairie, Texas, to pick up a new AT-6. I did all the paperwork and climbed into the cockpit confidently, expecting nothing but pure pleasure out of everybody's favorite airplane, the AT-6 Texan. I had tentatively "bought" it for the government, but the first fifteen minutes or so of flying would be the final check flight, if it could be called that. If anything was amiss during that time, I'd return the plane to the factory.

I climbed into the beautiful, brand-new silver Six and went through the cockpit check while two mechanics stood by, waiting with fire extinguishers. I started the plane, and the engine burst into flames. I didn't have time to be afraid.

We had been taught that if a plane caught on fire when we started it to quickly shove the throttle all the way forward to blast out the flames. So with an automatic reaction, I jammed the throttle forward while holding the stick all the way back and pushing with all my might on the toe brakes. Chocks were still under the wheels also.

I expected the prescribed move to blow out the fire as promised, but it didn't work—even with the mechanics' quick response with their extinguishers. The flames leapt higher, reaching all the way back to the open canopy of the cockpit where I sat. They were darting across the wings, to where the gas tanks were. Now I was scared.

One of the men jumped up on the wing beside me, screaming for me to get out. But I was already on my way, having throttled back at the last minute. I jumped down and raced away from the plane.

The brave mechanic jumped into the cockpit with flames leaping all around the canopy, and worked the throttle back and forth while the second man continued to spray the source of flames in the engine. Between them, they got the fire out. How they did it, I will never know. I watched them from a cowardly distance. Miraculously, no one was burned.

I was awed by the courage of those men and suddenly realized that there must be unsung heroes like them everywhere, who instinctively committed brave acts, risking their lives in the process. I wanted to present them with the Carnegie hero's medal.

That was one AT-6 I didn't buy for the government. But I almost bought the farm.

28

Ned and I finally got to see each other. I routed a trip through Richmond and made an illegal stop at Richmond Army Air Base, which was supposed to be closed to ferry traffic. I RON'd—sent a telegram back to my home base at Love Field, telling them my airplane was remaining overnight in Richmond. Then, as fast as I could, I hopped a ferry to Norfolk to see Ned.

Terrible weather was predicted for the area, so I thought surely I'd be weathered in and it would be safe to spend the night at his cousins' house in Norfolk. The cousins had thoughtfully gone to bed early and left a note for us by the time Ned and I made it to their house after dinner at a restaurant. So we sat in their dimly lit living room and talked and smooched half the night away, during which time Ned pinned a pair of Navy wings on me. "They're just a twenty-five-cent replica," he apologized. But if they'd been solid gold, they couldn't have been more beautiful. Finally he kissed me goodnight and headed back to the Navy base.

I was awakened the next morning by polite knocking at my door. It was Ned's cousin, saying Ned was on his way over to pick me up. Brilliant sunshine streamed through my windows and I could hear birds singing. Where was that bad weather that had been predicted? I was in Norfolk and my airplane was in Richmond! The weatherman had been wrong in his forecast. Ned had seen this unfortunate development and was coming to get me so I could make it back to Richmond pronto.

In a panic, I threw my things into my B-4 bag. Ned was there by the time I'd brushed my teeth. There was no time for even a cup of coffee, just a hasty introduction to the bewildered cousins, who were eating breakfast. I apologized, thanked them profusely, and whisk!—Ned rushed me out the door to his waiting car, which sped me to the bus that would board the ferry for Richmond and, hopefully, save my hide.

March 13, 1944

Ned, my darling,

So THIS is what it feels like! Honey, if there was ever any doubt in either of our minds about whether I really love you, let me tell you something: that was you last night, wasn't it? I really was in Norfolk, beaming across my roast beef like a goon at dinner, wasn't I? That was really you, not a dream I was talking to and kissing, wasn't it? Honey, I loves ya!! Won't it be just too bad if they kick me out of the Ferry Command and I have to marry you! Speaking of that, though, I was saved by the bell today. It's too turbulent for a C-78, according to the weather man and also pilot reports. I've never been so relieved in my life, because even though I could've delivered [my plane] on the same day (today) as though I'd been really conscientious, I've never felt so guilty over the matter of hours I lost. Don't know why I have such a terrific conscience on that score; maybe I'm just afraid I'll get caught.

Darling, I'm so proud of my wings I could die! Before I put my overcoat or leather jacket on, I pin them on my uniform. And of course I wear the darling tiny lapel wings on my overcoat, in plain view at all times [until my squadron CO made me take them off]. I feel much more like a Marine now than a WASP.

Can't wait until tonight so's I can wear the sentimental 25¢ job on a dress, for all to see. I feel absolutely slap-happy, drunk, and crazy as a loon.

That smacker you gave me as I boarded the bus was about enough to finish me. I just sat there, after you had waved good-bye, and gulped back the tears.

Ned, you are the most wonderful person who ever lived. The fact that I'm taller than you and [you say] you aint purdy in a bathing suit means less than nothing to me. You are everything I've ever wanted or dreamed of, and I'm so lucky to have you, I still can't believe it.

I love you.

P.S. Be sure and let me know what the board said.

Following is the letter Ned wrote me the next morning, with some surprising news.

[12 March 1944]

Baby, I won't mail this until tomorrow, when I hope I can add a wonderful last paragraph.

The record office called me to say that Bu.M.&S. is holding my survey until I appear before an Aviation Board who will determine my physical fitness for flight duty.

That word came as an unpleasant shock. I thought I could go to Cherry Point and take my physical there. I know the flight surgeons there, and was led by one of them to believe that if the doctors there would say I'm okay, they would put me back on flight status. I don't know any of the flight surgeons at the Naval Air Station here, and that's where I have to report tomorrow morning. If it's not you, it's the doctors who keep me on the "good behavior list." I was planning a little hell-raising tonight, and now I have to stay physically fit.

You have the distinct advantage of being in a position to see the future by turning the page.

[Later:] Here's the news. Everybody has seen me now, including the captain (flight surgeon). They surveyed me to duty within the U.S. as a Class II pilot. (I can be restricted to certain types of aircraft and am not to be considered for combat duty.) The best part is that in six months I go up for reclassification, and if I improve as much in the next six months as I have in the past six, there's a chance I'll get back to Class I status. (My skin will be the determining factor, as it changes so damn slowly, cuss it.) Anyway, darling, I'm happy as a fool and I love you.

Darling, I think you may know, but let me tell you again, that last evening was the happiest I've spent in my life! Thanks for coming to see me, honey. I hope if you are disciplined, it won't make you feel too bad—hell, baby, you're a civilian. They shouldn't discipline you. Tell them you conquered a Navy pilot and did a great work on bringing about closer cooperation between the Army and the Navy!

I love you.

In my lovesick state that March, I was unaware of a growing tide of resentment against the WASPs. Thousands of letters were pouring into Washington, D.C., protesting the government's employment of women pilots when there were now civilian men available who wanted our jobs. Civilian contract flying schools were beginning to close down, now that they had trained sufficient numbers of Air Force pilots. The instructors at those schools would soon be out of jobs, with many of them eligible for the draft.

It was the norm in the 1940s for the men to be the breadwinners of the families, and the mindset of the country was that women should not take jobs away from men. However, Ned and I were oblivious to what was happening on the national scene, as evidenced by his letter dated 14 March.

[Naval Hospital, Norfolk]

My darling,

I've just finished writing four pages on a letter to you only to discover that I've written so fast that I can't read it. You see, thinking of you gets me so excited that I not only can't talk, I can't write.

I've been thinking things over since you left. I miss you something fierce, guess that's why I can think of little else.

The thinking brought me to the conclusion [that we should get married now]. Married, we would stand a good chance of getting together from time to time, and as long as I am a Class II pilot, you could take your leaves visiting me and I could take mine visiting you, thus guaranteeing us about 20 days per year. Is there any reason why I couldn't ride as a passenger if I was on leave with you, and you were sent out on a trip? That would be a better set-up than loads of war husbands and wives have. . . .

To summarize it all [after twelve pages]: (1) I love you very much; (2) I don't think I could miss you much more married, than unmarried. (Might go mad from wanting to be with you, but I don't know about that now); (3) we could see each other as much or more than a whole hell of a lot of other war couples do; (4) We would have an interest in saving for our future; (5) We'd have to steer clear of entangling alliances; (6) We'd have to trust each other to operate pretty much as we do now, except no woo pitching [with others] or—for me, anyway—lustful eye glances; (7) I'd rather have you under a restricted set-up than not at all; (8) I'm afraid we are both susceptible [to other people, in our unprotected state]; and (9) I think this has more merit than "putting it on ice" [which is what we had agreed to do until we could get married].

[Love Field, Dallas]
March 14, 1944

Ned, my darling:

Just got back to DL after riding American all night.

If you could love me, honey, after seeing me as dirty and ugly as I was [Saturday] night, then it must be the real thing! I hadn't been able to get my clean uniform from the cleaners for a month, and I hadn't seen a bathtub for days! My hair was stringy, my nails were nubs, there were great bags under the eyes, and I was generally haggard, rundown, and worn out. And you! You said I was "beautiful!" Honey, ever since you said that, I've been feeling like the most exquisite creature in existence. Venus herself! A word of praise from you is like a shot in the arm, and I feel as though I could be beautiful—of face and soul—with you believing that I am.

29

All during March there were more rumblings on Capitol Hill about women pilots taking men's jobs away from them. On 15 March I was finally made aware of the situation, when I saw an Associated Press story in the *New York Times* stating that a House investigating committee was considering whether the WASP program should be discontinued.

The Army and Navy had now given official notice of their intention to abandon the War Training Service program, the article reported, thus releasing about nine hundred pilots and more than four thousand student instructors who would be looking for jobs. Indignation directed at the WASPs was building in male civilian flying circles, because many of these men were losing their draft deferment and abhorred the possibility of being put into the "walking army." In addition, the *Times* article said, about ten thousand of the twenty-five thousand Civil Air Patrol pilots could qualify for the work being done by WASPs.

I was shocked. I had thought we were indispensable to the war effort. We certainly had been sorely needed when I'd signed up. Mentally I shrugged. I was much too busy to worry about being viewed with displeasure by a bunch of jealous pilots, so I pushed the knowledge of their wrath to the back of my mind. When I sat down to write Ned on 17 March, I had temporarily forgotten all the hullabaloo and was in a frivolous mood.

Honey,

You complained that you didn't even know what I looked like in a bathing suit. If you'll have this negative developed, you'll see.

Nachully, I'm gonna have a real picture made for you real soon.

March 17, 1944

Ned, dear,

Here's another letter from Shreveport.

I have cholera and smallpox *à la présente,* and I'm sicker than a dog. D'ya realize what a bargain I'll be when you get me? Immune from typhoid, yellow fever, tetanus, typhus, smallpox, cholera, and THE PLAGUE! Maybe that's why you're marrying me, Mmmmm? Or is it my money?

Darling, I simply can't stand this much longer. My patriotism, sense of moral obligation, conscience and everything else are all shot to hell. Don't let me do anything I'd hate myself for later, hear? I don't want to be ignoble—and I know I have a debt to pay. But how can I stand being separated from you much longer?

March 19, 1944

[To Marion]

Hello, darling,

I had dinner with the wife of the guy that I flew to CG [Chicago] when I saw you—John Smith, first Marine aviation hero of the war. They both were awfully nice to me.

I told you once before that I have always envied big men their height 'cause I'm so partial to big gals—especially you. They never seem petty, are easier to get along with, are seldom shrews, are more thoughtful and generous. They seem to have, natively, qualities that are greatly to be desired. If you were a little gal, you'd probably be very nearly what you are but there would be a difference. There's something about a few inches that perfects the good qualities with which a gal started out in life.

The more I think about it, the better the idea seems, of getting married soon. Lordy, but I hope you see it the same way I do. I am good and blind to the virtues of any other arrangement.

Barksdale AAB, La.
March 19, 1944

Dearest Ned,

As you can see from el letterheado, I'm still in ZH [Shreveport] sweating out the weather. The weather man assures me I can get out by noon, but I'll never believe another weather man! However, I sure am glad I was gullible once't [back in Richmond].

I got the sweetest letter from your mother. Have you told them anything about us, or are you waiting until it's official? Would it be too hard to explain our predicament, and why we're waiting?

All I do when I'm up there is dream about you and drift off course, and that's no good at all! I'm going to get myself in hand, because as long as I have a job to do, I'd like the satisfaction of doing it well.

Honey, when the Army takes us over, naturally they can't force us to join. You know, of course, what I'm tempted to do. But how could I live with myself afterwards if I couldn't stick this thing out and try to help a little, so long as the war lasts? On the other hand, how can I go on living without you?

Please write and give me a little pep talk so that I can somehow go on enjoying my job while I'm waiting for the war to end. I have to, honey. Tell me that, hear?

March 23, 1944

[To Marion]

My darling,

One of the nice things about having been hurt is the pleasure and excitement of reacquiring former abilities. Convalescence becomes a long series of "red letter days."

For a long time I've been trying to run. I used to do it in the pool months ago, starting in deep water and gradually working down to shallower water. Finally I got outside and tried.

Anyway, I ran in place a few minutes and have been able to do this fairly well for some time, but since I don't have enough strength to be able to hop on one foot, we decided that running was probably mechanically impossible for a while longer, as well as muscularly impossible. Well, for no good reason, the running in place seemed easier today, so when I got my pants and socks back on, I went out into the hall and ran in place for a moment, then just leaned forward and, so help me, I actually ran!

Remember, I told you I ran a tiny bit some time ago. Well, one half of my body would almost stop when I put the rt. leg, with the stiff ankle, down; but this time, both sides seemed to move together.

It was only about ten short steps, but it was a start, and maybe I'll be able to run fast enough to convince the drs. that I can make it to a foxhole when my six months are up.

I'm always thinking of more reasons why we should get married soon. I hope I don't have to give you any more reasons, but here are two, if you need 'em. One, you would be better off if you had your status established before you are taken over by the Army. Two, we'd be about the only people in the world to have more than one honeymoon. Each time we saw each other, it would be virtually another honeymoon.

Darling, I buy so many of these cheap pads of paper [with United States Navy printed on them] that the clerks give me a peculiar eye. Let me tell you that I love you, darling.

Thurs. 23rd [March]

My darling [Marion],

I'm going to be forced to go to the Chaplain for a chit to cry on his shoulder if I don't hear from you before long. I don't mean that I haven't gotten any letters, it's just that you've been away and haven't gotten mine, so you can't answer.

My gosh, over a week has passed and I haven't heard from you [about the proposal that we get married now]. I doubt that I will today either, 'cause you haven't sent me your quarters address and phone number. I don't know why I should fret about it 'cause if you love me like you say, I think the plan should suit you, too.

Friday

[To Marion]

Don't dilly dally over answering my letter of the 14th. Spring's here! Now's the time! The sooner the better!

[23 March 1944]

[To Ned]

Just finished reading the sweetest letter I've gotten from you yet. I purposely skipped a day from writing you, though, because your letter of yesterday and then this one today (about marriage now) has really got me stumped. I've been going over and over the problem, and I can't make up my mind what the right thing to do is.

My main objection is this: when I become a wife, I want to be a *wife*. My marriage is going to be first and foremost in my mind and heart and actions. I don't want any career or miles between us to separate us.

Next objection: when on earth would we ever get to be together? They'd never let you go with me on trips, if you got a leave. They won't even let WASPs ride with WASPs when on leave. And

I won't have any more leave for a long time, so I couldn't be with you wherever you are. (It'll be Cherry Point, won't it?)

Next, I still maintain that [once I was] your wife, it would be twice as hard to bear the separation from you.

The paper today says Congress has passed the bill necessary to commission us, so it looks like the Army is getting closer and closer. They can't take us in without first giving us the right to resign, though, and naturally, I'm tempted. What should I do, darling?

Once I'm in the Army, though, they can do anything to me. I'm at their mercy as to where I'll go or what I'll do. And I don't like that! And I couldn't get out—ever—for any reason, until they were good and ready.

How long do you suppose this damn war will last? What will I do when the time comes to make my decision about the Army? We either have to go in or get out.

Allen (the Col. Remember him?) flew in three days ago with some general friend of his'n so he (Allen) could spend his leave with me. Imagine! I didn't get in until yesterday, so I only saw him last night. He came out here to our club for dinner and the regular Wednesday night dance afterwards, and I proceeded to alienate him. I was not very tactful, I'm afraid.

But I've told him about being in love with you before I even told you! So it's his own fault. Now! You've alienated all my friends, too. Hope you're satisfied. We're even!

I'm on a shuttle run between the Navy field here and the Army one (Love)—ferrying SNJs over to our side. I mean the Army's side. I'm a Marine!

Honey, please tell me what to do. I'm wiring you my phone number now. It's Justin 8-0078.

I love you very much.

M.

P.S. One other item on the disadvantage side of my resigning: they might draft me! Really, I'm not kidding. But the main thing still is my conscience.

30

Jefferson Davis Hotel
Montgomery, Alabama
March 24, 1944

Ned, my dearest,

Your "baby" is suffering from a bad case of jitters. I've just had the hell scared out of me. I delivered an AT-6 to Dothan, Alabama, today and they offered me an airplane ride up here to Montgomery with one of their lieutenants so's I could catch the airliner from here back to Dallas.

Well! The lieutenant looked like he was about 19 at the most, which made me a little wary to begin with. I knew before we took off that we were going to get lost. Naturally, I couldn't insult the guy by taking my maps [out], since he was the pilot— not I—and anyway, there were no earphones in the back seat where I sat. Also, the stick had been taken out and placed in a gadget on the side of the rear cockpit, but before the trip was over, I had replaced the stick in its proper place [so that I could take over the controls, if necessary].

Lord, honey, what a "flier" he was! He didn't hold one heading for five minutes at a time, so I knew we were in for it. He zig-zagged around until the sun set, then landed at the Tuskegee airport, where we saw lots of Tuskegee Airmen. First lieutenants, too!

I had not known until that moment that there were African-American pilots being trained by the Air Corps, and I doubt that many other people knew it. But black trainees had been at Tuskegee since 1941, despite the prejudice of some of those in the military who were skeptical.

Graduates of the flying school there formed the first all-black flying units in the Air Corps, and their 99th fighter group saw its first combat action in the spring of 1943. Their 332d painted the tails of their P-51s bright red, earning the moniker Red Tails. They flew bomber-escort missions and made strafing attacks on the Germans, who called them *Schwartze Vogelmenschen* (Black Birdmen). The 332d received the Distinguished Unit citation for extraordinary heroism in action.

But until we landed at Tuskegee that day, lost, I had been totally oblivious to their existence in the Army Air Forces, just as they seemed to be unaware of the WASPs' existence, judging by the mutual curiosity we exhibited. My letter about the confused young pilot who had landed us there continued:

The dope hadn't even switched gas tanks, and the one we were using was dry by the time we touched ground. I was about to switch them myself, out of sheer desperation, but we landed before I had to humiliate the pilot.

Then we left in the dark for the municipal airport here [Montgomery], and I'll never know how we got down. He made three passes at the field before we got in. I was about to take matters into my own hands. He obviously was scared to death, which didn't help my frame of mind any. Maybe he was just snarled up because of self-consciousness, resulting from my being a pilot, too. I dunno, but I sure don't want to ride with anybody like him again. In an emergency I'm sure he would've killed us both.

Darling, you've got to help me decide another question, besides the big one we've been discussing in our last several letters. We have our choice of whether to go to pursuit school or not. Should I? We'd fly P-47s, P-51s, P-39s (if I can fit into one), and P-40s—and after the course, we'll ferry them. I'm eligible now, so I have to decide. It would be a great thrill as far as I'm concerned, but I didn't think it would be fair to rush headlong into it without first asking you how you felt.

I love you, my wonderful boy.

March 24, 1944

[From Ned]

My darling,

I had the [bathing suit] negative printed and love it. You really are a beautiful creature, aren't you! Perhaps it's just as well I couldn't remember how you looked in anything but pants and shirt—you see, there was very little of the purely lustworthy, physical beauty to influence me. You were what I fell in love with, not your figure. Guess I was getting "a pig in a poke," so to speak, but I am not disappointed with my "pig" out of the poke.

Forgawdsake, darling, let me know that you think getting married *now* is a good idea. I've gotta write your mother and tell her, too, that I love you, baby, and I want to spend the rest of my life with you. Don't you dare mess me up at this point.

WESTERN UNION TELEGRAM

WU C88 NL NORFOLK VIR MAR 27
MISS MARION STEGEMAN WASP
5TH FERRY GP

MOST THINGS ARE RATIONED IN WAR TIME IT IS
BETTER TO HAVE A LITTLE THAN NOTHING AT ALL
PLEASE RECONSIDER LOVE

NED
742A

[Undated]

[From Ned]

Darling,

It's 1400 and I should be out exercising.

Angel, I appreciate your asking me how I feel about your change in ferry work. I think you have pretty well "come of age" on this flying deal and won't have the Air Corps 2nd Lt. attitude that "Now that I'm a pursuit pilot, I'm Jesus Christ and nothing can touch me." I think you have respect for your equipment and won't feel that you are a so-called hot pilot.

In the Navy they always tell us not to aspire to be the hottest pilot, but to be the oldest.

I respect your ability and I think you're level-headed enough not to get fighter pilot swagger or bravado. Besides, you won't stick your neck out unnecessarily if you love me as much as you say you do.

Hop to it, honey, if you think you want it! I know you can do a bang-up job of it. . . .

If you are qualified for pursuit school, aren't you qualified for multi-engine school, or does that come later?

If you have a choice, I'd like to see you take multi-engine! If you haven't, you have my blessings, darling. Shoot the works and be the best pursuit pilot the Army ever had 'cause you'll look at the flying of them as a business and not for the purpose of flattering your own ego. Develop confidence in your ability to handle the equipment, but have respect for it. Don't let familiarity breed contempt.

I'd like to do that myself. I only have about ten hours in an A-20. I loved flying it but I always felt like I was riding an unpredictable horse. Was afraid if I didn't fly it all the time, like the horse, it might try to throw me.

If it becomes a nervous strain that will make you old in a hurry, please don't let pride prevent you from asking for some other duty.

Lordy, but I hate to give you back to "the man in the sky." He'll really have you in his clutches, once you qualify in pursuits.

Baby, I know you know I'm disappointed as hell that you don't see [marriage now] my way. I'll try not to rub it in. I don't want to be unreasonable, and there's no point in trying to persuade an individual. I can simply present the picture, "rebut" your angles—the decision has absolutely got to be yours. If I try to sell you on it, you may feel that I blinded you to its bad points.

I just sent you a wire saying that most things are rationed. Well, love aint, but in our case, the fulfillment is rationed.

Mine is a selfish point of view in many respects. One of the selfish things is that I believe in the double standard. As long as I'm single I don't have the compulsion of honor to make me faithful to your memory. [However] I don't feel it's fair to bind you to any greater degree than I'm bound.

Now for #2: If you want to be my wife "first and foremost" that's exactly the way I'd like it to be, but your possibility of being drafted, your sense of obligation, etc., make it impossible to do that.

We'd get together more often than a great many other married people with both husband and wife in the service. What if it was only ten days a year! I'd rather have you ten days than zero days. What do other married WASPs do?

If they are going to take you into the Army, you could probably get "time out" before signing up, to complete your personal affairs (meaning marry me). I don't like the thought of the Army absorbing you, 'cause they get just as much work out of you now, if not more, than they would later. I don't like it at all—too much pettiness, jealousy, too many bigoted little people come into the picture.

I don't want you to resign, 'cause, as I said before, I don't want you living with me when you get a case of remorse over your conscience.

As far as joining the Army is concerned, I think you should each write a letter to the head (J. Cochran) and tell her what you don't like about the service idea.

When the time comes, the only thing to do is to go into the Army. Don't worry about being drafted, 'cause you aint resigning.

Darling, don't send me rebounding in the spring (of all times).

Goodnight, darling. I'll tell you what I'd do about anything but marrying me—that you've got to do yourself.

March 27, 1944

[To Marion]

Baby,

I hate to tell ya that ya got me under your thumb. Are you gonna do something about it or send me out on the godawfullest rebound I ever heard of?!

Aint I gonna get anywhere with you? Am I writing my heart out for nothing? Don't you agree with me on the get-married deal?

You let me know you were back by your telegram, but you were gone again before I could phone you the next morning. Honey, didn't you realize that it was and is terribly important to me to know what you think about it? YAS, IT IS! IT IS! IT IS!

Angel, it's spring, and "in the spring"—or did I tell you?—a young man's fancy turns him into the l.o.b. he's been all winter! If you play "hard to get" at this point, I'm afraid I'll just have to take my little .45 and shoot you. This aint Approach #1–7. It must be #8 'cause I'm not afraid to ask your mother for her baby. Don't be a "dog in the manger"!!!

Air mail now being 8¢ will make it cost you over $29 per year to write me every day. Get the war over in a hurry and move in with me—look at the money you can save.

March 29, 1944

[To Marion]

Sorry, angel, that I didn't get to talk to you. I'm going to check the weather in hopes you didn't get away today. We aint CAVU [ceiling and visibility unlimited] here. It's hardly possible you are in the same fix, but maybe.

The weather officer says the front has passed Shreveport this A.M. and that it will be followed by cold, turbulent air. Maybe the turbulence will keep you grounded and I'll be able to get you in the early A.M.

There seem to be a number of thinking people who figure the war in Europe will end in two months. That would suit me perfectly. If the invasion doesn't start in two days, Nostradamus' interpreter will be wrong. Last war, peace negotiations were started about four months before the armistice. I wish the massed power and potential Allied strength lying around Europe would be sufficient to awe Hitler into quitting.

Bye, beautiful baby. I still loves ya.

Lamar Hotel
Meridian, Miss.
March 29, 1944

Ned, darling,

I know what true love is!! It's after eleven P.M., and you aint home yet, according to SOQ, NOB, Norfolk; and even though I know you are probably out gadding, I'm not mad. Funny, I've always been very jealous of men I liked, but I must not have ever loved one until now, because, so help me, I'm not jealous! I guess love and trust go hand-in-hand.

Probably I feel this way because I'm often out after midnight, myself, and I know how effortless it is to be true,—or maybe that's just because I'm a woman. Anyway, whether it requires effort on your part or not, you're the first man I ever trusted or loved enough for me to be above petty jealousy. You seem to always bring out the best in me.

[Barksdale AAB]
March 29, 1944

Dearest Ned,

No news. Thunderstorms and more thunderstorms.

When are you going back to Cherry Point? Be sure and let me know ahead of time so I can address your letters there.

March 30

Miss Lovely,

Angel, how are we going to [work it so that you can] be "a real wife or not one at all"? You would always blame yourself if you quit. You can't do that. You'd be unhappy living with me, with that over your head. If I were stationed where you could do a vital aviation job (like putting Grummans through the 5-hour run in time; you know, the initial acceptance flight that is put on each plane), then I'd say this: when they ask you to go into the Army, say no. Then you could do a job that was just as essential to the war effort as a civilian as you would do as an Army pilot. I don't think that would be disloyal, if you felt that you just plain didn't want the Army. The services waste talent terribly.

The more I think about that test pilot job, the more it sounds like a good deal. Say you could work with Hellcats. That's the best job of all and safest. You'd be in one place, do an essential job. It wouldn't be as dangerous as ferrying pursuits. You'd be a civilian and still fly and contribute to the war effort, and we could swing the deal. Am I taking a biased view 'cause it's a way out? Would that be disloyal? You would have the half-wife, half-career girl setup you seem to distinctly abhor. Maybe I'm short-sighted, but a "half-wife" setup with you I think would be better than the zero wife setup and/or the "freeze" till after the war.

They keep putting my light out. Gotta quit so I won't embarrass the corpsman.

Don't let me persuade you to do anything your conscience and best judgment dictate against. That would be wrong, no matter how much I want you!!

What is your chief objection to the half-wife deal?

My objection to the "half-wife deal" was clear in my own mind, but I didn't know how to explain it to Ned without losing his trust. I simply wanted to remove myself from temptation if I were married.

So far, since falling in love with Ned I had resisted the constant temptation everywhere without too much effort. But I didn't want to push my luck too far. I had a history of being highly susceptible to attractive men, and in truth, I still responded to them—only now I had no intention of doing anything about the mutual attraction. But how could I be sure my willpower would remain strong under all circumstances? I was like an alcoholic who knew better than to work in bars.

I yearned with all my being to marry Ned, and I certainly intended to be true to him. But I wanted to make it easier on myself than it would be if I stayed in the Ferry Command, in a different port every night, lonely and bored, surrounded by good-looking single men who were eager to assuage that loneliness! How could I explain all that to Ned without sounding like a "bitch wolf?"

And how could I resign and marry him if my country still needed my services as a pilot? I didn't yet believe the jealous male civilian pilots who said we were no longer needed. The only solution, unsatisfactory as it was, seemed to be to wait.

Yet Ned was pressuring me to marry him now.

31

Hotel Floridan
Tallahassee, Florida

Hi, [Ned] honey,

What's cookin' in Norfolk? I tried for the third consecutive night to call my darlin'—but no soap. Tonight they said Norfolk was closed to all calls—incoming and outgoing. Spies?

Tomorrow night, weather willing, I'll be back in DL, and I can't very well call you from there unless'n I want every WASP in the BOQ to hear what I say. But I'll call again soon, because I must talk to you.

Honey, am I rationalizing when I look at my problem this way?: the only asset I have to offer the Army is my flying ability (?)—and General Arnold [now] says we now have more pilots than we need. [This was the first time the Army had publicly stated that, to my knowledge.] Therefore, should I have a guilty conscience if I resign when l'Army takes over, knowing that there is no longer a shortage of pilots? I'm so hopelessly in love with you that I can't tell when I'm rationalizing or thinking the truth any longer. I want to marry you so bad!! The sooner the better—but it's whole hog or nothin', as I done said before.

I'm chasing a cold front and aint making much progress. A state a day is all.

There's nothing to say except I love you, I'm confused, I want to be your wife, but what'm I gonna do about the Army? I want to be a Marine!

By the end of March, when I wrote the following letter, it had become obvious that WASPs were considered a surplus commodity.

Hotel Floridan
Tallahassee, Florida

Mother, dear,

(1) General Arnold says openly that the Army Air Forces has more than enough pilots.

(2) There are experienced instructors now being forced into the foot army—and others out of jobs.

(3) If I go into the Army, they could chain me to a typewriter for "the duration plus six months," in spite of anything they might promise.

(4) I can't see myself running around saluting and kowtowing and obeying orders from [nonflying] females who will really dish out the works to those of us who have been in only a year [or so] and will be mere second lieutenants. I can do what I'm told gracefully now only because—underneath it all—I know I don't have to.

Summary: All this adds up to a great deal of rationalization that has been taking place since I last saw my love. I want to marry him—now! Since the Army is forcing me to become a puppet or resign, I'm tempted to go my own way—mine and Ned's.

It may be days, weeks, or months before it is necessary for me to decide. How's about a long letter of advice from you—and also please ask Aunt Heluiz and Grannie what they think.

[Naval Hospital, Norfolk, *undated*]

Marion, darling,

If the half-wife position is untenable to you, this "lovesick pup" business is untenable to me. I want you any way you are willing to come—under any circumstances that your conscience and the war will permit! I don't want you to get away from me. I don't want to give you an opportunity to change your mind.

Ma says I'm stubborn (that's only one thing; she also says I'm an old maid and other things). I guess she's right. You are a rather determined young lady, too. We are both going to insist on our own suggested way and lock horns, I'm sure of that. So you say "whole or nothing." I say "anything or ice." What's it gonna be, darling?

Wire me when you expect to be in Dallas or elsewhere. I've had a fistful of quarters for weeks with which to call you.

March 31

[To Marion]

Hello, darling,

It would be nice if I could keep up with your travels. When I know where you're going, a weather map allows me to gauge your travels somewhat. If my complete guess is right, you should be back in DL tonight or tomorrow, so I'll try to get rid of my quarters.

Did I tell you that I pedaled around in a high wind and had to buck it for 3$\frac{1}{2}$ miles coming home? I got myself so stiff that I thought I must have busted something. Well, I didn't, but I couldn't straighten my knee. Anyway, it worked itself out and strangely enough, it looks like the hyperextension of my knee is being corrected through the muscles becoming tighter and taking up the slack. Sometimes it amazes me, what Ma Nature will do for her children.

April 1, 1944

[To Marion]

Oh, darling! If you don't love me, you better get the hell out of Texas fast, 'cause I'm coming down there and marry you!

Just got a call from Washington that my orders will be out right away. They asked me if I wanted to go to Texas, and before I could even think, my subconscious mind replied, audibly, Yes! Hell, yes. . . . I found out where in Texas: Eagle Mt. Lake Air Station, 14 air miles N. of the Ft. Worth range station. The job [is] to be Ex. O. [executive officer] of the station. The C.O., Sidney Williamson, is a friend, a good Joe I don't see eye-to-eye with. Strictly regulation. Twice divorced. Broken-down pilot, also. He's smart as hell and I will either learn a hell of a lot or get fired. I'll really have to work harder than I ever dreamed of. I know the job is well over my head, but I couldn't have a better guy to learn from.

The bad part is that I might as well be in Africa for all I'll see of you. Sidney never quits work and I'll have to keep the same hours he does.

Baby, I'd like you to make your mind up before you have an opportunity to compare me, in person, with other people.

The most horrible thought just struck me! Here I am practically on my way to Texas, and I told you to go to pursuit school, which means you'll leave DL and won't come back after you finish training! What a blow. If I ask you not to go now, I know it'll be for purely selfish reasons. I can't do that. Why did you ever have to answer my letter! Why did I ever get involved with a female pilot!!

Love Field, Texas
April 2, 1944

Mother, dear,

The solution has arrived! Ned himself thought of it. A way to marry him, yet continue to use my Army training so that it will be of benefit so long as the war lasts, and yet not actually go into the Army. Guess what? Test piloting! They have girls doing it now for the WASPs, on old, formerly wrecked ships that have supposedly been fixed, but mine will be lots less dangerous—because I'll be dealing with brand new ships. And I'll have definite days off when I can see Ned. I'll be at one place, and I'll be on contract—and not in the Army! (Of course I'll no longer be a WASP, because they will all be in the Army when I resign).

I'm so happy! An answer at last!

Thanks for your letter, dear. All of it was sound advice and I appreciated what you had to say. That is, all of it was sound except one thing: you didn't mean it when you suggested going back to being a stenographer??!! MOTHER!! If I resign, it'll be only to marry Ned or get another flying job—or both. In any case, I'm gonna marry Ned, because it's like Grannie always told me it would be: I can't help myself!

WESTERN UNION TELEGRAM

WU C57 21 NORFOLK VIR APR 4 739A

MISS MARION STEGEMAN
WASP 5TH FERRYING GP

ARRIVING TEXAS WITHIN TEN DAYS LEAVING TODAY VIA CHERRY POINT WRITE ME ATHENS PHONED YOU THREE TIMES CANT GET YOU LOVE

NED.
732A

Hilton Hotel
El Paso, Texas
April 4, 1944

Ned, darling,

Oh, honey!!! You're coming to Texas! Ned!! Do you realize what that means?! Darling, how can I possibly wait? And I'm so proud of you for what you're slated to do. When can I tell everybody?

You told me if I definitely didn't want the half-wife deal to write it down. I can't. I could no more put you on ice than ["I could fly" was scratched out] the man in the moon.

Love Field

April 6, 1944

Ned, honey,

Of course it may be many weeks or a few months (though I doubt it) before the Army takes over and I'm in a position to resign and marry you—but anyway, it's definite, and I'm your'n! You really cooked yourself up a marriage when you suggested that test pilot setup, because at last I can see my way clear to work off my obligation and also be married to you.

[Love Field]

April 10, 1944

[Mailed to Eagle Mt. Lake]

Ned, dear,

Yesterday was the best Easter Sunday yet! It was really wonderful to see you and be with you. I sure hope we can have a repeat performance this weekend. I'll let you know as soon as I myself know.

I'm so glad you think you're going to like Eagle Mt. Lake. Although it'll undoubtedly be awfully hard work at first, methinks you will be a thoroughly capable and well-liked Ex. O.

Ned, please don't worry yet about when we'll be able to get married. I know how much you have on your hands now and how it'll require your undivided attention for many weeks, and also how Sidney feels about matrimony [disapproving]. There's no hurry, because I'll still be here, and besides, it may be longer than we'd planned before the Army absorbs the WASPs. To make the waiting easier, though, let's go out with other people and not be alone so much.

P.S. I wasn't going to say it, dammit, because you're getting so stingy with the forthcoming three words, but I love you.

> [Love Field]
> *April 13, 1944*

[To Ned]

Hello, my darling—

Just wanted to say again how perfect it was, being with you last night. Thank you for coming over. It's lucky, too, that you did, because I'll almost certainly be away Saturday night. I just got word that I'm to go to Wichita to pick up a C-45 (twin Beech), and that means either California or New York—or, possibly, Canada. I'll wire you if I am going to be here. Otherwise, I won't be in Dallas—sniff. . . .

Ned, grab onto that house [on the base] for us! I believe I could become quite domestic, with a setup like that—and just incidentally, you.

You've sold me on a gold wedding ring. I didn't know its significance until you told me.

Please, darling, don't neglect your legs. Until I'm there to take care of you, remember your promise, and keep them in good shape. Now is the most important time of all.

> [USMC Air Station
> Eagle Mt. Lake, Texas]
> *Apr. 14, 1944*

Marion, darling,

Last night driving home I had a wonderful time, just daydreaming away the miles, about you. You are certainly one of the chosen few to be endowed with so much beauty and such an understanding heart.

8 A.M. to 9 P.M. has robbed me of the ability to recall [the letter

I wrote you in my mind, but] let's do go out with your friends when I'm there, and you pursue all the big, handsome men you meet between my visits. Baby, please take advantage of every opportunity to compare your "little fellow" with all the swains. I want you to have every opportunity to know what you're doing.

Allis Hotel
Wichita, Kansas
April 17, 1944

Ned, dear,

It still seems like a dream, having had you and Shirley [at Love Field] at the same time. I'm so glad you like her, and it's wonderful that she is so enthusiastic about you. This morning when I told her good-bye, she said that when she saw Sandy (which will be when she gets back to Harlingen [where they were towing targets in B-26s]), she'd tell her that she not only approved, but thought that it was the most perfect match she had ever seen. Will you really like her for an attendant? Sandy, too? Good!

I was in Fort Worth this morning [delivering an AT-7, a twin-engine Beech, to Tarrant Field], a little after nine, but I didn't call you because I'm gonna try not to interrupt your work.

A lieutenant flew me back to catch the first airliner to Wichita, and I'm going to be terribly conscientious for a while, to make up for my lack of conscience since you've been [in Texas]. Speaking of above-mentioned lieutenant, I wish you could have seen the landing he made in an AT-11. It was so bad, we had to go around.

I flew over Eagle Mountain Lake Marine Corps Air Station this morning. If I hadn't been so naughty lately, I'd have buzzed the very hell out of the place! I got a good look, though, and thought I spotted our house.

Got my first wedding present today. Mac [my friend who later married Ned's brother] sent me a beautiful chiffon gown—but it's so sheer that I'll have to be married to you awhile before I have the brass to wear it.

32

While I was opening my first wedding present, the WASPs were rapidly becoming an endangered species. The 19 April 1944 issue of *Time* magazine had a half-page article with the caption, "Saved from Official Fate." It stated that General Arnold had saved the official lives of the WASPs, who had been "wondering whether they were going to become unwanted women." The article went on to claim that Hap Arnold had once privately said that he did not want women in the AAF but was now backing a bill to put them in the military "with the same kind of status as the WACs, WAVES, SPARS, and Women Marines."

Ned saw it and saved it for me, but his thoughts were more nervously centered on our upcoming marriage. He seemed to be getting cold feet as he wrote the following letter:

[Postmarked 21 April 1944]

[To Marion]

Baby, please don't think I've gone nuts, writing on this [at the bottom of some old orders]. It's just that I'm home and still haven't unpacked—have no paper on which to write.

It's now about 11:00, and I'm in bed, having quit the office at 10:00. Tried to phone you, and talked to Helen [Anne] Turner.

Got a leg soak at the dispensary. Have been treating my leg like I promised approx. every day. It's gonna mean rising 40 minutes early or going at night for a leg soaking, however.

Got a letter from you telling me you'd marry up with me. Why does it seem to scare me when I'm faced with it? I'm not much scared when I think about it and wasn't scared when it first got started. When I think about it, I'm always amazed you'd consider me. When I think about you, I want to be with you all the time, but the thought of marriage really is a sort of scary thing, isn't it?

Got a letter off to a Red Cross gal in Norfolk, telling her I have a, shall we say, "matrimonial alliance" or "understanding" with you. Will have to write the others, one or two at a time, as time permits.

His letter hit me like a jab in the stomach. I had thought he'd be turning cartwheels at my acceptance of his persistent proposals, and now it sounded as if he was suffering from buyer's remorse. When I sat down to reply, I tried not to let the shock and hurt show.

Wichita, Kansas
April 19, 1944

Darling [Ned],

Got your two-in-one letter early this morning (about 4 A.M. to be exact) while I was killing a few hours in DL between airliners. Glad you found time to write, but don't forget—I'll understand when you don't, so please don't take time out when you shouldn't.

I'm quite content to wait for the marriage part. The only thing that worries me is when you say you're scared. Honey, I'm the only one who is supposed to be scared! (And I yam.) Men aren't supposed to realize what they're getting into—until it's too late. Who told you!?

You said, "Don't make me commit myself on your P.S. on the 13th about getting married before the Army takes over. To be married and together for one day and night and then go our separate ways wouldn't be too good, do you think?" (End quote.) My, how the tables have turned! Who was saying that, vehemently, over and over again before you came to Texas? And who was trying to convince me otherwise? Eh, eh, eh. At last you see it my way. Because I still see it that way, in spite of aforementioned "P.S." Please scratch that out or tear it up (if you haven't already) because it's just when I get moonstruck that I think it would work, with me still in the Ferry Command. In the cold, clear light of day, as you are always saying, I know in my heart that with traveling all the time, no marriage could be really successful.

But, Ned, how about that test pilot job? I wouldn't get to be with you except on weekends then. Have you thought of that? Do you still want to go through with it?

Don't ever forget that if you have a change of heart or change of mind, it's never too late to plot another course. I love you, darling, but I don't want you—now or ever—as long as there is a single reservation in your mind.

Marriage, at best, is difficult enough without any misgivings to begin with. So let's not rush into anything until we are both sure and there is no scaredness or doubt in anyone's mind. Okay?

[Love Field]
April 22, 1944

Mother, dear,

Ned came over last night and brought me a beautiful pair of 14K gold wings. He originally planned to save 'em as a wedding present.

The weather is stinko here and I'm going over to Fort Worth tonight to see my boy. Thank the Lord I couldn't get out today.

Tell Grannie mum's the word from now on.

Allis Hotel
Wichita, Kansas
April 24, 1944

Ned, darling,

It was sho wonderful, visiting you at Eagle Mt. Lake. I thought the place was swell, and Sidney couldn't have made a bigger hit. He certainly is a lot of fun to be around, and if he liked me half as much as I did him, then things should be okay on that score.

Nacherly the Fort Worth forecaster was right. I got off about 9:45 A.M. from Love, so nobody will say anything. The air traffic was too heavy to have made it any sooner, anyway. The trip to San Antone just lasted an hour plus 40, but it seemed like 10. I let "George" [automatic pilot] do most of the work, while I sat there dreaming about my man.

In San Antonio, I'd had to wait from 11:45 A.M. to 9:45 P.M. for a flight back to Wichita. As I handed over the papers to the handsome, smiling Mexican officer who was waiting to fly my C-45 on to Mexico City, he bowed and said, *"Gracias."*

With my "You're welcome," he looked puzzled. He seemed to be waiting for me to say or do something more. "Do you speak English?" I asked.

He shook his head and shrugged his shoulders.

"Parlez-vous français?" I tried.

"Oui, oui!" He nodded enthusiastically.

"Moi aussi—un petit peu," I said in my thick American imitation of the language.

"Moi aussi, un petit peu," he repeated with a Spanish accent, measuring with thumb and forefinger the small amount of French he knew. We went on this way in a few halting phrases until he flourished pencil and paper and began printing an invitation to lunch in French. I produced the picture of Ned that I always carried in my billfold, then made fluttering gestures with

my hand over my heart so he would understand how things were.

He countered by producing a picture of the mansion he lived in. We both laughed. He could afford lunch! Since I had all day to kill, I accepted the invitation. We rode on a festive barge that cruised beneath curved stone bridges on the river, which wound its way through the heart of that picturesque city. Then we stopped at a sidewalk cafe next to the water for lunch. I asked César—that was his name—if he didn't have to get his C-45 to Mexico that day, and like a true Latin, he replied, "*Mañana, mañana.*"

After lunch we visited the Alamo. As I read the account of the heroism there, I was overcome with admiration. It was ironic that I should learn details about this particular chapter of American history with a member of the Mexican military. When I came out blinking in the brilliant sunlight, César ceased to exist for a few minutes. I was ready to volunteer for the Republic of Texas.

Then he bought me flowers—ridiculous with my uniform—but it made us friendly neighbors again. We put them on the table when we had dinner together that night. After a leisurely, sumptuous meal with wine, I looked at my watch and printed on the piece of paper that lay between us (we couldn't even read each other's handwriting) that it was time for me to get back to the airport.

In the taxicab, I was forced to say, "*César, vous êtes un wolf,*" as I pushed him away, embarrassed for both of us.

"*Eh? Quoi? Comment?*" he asked, puzzled, insisting with injured innocence that he had been looking for me all his life. "*Je t'aime toujours, TOUJOURS!*" he cried mournfully, and I cried, "*Oh, non, non!*"

He looked at me with sad eyes and murmured, "*Quel domage.*" What a pity.

César didn't want to let me out of the cab at the airport without further cementing international relations. "Do you speak

Spanish?" I implored the cabbie, leaning forward to escape César's embrace.

"Sure."

"Then please tell the lieutenant what a wolf is."

There were several exchanges in Spanish, in the middle of which the cabbie gave the classic wolf whistle. César had to laugh, even though he feigned a wounded look. He was still protesting his innocence and undying love, in French, as I told him *au revoir*. He gave me his photo with his address on the back and waved good-bye, looking suitably grief-stricken.

I arrived back at Wichita on Braniff about four A.M. and, for once, could sleep till noon.

Ned seemed to have gotten over his pre-nuptial jitters long enough to talk about getting a marriage license. In a letter post-marked 26 April, he wrote:

> Baby, why don't you send me your full name, age, height, weight, and any other info so I can see about getting a license to marry up with you. Oh, yes, some evidence that such is your age so I can get a friend to swear you're over 18. Any old document will do. They require a physical on me but not you.
>
> Just have a minute.
>
> I love you.
>
> P.S. The license is a bit previous, but I'd like to have the dope so I can get it done if I ever get to town.

While we were talking marriage licenses and still working out the kinks in our conflicting ideas about a wedding, Soviet forces reached the Czech and Romanian frontiers. They vanquished German strongholds in the Crimea. At the same time MacArthur's naval, air, and ground forces eliminated a Japanese base in New Guinea. British and American forces continued to pound Germany.

U.S. losses of military pilots overseas were not as high as predicted, and our victories brought a reduction in the requirements
for military pilots at the same time that flying schools in the
United States had been turning out huge numbers of them. The
number of WASPs in the Ferry Command alone reached its peak
in April 1944: 303 women.

Meanwhile, Ned was having another attack of nerves about
getting married. After a bewildering evening with him, I wrote the
following letter:

> The Washington Youree
> Shreveport, Louisiana
> *May 5, 1944*

Ned, dear,

You must be completely worn out today. I'm really sorry I kept
you up so late two nights in a row.

Last night was a little confusing, but I'm awfully glad we had
that talk. You are a brave darling to be so frank with me and I
love you for your honesty. I do hope, however, that your very
severe analysis of everything—including our hearts—won't tear
us apart. I have just enough rebellion in me to revolt when I see
you taking our love apart bit by bit and coldly going over every
related item, trying to be sure in your heart of hearts that This Is
It. What I mean is this: if it is necessary, even now, for you to do
that, then you don't feel the way I do. I like your analytical mind
and your honesty with yourself and me, but I don't like the fact
that analysis of our love is still necessary.

I'm so sure that I disregard the qualms and snatches of panic
that I, too, get when I think about marriage, and cast them aside
as being the natural reaction of any person who has lived inde-
pendently for more than a score of years and is about to give up
complete and accustomed freedom and independence forever—
or I hope forever.

Wedlock is no small step, and anything that is so big and important a step as marriage involves giving up much, as well as gaining much more, and everybody surely must inwardly balk at giving up personal liberty and taking on all the responsibilities and problems that becoming husband and wife involves. But there are obstacles in any course of life, and when I feel myself balking I remember the goal ahead and know that nothing is important enough to stand in the way, if the goal to be attained is desirable enough—and you certainly are that.

Until you feel the same way, I think we should wait. Maybe I'm not the right girl for you, after all. (Maybe no girl is?) You are certainly the boy for me, and it's hard to say this, but: I hereby release you from any obligation you feel that you have as far as I'm concerned. Don't worry about hurting me, because there's plenty of fight in the old girl yet, and I won't go under.

I'm putting myself on the available list again and will try to remember that it once was possible to live with zest without you, so that I'll be prepared to plan another life if you want it that way.

I hope nobody notices how vulnerable I'll undoubtedly be, if a rebound is necessary—but I'm sure I won't do anything foolish, even so. I'll watch my step, because I know that susceptibility is at its height when someone is trying to get over anything as terrific as our romance has been.

You may as well put yourself on the market again, too, Ned. Give yourself every test known to man! Then, if you decide you want me—without mental reservation—I hope I'll still be around, though I can't promise.

I'm going to conscientiously do my best at my job—really this time—so there will be fewer stops at DL. When there are legitimate RONs [in Dallas], however, I'll let you know so that you can come over if you don't have anything else planned. And—brother! Talk about playing hard to get!! If you want me back, you are truly going to have to work to convince me this time—

because I'm not in the market for heartbreak any longer, and you are going to have competition once more, me lad.

As soon as he got that letter, Ned rushed over to Dallas. I had Saturday and part of Sunday off before going back to Wichita for further orders, so he came to talk things over. Apparently he had been as miserable as I had. The following letter tells what happened when we got together.

Allis Hotel
Wichita, Kansas
Sunday afternoon

Ned, darling,

This afternoon, as we took off and I realized I was leaving you, I suddenly got weak all over.

I really meant it yesterday when I said that what I had written in that last letter still goes. I meant it until last night at the dinner table, when you looked over at me and said, "The food won't go down." Then I suddenly realized that you must love me a lot after all, if it affected you that way. So I won't go through with it, after all, if you're sure the shoe is on the right foot now. If ever a doubt comes into your mind again, though, about who the originator, persuader, pursuer, and aggressor was, is, and always will be (as long as I have anything to do with it), then promise you'll let me know—and I'll go through with my plans so thoroughly that you'll have to make the biggest offensive of the war to get me back! Okay? Okay!!! I'm glad we see eye to eye on that.

My love and my life are yours.

Ned had finally convinced me that he really did want to get married—now. He seemed to be over his pre-nuptial qualms.

May 6, 1944

Mother, dear,

I'm on my way back to Dallas, where I'll spend the night before returning to Wichita. I hope Ned'll be waiting for me when I get off the plane. I wired him I was coming.

He has written his mother to go ahead and tell everybody, so I'm giving you permission, too. Hope you and Grannie have a field day. I have a sneaking suspicion that you will.

I spent the night in Fort Worth night before last. Ned slept on the couch and I slept in his room, and Sidney slept in his'n. But everything was strictly on the up-and-up, for your information, Mrs. Stegglepuss.

I delivered an AT-11 to Midland this afternoon. I've really put in a lot of flying time in the last couple of weeks, thanks to good weather.

It's so bumpy right now, though, that three or four of the passengers are ooping in their ooping cups. I better stop writing before I join them (using one's eyes makes it worse).

Sorry I'm such a sorry letter-writer lately. I don't know what's wrong with me, unless it's love!

May 7, 1944

Private

Mother, dearest,

Yesterday when I got off the plane at Dallas, Ned was waiting there to meet me. We had a wonderful time together—went out to dinner and then went to a park where we sat under a tree and looked out on the moonlit lake and talked [and smooched] away the hours. The lake is near Love Field, and we could see the blinking lights of the planes about to land and the revolving sheath of light put out by the beacon.

Ned stayed in the BOQ at the field and we had breakfast together this morning at the airport terminal, while I waited for the airliner to take me back to Wichita [to pick up another plane for delivery].

I looked at his poor legs today in the sunlight, and nothing in me was offended. They are pretty pitiful, but I think I'd love Ned if he had no legs at all. Naturally I can't say that I don't care if his legs are [burned], or that it doesn't matter, but I can truthfully say that I love him—all of him—with my whole heart and soul.

Ned wants to get married while [his sister] Marjorie is in Texas. So, since she will be leaving soon, you and the Hodgsons may get a wire some day this month saying to come on out and help us tie the knot. But we may wait for the Army to take over [at which time I planned to resign].

33

The uncertainty of things began to take its toll. Ned suddenly began to get extremely nervous about wedding details. He fretted and stewed over things I didn't consider important. I had never seen this side of him and it alarmed me.

One night, when we were feeling the strain of unconsummated love, I said to him, "Why don't we just go to the justice of the peace and get it over with?" I was not only frustrated, I was scared. Ned seemed to care too much what other people thought. And he was afraid our families would be hurt if we just ran off and had a civil ceremony, even though it was wartime, and gas rationing and travel restrictions would probably prevent our families from joining us for our wedding, anyway.

We came to an impasse with a conflict of wills, and by the time the evening ended we both seemed to feel that maybe we were all wrong for each other, after all. After Ned put me on the bus for Dallas, he wrote the following letter before going to bed:

May 16 0050

Marion, my darling:

At this point I have the comfort of the remains of the bottle we were working on.

Baby, let me put one thing straight. To my way of thinking, tonight's unfortunate experience [heated disagreement] was not a matter of personalities, but rather a conflict between that which is conventional and that which is not.

My quarrel is not with the simple ceremony as much as it is with the fact that we'll have to live with our families and friends forever—tonight is long gone, but the future is ever present.

When you boarded the bus tonight and would not look up [out of the window] to see if I was there, you just about broke my heart. The noise of the bus starter I mistook for the pieces of my heart rattling against the bottom of my stomach.

Of all the gals I've ever known in my life, none has ever been your equal. I can't lie to you because I love you. Some have had qualities which exceeded yours, but only in very limited respects. No lady I have ever met has your beauty, personality, background, brains and talent. I love you, my darling, with the most selfish love I've ever known—I'd still hurt my family and friends and marry you in a thoroughly unconventional manner if you wish it.

My preference [however] is to have a simple service with one or two friends, minimum, any time after you have notified the public of our intention to marry at an undetermined date—hell, two yokels off the street would be all right [as witnesses] so long as your mother didn't have to spend the remaining years of her life explaining away the marriage of her most beautiful daughter.

My writing is probably becoming less legible as a result of having drained the bottle, but my thoughts are no less clear.

There is one other point that I would like to try to put across. You are obligated to me or my family and friends in absolutely no respect. I say this cold-bloodedly and frankly with no great fear of equivocation on the point. I am old enough to take care of myself; I've had heartaches before, and I feel I'm better qualified to have you decide that we are not suited for each other at this point in my life than at any other previous time. I agree with you that if it's "no go" it is better for all concerned that it be decreed "no go" now.

Divorce has its place, but I'll not countenance the thought of marriage with the proviso that if it doesn't work, we can get a divorce. I'd love to have you as the mother of my children. I love you with all that there is in me, but if you don't like my sense of propriety, take exception to my thought of convention, with relation to your family and mine, plus our progeny, for God's sake, forget about me and I'll find ways to rid myself of you and thoughts of you.

Darling, a man can only happily marry a lady who wants him for what he is, and not for the "best foot forward" that he may present.

I love you, darling, with every cell that has response. It's either goodnight, my love, or goodbye.

That night, when I left Ned without looking up, was one of the bleakest of my life, ranking right next to the night my father died. I didn't think anything else could happen to make me feel any worse, until I got a telegram the next day saying Grannie had died. Even though Ned and I were estranged, I knew I had to notify him of Grannie's death. Grannie had adored him and he loved her, so I swallowed my pride and called him.

He rushed right over. We fell into each other's arms, just as Grannie had known we would. He just held me close, without words, for a long time. His embrace told me that he understood what I was feeling, that he felt it too. And I was sure he remembered that Grannie had encouraged us to declare our love and to welcome it. To her it was right.

I will always believe she chose that exact time to die in order to get us back together. Her strategy worked. But how could she have known? She just knew!

Ned and I stayed up half the night, reconciling and blessing Grannie.

[To Marion from Ned]

Darling,

Thank you for your wire. Lordy, angel, I miss you too. I didn't know I could ever miss anyone the way I miss you. Was as restless as a wild animal and realized that missing you is the foundation for it.

Went to talk to the doctor about "what every young man should know." I'm very glad I went. Felt sorta awkward but I could never have talked sober to anyone like that if I weren't on the threshold of matrimony. It gave a strange sort of confidence, so that I could just ask what would otherwise be the most embarrassing questions. The doctor seemed more hacked than I was at first.

[I had suggested to Ned that we each read a book about the physical side of marriage.] I was very happy to discover that I wasn't as ignorant as you had made me feel I must be. I know I should read some book and will try to do so right away, but over a period of years I've read parts of good books and in school took embryology, comparative anatomy, human anatomy, and cut up a cadaver in lab, so maybe I can get by for a little while in case I don't get the book read before we get married. That okay?

Your call came through right here. Damn, but it was almost like a paralyzing electric shock to hear your voice. To get back: the Episcopal church out here seems to want three days' notice before the ceremony. We can get the man here [Sherwood Clayton]—a really amazingly outstanding man. Met him. Some friends of mine spoke about us and he told them okay, that today would be the first day of the three days "banns" (public announcement of a proposed marriage).

You should have some annual leave coming. Baby, the wedding is yours, but I'd like not to have to do one damn thing in the world the day after we're married, at least. Two days are about all I can hope for, but I'll have to plan it a little, for even one day.

Darling, we're making our flight plan for life. We've mulled over all the hazards en route and I'm satisfied that it will be "tail winds and happy landings, with a minimum of turbulence en route."

Let us plan when to start the flight, be it in the morning or at night, quietly or with fanfare. Let's file our flight plan, get our clearance, and say a little prayer that our flight together be the most joyous and successful ever.

While Ned and I contemplated a wedding for June 1944, the war in Europe was winding down and D-Day was on the horizon. In spite of terrible losses, the total number of casualties of American pilots had been far less than had been anticipated.

This was a happy factor that augmented the lessening need for WASPs. But even with the decreasing need for us, in May 1944 it seemed certain that WASPs would be absorbed into the Army, even though the training of new classes might be halted. The next month they were, and on the first of October it was announced that all WASPs still on duty would be released and sent home in December.

All the hullabaloo caused by unemployed male pilots simplified my decision in May about what to do. I had volunteered for the WASPs because pilots were desperately needed—and also for less noble reasons: I wanted to be where the action was, and I wanted to fly. Our purpose, as I understood it and as stated by General Arnold, was to release men, not to replace them. I had done my job and done it well, if I did say so myself. Now I could resign and marry Ned!

I could still serve my country as a civilian, if needed. Since I wanted to keep on flying, I definitely would check out that test-pilot job that Ned had suggested. But my number-one objective was to become Ned's wife, and now there was no obstacle in the way. Hallelujah!

Resigning was surprisingly easy. I just stated my reasons on paper: (1) I did not want to go into the Army; and (2) marriage. Two other girls at Love Field resigned at the same time, and a telegram from the office of the commanding general of the Ferrying Division of the ATC, General Tunner, advised:

HENCEFORTH RESIGNATIONS SUBMITTED BY WASP PERSONNEL MAY BE ACCEPTED BY GROUP CO WITHOUT PRIOR AUTH FROM THIS HDQS. NOTICE OF SUCH ACCEPTED RESIGNATIONS SHOULD BE TRANSMITTED TO THIS HQS FOR RECORD PURPOSES.

I had only two more weeks to fly as a WASP. Bittersweet weeks. And Ned had a hard time keeping up with me. Our phone calls just missed each other, so he wrote out tentative wedding plans.

[Late May, 1944]

Marion, my beautiful darling, when you coming back? Last night your call came through about 9:15, but you could not be located.

Honey, if it suits, why don't we try to make the wedding this weekend, say Thurs. or Fri. Mary Van Zandt Violette [Sidney's new love, a Fort Worth woman] has offered to give us a hand. [She and Sidney later were married and became two of our best friends.] It would be swell if Shirley and Sandy could come up.

Baby, I'm so delighted you were stuck in AG [Atlanta] and got a chance to see your family and mine. Dad and Mother really hardly knew you 'cause they have seen so little of you in recent years. I don't think you'll ever have to worry about in-law trouble, 'cause they think you're wonderful, too.

[Richmond, Virginia]
May 25, 1944

Mother, precious,

It was so wonderful to see my darling Mother again! Did you call the airport to find out whether I had landed okay? I guess they informed you that I landed at Greenville, S.C., instead of Spartanburg. I didn't know they had such a nice field at Greenville, and since Spartanburg has no Army facilities, I thought I'd better land where I could get GI service. And it was sure lucky I did!! The left hydraulic system on my landing gear went out (luckily on the ground) and I had to stay there nearly all day to get it fixed.

I'm stuck in Richmond, as you can see. I tried to get here the day after I left you, but I ran into a big thunderstorm and had to turn around and land at Greensboro, N.C. Got here the next day and have stayed here ever since because of the **!!**##!! weather [ahead on my route].

I'm staying at the Nurses' Quarters and they are a nice bunch of gals—real sweet to me. Also, a young lieutenant has been taking care of me and keeping me occupied. He's a darling looking boy, but I feel so much older than he seems. He's flying fighters here and will be shipped out any day. [He was shot down over Avignon, France, a few weeks later and declared missing in action. His body was never found.]

I get all lump-in-the-throaty every time I go out with some nice young kid about to go out and get shot at. He's been trying to talk me out of getting married.

Honey, when you get the wedding announcements, no matter how expensive they are, please get plenty. Either send me about a hundred to address to my friends (just send me the envelopes) or I'll send you a list—whichever will be easier for you.

I love you, Mother.

[USMCAS, Eagle Mt. Lake,
25 May 1944]

[To Marion]

Darlin' I'm beginning to wonder what in the hell has happened to you. You called from Athens Fri. night, so figured you'd make N.Y. Sun. at the latest and be back here Tues. at the latest. Guess you must have had engine trouble again. Here I've been aboard every night this week, hoping to hear from you from DL, but no word.

Went flying today in what was hardly "Field Officer's weather." Rain all the time. It's embarrassing to discover that you do green pilot stunts, like making a turn in the wrong direction to come to a heading—you know how the compass needle moves the wrong way at the start of a turn. Landed in a fairly light, shifting wind and damn near ground looped, 'cause it switched 45 degrees in a gust and caught us pretty flatfooted. 'Tis fun to fly and frighten one's self again.

Just want to say I love you and let's get married, darling. I'll make you the best husband you ever had.

34

I delivered my last airplane to West Point, New York, home of the nation's Military Academy. What a fitting way, I thought, to end my flying career with the Army: with the safe delivery of that beautiful dreamboat, the AT-6, to West Point. All I felt was relief at having delivered my last plane without so much as a scratch. I had been terrified that I might mess up at the last minute on my very last flight and ruin my record. What a sense of elation! A clean slate, from beginning to end.

After parking the plane and filling out the Form One, I climbed out on the wing. I patted the side of the ship affectionately, the way I'd pat a nice horse after a good ride. Jumping down with my parachute still on, I retrieved my B-4 bag from the baggage compartment, handed it to the driver of the jeep that was waiting for me, and started to climb in.

Then it hit me. This was good-bye. Not just to the AT-6 that I had lost my heart to, but good-bye to my military flying career. It was over.

"Just a minute; I'll be right back," I told the driver.

I turned and walked a few steps to the AT-6. It stood waiting, gleaming silver in the sunlight, sleek and gorgeous, aerodynamically close to perfect, a pilot's dream. I knew I would never fly it again. I rubbed its smooth side, warm from the sun. Then I put my cheek against it for a moment before giving it a farewell kiss.

When I turned back to the jeep, the driver's look said, "Women!" But he was smiling.

My next-to-last transportation request was written for a ferry-boat ride down the Hudson River to New York City, to catch the first available airliner back to Love Field. It was a brilliant day, just warm enough, and the ferry took us past lovely rock cliffs and wooded hillsides. I wasn't fully aware of anything but peace and beauty. I didn't let myself think about what I was leaving behind in my life; I tried only to think of what lay ahead. But I was in a daze, my emotions in neutral.

Ned called me on Monday night, after I got back to Texas. "Your last day at Love Field is Wednesday," he said, "so why don't we get married Thursday [1 June]? Mary says you can spend the night with her Wednesday night."

Mary Van Zandt Violette was one of those totally open, warm, and genuine people to whom I felt close almost instantly. I'd already asked her to stand up with me when the chaplain married us, and Ned had asked Sidney to be the other witness. Shirley and Sandy weren't going to be able to come, and none of my friends at Love Field knew from minute to minute when they'd be called out on a trip. Our families couldn't come on such short notice, especially with the travel situation so iffy.

"Will the chaplain be available on Thursday?" I asked.

"That's another thing, Missy. Remember that great guy I wrote you about—the Episcopal priest? Well, he's a friend of Mary's, Sherwood Clayton. She has him lined up for us. And she wants us to have a home wedding, with all the trimmings. At the Van Zandt farm."

"Bless her bones. But that would be a lot of trouble for her."

"She wants to do it. Says she's going to invite all her friends, since we don't know anybody yet. I've given her a check for champagne afterwards. I'll bring my car over again tomorrow and leave it with you, so you can start loading it up," he said.

"I don't have much to load. I'll have to clear the post—turn in all my gear—tomorrow and the next day, but I can get out of here by 1800 Wednesday."

The night before the wedding, Mary and I lay awake in the huge Victorian bed that so many Van Zandts before her had slept in. We talked and giggled, confiding in each other.

The next day, while I washed my hair, Mary transformed the living room of the farmhouse into a fragrant bower. In front of the stone fireplace where Ned and I were to say our vows, she placed great sprays of greenery to which she tied gardenia blooms cut from a friend's bushes. She spread the dining-room table with her mother's best lace tablecloth and put a silver wine cooler at each end for the champagne, with silver candelabra in the center.

She asked a friend, Dr. Jagoda, an MD who played the violin, to bring his instrument. A professor from the music department at Texas Christian University played the piano. Mary invited all her best friends, including Elliott (son of the president) Roosevelt's recently divorced wife, Ruth. She asked me to wear her wedding ring on my right hand; she'd heard it would bring a divorced woman good luck in love if a bride wore her ring during her wedding ceremony. (It worked for her.)

Ned and I both were teary-eyed as we faced each other in front of the greenery-bedecked fireplace and exchanged vows. Then it was over, and I was Mrs. Ned Hodgson.

We stayed at the reception long enough to determine that we were going to love our new Fort Worth friends (most of them became our best friends, too, over the next fifty-odd years), and then we departed for the bridal suite at the Blackstone Hotel. There we found a white-gloved waiter presiding over a table laden with a cold turkey feast and more champagne, ordered by my thoughtful bridegroom. Ned thanked the waiter, tipped him, and dismissed him.

We drank the champagne, but the food was never touched.

Epilogue ————————————————

It has now been more than fifty years since I made that transition from pilot to bride—the easiest leap I ever made. I can still see Ned's face on our wedding day, when I turned toward him to exchange vows. I saw him then through a blur of tears—the strong, sensitive face, the brown eyes filled with feeling, shining with an indomitable spirit that no earthly fire could extinguish. Full of love for me.

I didn't get that test pilot's job. Nobody was hiring women when men were available. So I took on the job of helpmate to my love, eager to make his home and bear his children. I worked at part-time jobs and wrote memoirs of the WASPs (which I filed away for grandchildren, since no one was interested in us right after the war).

We spent a happy year at Eagle Mt. Lake, where Ned worked hard and grew stronger. We were then transferred to Miramar Marine Corps Air Station, California. There we opened our tiny garage apartment, which we dubbed Hodgson Hotel, to any and all war-weary military friends passing through on their way home.

After V-J day, Ned had surgery for his shattered ankle at the Navy hospital in San Diego. Doctors ankylosed the joint, giving him a permanently rigid ankle. He walked on crutches (and on the beach, he walked on his hands!) for many months, but his ankle no longer caused him pain.

Since the war was over, Ned got a medical retirement from the Marine Corps and we headed back to Atlanta. Because of the stiff ankle he couldn't return to Eastern Air Lines as a pilot, so he went to work for them on the ground as an aircraft dispatcher. And I finally got pregnant.

Ned wasn't happy with his job, which was shift work, and when the opportunity arose to return to Texas, we grabbed it. Mary's good friend Thomas Ryan was starting a life insurance company and asked Ned to come out and help get it going. "Why me?" Ned asked. "I don't know anything about life insurance."

"I can hire an actuary and a lawyer to help us," Tom said, "but I want you because I want my company to have integrity."

So we bundled up our new little Hodgson, Edward Sheldon, and moved to Fort Worth. Two years later I presented Ned with a daughter, Marjorie, and ten years after that, John arrived.

Having a new baby at age forty was more challenging and thrilling than my first airplane ride with Mr. Wade. It instilled in me a new appreciation for Ned, too, who was still as supportive and excited as when we had our first baby. In my third trimester, when I was extremely large with child, I penned these lines to Ned's mother (whom her grandchildren called Momoo):

Dearest Momoo,

I shouldn't wait until Mother's Day to tell you how much I love you, but it is less embarrassing on Mother's Day! Really, I don't know how I can ever thank you for being the kind of mother that you were to Ned (and are now to both of us)— because his early training and environment of love and understanding stand out all over him now! He makes just about the sweetest husband and father in the world—and things like that don't just happen—they were made to happen years ago when he was your little boy and receiving all his early impressions and attitudes.

If we can do half as good a job on our children, then our life's goal will be realized.

You just can't imagine how tender and helpful and understanding your son is to me during these uncomfortable days. I look like a freak from the side show [when the baby was born, he weighed over ten pounds] and Ned makes me feel like Miss

America! Seriously, he just couldn't be more darling in every way, and gives of himself without stint, to me and the children. They are reflecting all this by growing into beautiful, happy, loving children—and just think!—all this really goes back to you, Momoo! So happy Mother's Day and all my thanks and love—

Marion

After becoming a parent, not only did I have a new appreciation for the sacrifices made by our parents and the love they had given us, I also changed inwardly. When our firstborn, Sheldon, was placed in my arms, I instantly lost my agnosticism forever. I knew there had to be an almighty God to create this miracle, this new life. And the hormones of motherhood flooded my being with overwhelming delight. Soon after the birth of John thirteen years later, I became a Christian. This step added more to my already blessed life than anything else that had ever happened to me, deepening my love for Ned and the children, making life even more joyous, and giving me a peace I had never dreamed possible.

I stayed home by choice with all three children. I kept the typewriter hot, turning out short stories, articles, four cookbooks, and a novel. I sold only a fraction of what I produced, but it was enough to treat the family to several trips to Europe.

Sheldon got his pilot's license when he was eighteen. He and John are both engineers. Marjorie is a journalist and author of children's books. All three are happily married and have presented us with five (to date) grandchildren who are the delight of our old age.

Before Ned retired, he had worked his way up to being president of the life insurance company. We've lived in the same little house, adding a room every time we added another member to the family. Hodgson Hotel is always open.

Sandy and Shirley (and Helen Anne, until her death in 1995) and I have remained close friends despite living hundreds of miles apart. We attend WASP reunions every chance we get. The best reunion of all was when a group of us went to the USSR in May 1990 to meet Soviet women pilots, our sisters in World War II who flew combat. For us, the Cold War ended that May.

Thirteen years before that memorable trip, President Jimmy Carter had signed a bill making WASPs members of the United States Air Force, retroactively. Even though I hadn't wanted us to be militarized back in 1944, by the time it actually happened in 1977, I was glad. Glad because the year before, the U.S. Air Force had decided to train ten women as pilots. And with a roll of drums, the Pentagon announced to the world that those ten would be this country's first women to fly military planes. Humph! They had already forgotten the WASPs of World War II.

So I was happy when the oversight was corrected by an act of Congress, especially since so many people had worked so hard to get veterans' rights for the WASPs. I framed my honorable discharge along with my Victory medal and the American Theater medal, for having been on duty for more than a year. I hung them alongside Ned's identical medals, thinking how much more they had cost him than they did, me.

Life has had its ups and downs, but Ned and I have been blessed. Our love and shared faith have held us up when troubles clouded our horizon. We know, as all pilots do, that the sun is still shining up there above any overcast, if you climb high enough.

And it shines on us warmly as we sit together now on the porch of a large beach house we've rented for a family reunion with our children and grandchildren. Ned is in his early eighties; our youngest grandchild is a preschooler. Ned's face is bronzed from the sun and his looks belie his age. I sometimes gaze at him and marvel. In 1943 he was not expected to live.

He catches me looking at him, smiles, and reaches for my hand. A plane flies overhead and we crane our necks to see it. Here we sit, two old World War II aviators, not feeling old at all, rejuvenated by sun and surf and happiness.

"What do you think the weather will be like tomorrow?" I ask (we're planning a fishing trip), looking at little puffs of clouds on the horizon.

"CAVU."

Pilot talk. But it's also Ned's way of looking at life. And it's become my way, too. Ceiling And Visibility Unlimited.

About the Author

Marion Stegeman Hodgson, a former WASP who graduated from flight school in 1943 with the Army Air Force's Flying Training Detachment in Sweetwater, Texas, has published one novel, four cookbooks, and numerous magazine articles. She now resides in Fort Worth, Texas, with her husband, Ned.